MOVE

Also by Greg L. Hawkins and Cally Parkinson

Reveal: Where Are You?

Follow Me: What's Next for You?

*Focus: The Top Ten Things People Want and Need
from You and Your Church*

MOVE

What 1,000 Churches REVEAL about Spiritual Growth

GREG L. HAWKINS
& CALLY PARKINSON

ZONDERVAN®

WILLOW
Willow Creek Resources

ZONDERVAN.com/
AUTHORTRACKER
follow your favorite authors

ZONDERVAN

Move
Copyright © 2011 by the Willow Creek Association

This title is also available as a Zondervan ebook.
Visit www.zondervan.com/ebooks.

This title is also available in a Zondervan audio edition.
Visit www.zondervan.fm.

Requests for information should be addressed to:

Zondervan, *Grand Rapids, Michigan 49530*

Library of Congress Cataloging-in-Publication Data

Hawkins, Greg L.
    Move : what 1,000 churches reveal about spiritual growth / Greg L. Hawkins and Cally
Parkinson
      p. cm.
      Includes index.
      ISBN 978-0-310-32525-3
      1. Spiritual formation. 2. Christian life — United States — Statistics. I. Parkinson, Cally. II.
Title.
BV4511.H39 2011
    248.4 — dc22   2011008910

Cover design: *Rob Monacelli*
Interior illustration: *Dan Van Loon*
Interior design: *Ben Fetterley, Greg Johnson/Textbook Perfect*

Printed in the United States of America

11 12 13 14 15 /DCI/ 21 20 19 18 17 16 15 14 13 12 11 10 9 8 7 6 5 4 3 2 1

For Eric Arnson

"It's amazing, in fact, what one highly charged, crazy man can do."

—Peters and Waterman, *In Search of Excellence*

About the Authors

Greg L. Hawkins is executive pastor of Willow Creek Community Church in South Barrington, Illinois. Since 1996, he has assisted senior pastor Bill Hybels in providing strategic leadership to Willow Creek's six campuses. Prior to joining the staff of Willow Creek in 1991, Greg spent five years as a consultant for McKinsey & Company. He has an undergraduate degree in civil engineering from Texas A&M University and an MBA from Stanford University. Greg and his wife, Lynn, live in the Chicago suburbs with their three children.

Cally Parkinson is brand manager for REVEAL, an initiative within Willow Creek Association that utilizes research tools and discoveries to help churches better understand spiritual growth in their congregations. She previously served as the director of communication services at Willow Creek Community Church, a role she took on following a twenty-five-year career at Allstate Insurance Company. She has a bachelor's degree from DePauw University and a master's degree from the American Graduate School of International Management. Cally and her husband, Rich, live in the Chicago suburbs and have two grown children.

Contents

Acknowledgments

Foreword:
Facts Are Our Friends

They wrecked my day.

Three colleagues I trust and respect had just walked me through the findings of an elaborate—and quite expensive—congregational survey, and the results weren't at all what I'd expected.

I've always believed the local church is the hope of the world. I still do. But what I learned from the survey on that day was that the local church I'd led for more than thirty years was not doing as well as I thought when it came to helping people grow spiritually.

Greg Hawkins, our executive pastor, and Cally Parkinson, our director of communications, had been working on the survey—a project that had my full support and interest. They recruited Eric Arnson, a research specialist who helped them develop and interpret the survey. Their goal was to find out which of the many activities and programs we offer delivered the greatest spiritual growth in our people. In other words, we wanted to identify which activities were most effective in helping people grow in their love of God and love of others (Matthew 22:37–40). The results of our survey would help fine tune our various ministries so that even more people could grow deeper in their faith.

What they discovered challenged some of our core assumptions about our effectiveness as a church. For example, 18 percent of our congregation—more than 1,000 people—had stalled spiritually and didn't know what to do about it. Many were considering leaving. And some of our most mature and fired-up Christians wanted to go deeper in their faith and be challenged more but felt as if our church wasn't helping them get to the next level.

I was shocked. I had thought that helping people become fully devoted followers of Christ was what we were all about at Willow, but the facts told us we could do better.

After the team finished sharing the results of the survey, I thanked them and then told them I needed some time to process all their data and analysis. For the next several days I couldn't stop thinking about all I had learned. I reassured myself with the findings that 50 percent of our congregation indicated they "loved God more than anything else" and were expressing that love by reaching out to their unchurched friends and serving the poor on a regular basis. But the disconnect between what we thought we were doing and what we were actually accomplishing was troubling and unacceptable.

We made the survey the focus of our annual strategic planning event that year, and like me, many on our leadership team found the results disturbing. I shared with them some of my own misgivings when I first saw the results of the survey, but I reminded them of something I had learned a long time ago: facts are our friends. One of the worst things we can do as leaders is to ignore news that we don't like to hear. To their credit, the leadership team kept at it with open minds and hearts as they sought ways to improve the way we do ministry at Willow.

Here's one simple yet profound fix that came from this survey. We learned that the most effective strategy for moving people forward in their journey of faith is biblical engagement. Not just getting people into the Bible when they're in church—which we do quite well—but helping them engage the Bible on their own outside of church. We also completely restructured our Wednesday night service into a university format to better serve the varying needs of our people.

The changes we have made based on what we learned from this survey have made our church better. In recent years, we have baptized record numbers of people. We are healthier and more vibrant, and we are leading more people to faith. Most important, we are seeing more people growing into fully devoted followers of Christ.

As we saw how much the results of the survey changed the way we approach ministry, we decided to roll it out to a wider audience because we suspected that the issues we found weren't just Willow issues—other churches would likely benefit from it as well. Working closely with their colleagues at the Willow Creek Association, Greg and Cally's team expanded this survey to include 1,000 churches and over 250,000 congregants over a four-year period. This expanded database confirmed the findings from our own survey at Willow, and the result is *Move*, a book that will transform how you lead your church.

As you begin your own journey through this book, be open to hearing God speak to you. I offer the same encouragement to you that I gave to my leadership team: facts are our friends—challenging friends at times, yet friends nonetheless. My prayer is that the information you wrestle with in this book begins an ongoing dialogue about how *your* church can reach its full redemptive potential.

Because the local church *is* the hope of the world, and it deserves our very best.

Bill Hybels

Founder and Senior Pastor
Willow Creek Community Church

Chairman of the Board
Willow Creek Association

Is It Possible to Measure the Heart?

Church work is extremely easy and incredibly hard. It's easy because Jesus was crystal clear about the mission of the church: "Go and make disciples of all nations," he said, "baptizing them in the name of the Father and of the Son and of the Holy Spirit, and teaching them to obey everything I have commanded you" (Matthew 28:19–20).

He left no ambiguity when it came to those commands he cited, either, as he responded to the Pharisees' question to name the most important commandment: " 'You must love the Lord your God with all your heart, all your soul, and all your mind.' This is the first and greatest commandment. A second is equally important: 'Love your neighbor as yourself' " (Matthew 22:37–40 NLT). And what about that love he refers to? Did he leave *that* open to interpretation? Hardly. "Those who accept my commandments and obey them are the ones who love me" (John 14:21 NLT).

So the purpose of our churches — our commission, as church leaders — is to help the people in our congregations to become disciples who obey Jesus by loving God and loving others. That's what Jesus wants us to achieve, and it's pretty straightforward, making the *what* the easy part of church leadership. For close to two thousand years, however, each new generation of Christian leaders has struggled to get a handle on the *how*: How do we foster the transformation of our people into disciples of Christ? How do we know if those we lead are truly growing more in love with God and extending that love to other people? It sure would help if we had a way to measure changed hearts.

The 1962 movie version of *How the Grinch Stole Christmas* by Dr. Seuss is a Christmas classic. If you remember the story, the Grinch is a grouch. No one really knows why he is the way he is, but the storyteller suggests that perhaps his heart is too small.

How do we verify that? Well, when we watch the animated movie, a magic X-ray screen shows us that indeed the Grinch's heart is two sizes too small. Fortunately, that's not the end of the story. After doing a lot of really bad stuff to the town of Whoville — and poor Cindy Lou Who — the Grinch has a life-changing experience. We actually get to see the transformation of his heart. Thanks, again, to the magic X-ray screen, we watch as the Grinch's heart grows *three* sizes that Christmas Day!

If church leaders had access to Dr. Seuss's magic X-ray screen, measuring progress in making disciples might be a whole lot easier. Jesus said, "Your love for one another will prove to the world that you are my disciples" (John 13:35 NLT). So we could line folks up each week as they file into church and measure how full of love their hearts are. Then we could compare their X-rays from week to week and we'd know whether their love for God and others was growing and active. With such knowledge at hand we could determine, with a great deal of certainty, which of our church's ministries really support spiritual growth. We'd have a far better idea of how to best spend our time and resources in order to maximize heart change. And we would know for sure if what we're doing was helping our people become disciples who obey Jesus by loving God and loving others.

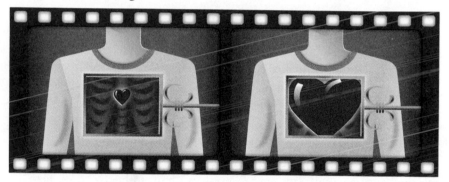

Alas, there is no such contraption at our disposal. That fact doesn't quell our need to know, however, so we just do our best. We measure what we can. And we follow the lead of generations of church leaders, whose unspoken measurement of success has typically revolved around church activities.

We hear stories of great preachers, so we work on our teaching. Sunday mornings. Wednesday evenings. We teach as best we can — and encourage others to do the same. We realize too that our people have pressing needs: they are lonely, facing tough decisions, experiencing loss. So we offer counseling and spiritual guidance. We organize care ministries to provide assistance; then, as the need expands, we recruit, train, and organize volunteers. Understandably, people want to feel connected, so we launch small groups and wrestle with who is qualified to lead them and how these individuals should be trained and equipped. And then there are the needy in our larger communities: the hungry and thirsty, the strangers and the prisoners, the naked and the sick. Christ's admonition rings in our ears: "I tell you the truth, when you [cared for] one of the least of these my brothers and sisters, you were doing it to me!" (Matthew 25:40 NLT).

From time to time, we step back to review all we have done. All the work. All the hours. All the decisions and challenging conversations. It may look quite impressive. In our quiet moments, though, most of us still find ourselves wondering, "How are we *really* doing? How much impact is our church making on people's lives? Are they closer to Christ? Do they exhibit more love and compassion? Are they more like Jesus in word and deed?" We've hoped the answer was yes, but there has been no way we could be sure. (Did we mention this was hard?)

It was that very difficulty—and church leaders' long-standing desire to know whether they were taking kingdom ground or just staying busy—that led, in 2003, to unprecedented efforts to answer those important questions. What began as a survey of a single church—a questionnaire based primarily on conventional wisdom among church leaders—yielded some surprising initial results. Then, over the next several years, persistence prevailed, research tools were professionally honed, more than a thousand congregations provided their input, and unprecedented breakthroughs surged to the fore.

The results have been astounding. Paradigm busting. Hope generating. (In fact, who *needs* a magic X-ray screen?) Yes, there actually *are* ways to know whether the people in our congregations are truly growing more in love with God and extending that love to other people. Yes, there *are* churches among us that are experiencing significant and authentic spiritual growth within their people. Yes, there really *are* ways to measure changed hearts. And, perhaps most important for church leaders: yes, there *are* lessons we can learn, attitudes we can incorporate, successes we can emulate, and spiritual-growth milestones we can help our congregations reach.

We are thrilled to be able to share all this and more with you through the pages of *Move*. We predict you will be surprised by a number of findings that will appear, at least initially, to be quite counterintuitive. We know you will enjoy meeting and learning from pastors who shepherd hearts that are indeed on fire for Jesus. And we anticipate that people in your own congregation will benefit from your expanded knowledge, as they experience unprecedented growth in their love of both God and others. That is, in fact, our fervent prayer.

CHAPTER 1

The Truth about Church

I (Greg) should have been ecstatic.

Our numbers over the past five years weren't just good, they were great. Twenty-six percent increase in church attendance. I know—bigger doesn't always mean better, but our people were not just showing up on weekends. Participation in small groups had increased by 200 percent. We were also seeing more people than ever before spreading Christ's love in local compassion initiatives throughout the greater Chicago area.

It wasn't just the numbers, though. Behind every number is a person, and I saw so much evidence of life change in our congregation. Marriages put back together. People finding purpose for their lives. Students taking a stand for God. The look on a guy's face when he finally gets what grace is all about.

This is why I do what I do. This is what keeps me going.

And yet.

One Sunday in 2003 I was sitting with my wife in the same spot in our auditorium where we always sit. As people streamed in, my heart was full of gratitude at the sight of so many people eager to worship God and learn from his Word. The weekend services are a visual reminder of all that has gone on during the week—small groups, special classes, serving opportunities, outreach experiences, and other events designed to help people grow. It's hard not to get excited about ministry when you're surrounded by people hungry to know God.

That's when it hit me—a haunting question so jarring I couldn't shake it off: Are all the things that we do here at Willow that these people so generously support *really* helping them become fully devoted followers of Christ—which is our mission—or are we just giving them a nice place to go to church? For all the work, all the financial investment, all the programming, and all the planning we pour into "church," is it really making a significant difference in people's lives?

As I looked out over the crowd, I imagined every family returning to their neighborhoods after the service and I wondered, "Is our corner of the world here in the Chicago suburbs a better place because of what we do at Willow, or does life pretty much go on here as it does everywhere else?"

I love being a pastor, even though that's not what I set out to do. I had my MBA and was working for a world-class management consulting firm, but God's call on my life was so radical and so clear that I knew this was where I should be. This was what I should be doing.

But I couldn't shake that nagging question rattling around somewhere between my heart and my head. *You think you're doing all the right things. You pour yourself into ministry because you love helping people grow in their faith. But are you really?* I wasn't so sure, and that's what makes ministry so unsettling for me: not knowing if the work I do is really helping the people I love move closer to God.

If you know anything about Willow Creek, you know that we love guiding people on a journey from standing on the sidelines to becoming fully devoted followers of Christ. We've designed programs and activities to keep them engaged so that they grow in their relationship with Jesus and find ways to share his love with others (Matthew 22:37–40). From the very beginning in 1975 when founding pastor Bill Hybels and a small band of volunteers started this church, that's been our focus. The fact that our church has grown from a few hundred people in 1975 to more than 25,000 today is humbling, and we've taken it as one indication that our way of doing church is having an impact.

At least that's what we thought.

But when we surveyed our people in 2004, we got one of those wake-up calls that you'd rather not get but you know you can't ignore. Our initial interest in conducting the survey was based on our long-held, overarching hypothesis that increased participation in church activities—small groups, weekend worship services, and volunteering—increases a person's love of God and others. Said another way: Church Activity = Spiritual Growth (chart 1-1).

That's what we believed at Willow Creek. Actually, our bias was so strong we would have said that we *knew* this was true.

We never questioned the validity of this approach to helping people grow in their faith. So what we really wanted to know when we conducted our initial survey was *which* activities produced the *most* spiritual growth. In other words, which activities were most effective in helping people grow in their love of God and love of others? We considered this the mother lode of church-leader

CHART 1-1: Many churches work from a model similar to this: the more a person far from God participates in church activities, the more likely it is those activities will produce a person who loves God and loves others.

questions. If we could figure that out, we could make better decisions. Spend money more judiciously. Minister more effectively. Cut those programs that don't help people grow and beef up the ones that do. We felt that we were doing a pretty good job of moving people toward spiritual maturity. The results of our survey would help us do much better.

Initially, we were very encouraged by the congregation's response to the survey—a 40 percent return rate on the fifteen thousand surveys distributed. But despite questions designed to measure everything from church participation to spiritual maturity, and despite the application of state-of-the-art research techniques, the answers we were looking for just weren't showing up.

Weeks went by, but the data still was not making sense to us. In fact, the data *itself* was perfectly fine. We were just blinded by our bias that increased participation in church leads to spiritual growth. Once we got over ourselves and let the data do the talking, we learned three shocking facts about our congregation: (1) Increased participation in church activities by themselves *barely moved* our people to love God and others more; (2) We had a lot of dissatisfied people; (3) We had a lot of people so dissatisfied that they were ready to leave.

All the great things we were doing and our people *barely moved*! The haunting feeling that came over me that Sunday had now been confirmed by cold, hard facts.

That's the bad news, and I have to admit, it was hard to take. But the good news that came from this survey has not only transformed how we do church at Willow, but it dramatically revitalized my own commitment to ministry. Here's what happened.

What began as a survey to inform the direction of Willow Creek, a single church, slowly evolved into the REVEAL Spiritual Life Survey—a tool that has been used by over 1,000 diverse congregations. Based on the responses of over 250,000 people who attend those churches, we discovered not only a new lens through which to view spiritual growth, but also a new way of understanding what it takes to lead a spiritually vibrant church. That's what the rest of *Move* is all about: an opportunity to face the facts about what is really going on in churches just like yours and to make the changes that will most enhance your congregation's ability to reach its full redemptive potential. And based on what we learned, we will share practical insights into how to get your people moving on a dynamic journey to spiritual maturity.

One important caveat: surveys and data are never the deciding factor in determining spiritual growth. In his sovereignty and providence, God often moves mysteriously in the hearts of people, which is why we continually sought his wisdom and guidance throughout the REVEAL experience.

At the foundation of this new way of understanding how people grow spiritually are eight significant discoveries—discoveries relevant to all churches and helpful to all ministry leaders willing to act boldly on strategies designed to move their people closer to Christ. Despite the fact that these findings are both universal (at least in the North American context) and verifiable, however, they are also surprising and sometimes even counterintuitive:

* **It *is* possible to measure spiritual growth.** Measuring spiritual growth is not something the REVEAL team set out to do. But in analyzing the results of our first survey in 2004, a framework emerged—based on how people describe their relationship with Jesus Christ—that predicts spiritual growth (defined by increasing love of God and increasing love of others—Matthew 22:37 – 40).

* **Church activities do not predict or drive long-term spiritual growth.** More precisely, increasing church attendance and participation in organized ministry activities do not predict or drive spiritual growth

for people who are in the more advanced stages of spiritual development. Church activities have the *greatest* influence in the *early* stages of
spiritual growth, but things like personal spiritual practices, including
prayer and Bible reading, have far more influence later in the spiritual
journey.

* **Lots of apathetic nonbelievers who attend church are unlikely to
ever accept Christ.** There are a significant number of people who have
not yet made a commitment to Christ but have still attended church
for more than five years. These people aren't actively exploring faith. In
fact, the longer they've attended church, the more likely they are to say
they are content with the pace of their spiritual growth, or to say they
are "stalled." This means that the longer they attend church without
making a commitment to Christ, the less likely they are to ever accept
Jesus as their Lord and Savior.

* **Even the most devoted Christians fall far short of living out the
mandates of Christ.** Mature believers serve the church, help the underresourced, evangelize, and tithe more than other Christians. However,
high percentages of them are still surprisingly inactive. For example,
even though most (almost 80 percent) very strongly agree that they
"love God more than anything," one-third do not serve the church and
50 percent do not serve the underresourced on a monthly basis. In the
past year, 60 percent had fewer than six spiritual conversations with
nonbelievers and 80 percent invited fewer than six people to church.
Forty percent do not tithe.

* **Nothing has a greater impact on spiritual growth than reflection
on Scripture.** If churches could do only one thing to help people at all
levels of spiritual maturity grow in their relationship with Christ, their
choice is clear. They would inspire, encourage, and equip their people to
read the Bible—specifically, to reflect on Scripture for meaning in their
lives. The numbers say most churches are missing the mark—because
only one out of five congregants reflects on Scripture every day.

* **Spiritually stalled or dissatisfied people account for one out of four
church congregants.** People who are stalled spiritually and/or dissatisfied with how the church is helping them grow *exist in all churches*. On
average, 13 percent of all congregants select the word *stalled* to describe
their pace of spiritual growth; 18 percent of those surveyed described

themselves as "dissatisfied"—in some churches the number was as high as 50 percent.

✳ **There is no "killer app" for spiritual growth.** While we did identify a number of churches that are spiritual powerhouses, we found no single "save the day" program that guarantees discipleship success. However, in the top REVEAL churches, we did find four best practices, which we'll discuss in part 3.

✳ **Leadership matters.** The leaders of the more highly successful churches who participated in the REVEAL survey have diverse personalities and styles—from quiet and reserved to self-assured and commanding. But they share one key attribute: an unrelenting, uncompromising focus and drive to help grow people into disciples of Christ. This matters—big time—because the strategies and programs they pursue are not radically different from those found in most churches. It's their hearts—consumed by Christ—that make the difference.

These eight discoveries set the stage for the spiritual-growth framework detailed in this book—a framework based on a new way to think about doing church and a new set of tools to help church leaders answer the question, "What should we be doing to help our people grow spiritually?"

REVEAL has helped us answer that question for Willow Creek, and we believe it will help you with your church as well. Just to be clear, what you will see in this book is not just one church's recommendations or opinions but a compilation of relevant, fact-based information. As my coauthor, Cally Parkinson, likes to tell people who question one finding or another from the research: "Listen, we did not make any of this stuff up!"

Such assurance is occasionally necessary, because many REVEAL discoveries take some getting used to. They don't always align with what we thought we knew. In short, the new lens we have talked about requires that we also use new eyes. Or at least old eyes, opened slightly wider.

A Quick Take on *Move*

In the pages ahead you will find a great deal for those eyes to take in—all arranged in a three-part progression of what this new, more relevant spiritual-growth framework looks like (part 1), how that framework best facilitates spiritual growth (part 2), and how pastors and church leaders can most effectively serve their congregants and Christ's church (part 3).

Part 1: The Spiritual Continuum

REVEAL identifies a spiritual continuum that includes four segments of church attenders (chart 1-2):

Exploring Christ: The people in this segment have a basic belief in God, but they are unsure about Christ and his role in their lives.

Growing in Christ: The people in this segment have a personal relationship with Christ. They've made a commitment to trust him with their souls' salvation and for eternity, but they are just beginning to learn what it means and what it takes to develop a relationship with him.

Close to Christ: The people in this segment depend on Christ every day. They see Christ as someone who assists them in life. On a daily basis, they turn to him for help and guidance for the issues they face.

Christ-Centered: The people in this segment would identify their relationship with Christ as the most important relationship in their entire lives.

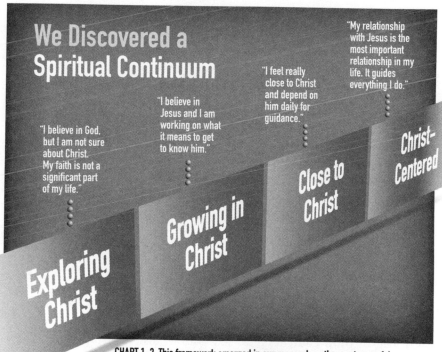

CHART 1-2: This framework emerged in our research as the most powerful predictive description of how people grow spiritually. This means that the strength of people's spiritual beliefs and their level of engagement with spiritual activities depend on (or can be predicted by) how they describe their relationship with Christ.

They see their lives as fully surrendered to Jesus and his agenda, subordinating everything to his will and his desires.

You will hear directly from people in each of these segments as they share their stories with you. And we imagine that, as you read about the segments along this spiritual continuum, names and faces within your own congregation may come to mind.

Part 2: Spiritual Movement

As people grow spiritually, they move from one segment to the next on the spiritual continuum. In part 2, we take a closer look at three movements of spiritual growth (chart 1-3):

Movement 1: *From Exploring Christ to Growing in Christ.* Movement 1 is all about Christian basics. Developing a firm foundation of spiritual beliefs and attitudes is critical during this trust-building phase. The impact of church activities on spiritual growth is most significant in this movement.

Movement 2: *From Growing in Christ to Close to Christ.* In Movement 2 people decide that their relationship with Jesus is *personal* to them. It hinges on developing a routine of personal spiritual practices that make space and time for a growing intimacy with Christ.

Movement 3: *From Close to Christ to Christ-Centered.* In Movement 3 believers replace secular self-centeredness with Christlike self-sacrifice. They pour out their increasing love for Jesus through spiritual outreach activities, especially evangelism.

Importantly, each of these movements is most effectively fostered through unique aspects of what the church has to offer—an "aha" for most of us, who have long believed that weekend services, small groups, and serving opportunities carried with them much the same potential impact for just about everyone in our congregations. But the reality is that people in different segments have different spiritual needs, and we'll take an in-depth look at how to meet the needs in each of the segments.

Part 3: Spiritual Leadership

Part 3 showcases those results in action. Once five hundred congregations had taken the REVEAL survey (we hit that mark in the fall of 2007), we could easily identify those churches most successful at fostering spiritual maturity. We performed a simple mathematical process, identifying what would become known as the "top-5 percent" churches. We wondered what those twenty-five

CHART 1–3: People progress across the spiritual continuum in three movements: Movement 1, early spiritual growth; Movement 2, intermediate spiritual growth; Movement 3; advanced spiritual growth.

congregations were doing. Why were their results so exceptional? And, most importantly, what could the rest of us learn from their leaders?

A lot, as it turns out.

Rather than being concept driven, the information these pastors and leaders shared is vitality driven. It works. And—best of all—it is simple and reproducible, whether you lead a church with great resources or one that scrapes by from week to week. These are their four best practices and one overarching principle of leadership, which we'll unpack in practical detail in part 3 (chart 1-4):

Practice 1: They get people moving. Instead of offering up a wide-ranging menu of ministry opportunities to newcomers, best-practice churches promote and provide a high-impact, nonnegotiable pathway of focused first steps—a pathway designed specifically to jumpstart a spiritual experience that gets people moving toward a Christ-centered life.

Practice 2: They embed the Bible in everything. At best-practice churches, the Bible goes well beyond its role as the foundation for teaching and life instruction. These churches *breathe* Scripture. Every encounter and

Four Best Practices Revolve around **Christ-Centered Leadership**

① GET PEOPLE MOVING

② EMBED THE BIBLE

③ CREATE OWNERSHIP

④ PASTOR THE COMMUNITY

LEADERSHIP TEAM

Regardless of size, denomination, or socioeconomic environment, churches that inspire spiritual growth most effectively demonstrate four best practices: (1) they get people moving on a spiritual pathway; (2) they embed the Bible in everything they do; (3) they create a church culture of ownership; and (4) they pastor their local communities. These four practices are derived from and depend on the same central source, which is Christ-Centered leadership.

experience within the church begins with the question, "What does the Bible have to say about that?" And church leaders model living life according to the answers to that question.

Practice 3: They create ownership. Best-practice congregants don't just *belong* to their church; they believe they *are* the church. They embrace its discipleship values as part of their identity. Best-practice churches inspire and hold people accountable for *changing their behavior*—for becoming more Christlike in their everyday lives as a reflection of their faith.

Practice 4: They pastor their local community. Best-practice churches don't simply *serve* their community. They act as its shepherd, becoming deeply involved in community issues and frequently serving in influential positions with local civic organizations. They often partner with nonprofits and other churches to secure whatever resources are necessary to address the most pressing local concerns.

In addition to these four practices, we identified one overarching leadership principle that emerged in our interaction with the senior pastors of these top-5 percent churches. These churches are led by individuals *consumed* with making disciples. Absolutely consumed. Making disciples of Christ was unquestionably their most important aspiration and the deepest desire of their hearts. And that characteristic fueled all four of the practices you will learn more about.

I don't know if you've ever had those nagging doubts that I had: Do I really know what's going on in the hearts and souls of my people? Is all this activity and programming moving them closer to God, or are we all just spinning our wheels? The REVEAL survey told us the truth about how our people experienced church, and some of what they told us wasn't pretty. But it also showed us how to do a better job of helping people grow spiritually, which, after all, is why all of us—you and me—do what we do. Now in *Move*, we'd like to share with you what we learned so that you can have greater confidence that what you are doing will make a difference in the lives of *your* people.

A few Sundays ago I sat in our auditorium watching people take their seats. This time the gnawing feelings of doubt about our ministries' effectiveness had been replaced with a settled peace. We might not be doing everything right, but I knew we were making a real difference in these folks' lives. Not because we came up with yet another creative program, but because we were willing to face, and act, on the truth: increased church activity does not lead to spiritual growth.

What does?

You might be surprised.

The Simplicity of Spiritual Growth

Spiritual growth is not linear or predict-able. It is a complex process as unique as each individual, and it progresses at a pace determined by each person's circumstances and the activity of the Holy Spirit. This observation, while true, can make spiritual growth feel very complicated – difficult to understand, hard to resource and support, impossible to measure. The findings in *Move* offer church leaders the encouragement that, while spiritual growth is complex, there appears to be a simplicity in its general progression that may help us to think about it differently, to resource it better, and to support it more productively.

The findings featured in *Move* suggest, in general, that spiritual growth progresses across a continuum of four segments, moving from those who are Exploring Christ to those who are Christ-Centered. Three movements of increasing spiritual maturity define this progression, and various spiritual catalysts, ranging from organized church activities to personal spiritual practices, influence how people advance from one segment to the next (chart 1-5).

Move unpacks these findings in the aggregate; it is not intended to describe how spiritual growth occurs at an individual level. As noted, that process is unique for each person and unlikely to follow a predictable path.

However, for church leaders who influence the spiritual growth of hundreds or thousands of people, we believe it is possible to think of spiritual growth in simpler terms. That's because, while each person's spiritual path is distinct, when we pool together thousands of individual surveys describing spiritual experiences, a general pattern emerges that transcends individual results.

This is similar to the progression of an entering freshman class to eventual graduation. The paths of individual students will be unique – some may transfer or drop out, others may change their major fields of study more than once. But, in general, the class will progress as a group through similar but varied learning experiences and graduate within a predictable time frame. The individual pathways are distinct and difficult to forecast, but the progression of the group overall is more dependable, and consequently, easier to predict.

So while the process of spiritual growth is unique for each person and will always have an enormous Spirit-led component, the simplicity of the findings described in *Move* offer insights and strategies church leaders can act on with a high level of confidence that their decisions will make a difference in the lives of those they serve.

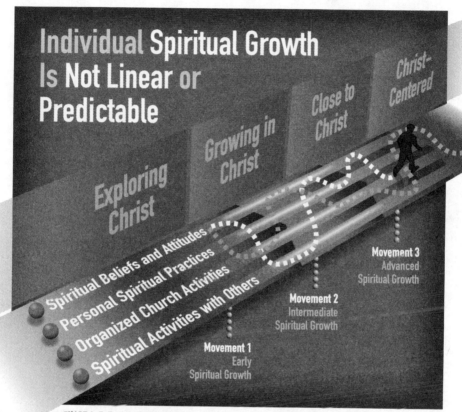

CHART 1-5: Each individual follows a unique spiritual growth pathway.

PART 1

The Spiritual Continuum

CHAPTER 2

Exploring Christ: Getting to Know Those Who Are Searching for God

While driving through their small town on a Saturday afternoon, Marcia and her husband Rick passed by a local church where they had recently attended a wedding. This prompted Rick, a self-described agnostic, to turn to his wife and ask, "Would you be surprised if I told you I wanted to go to church tomorrow?"

Marcia took her husband's question in stride. She wasn't all that surprised at his sudden interest in the church. After all, Rick had recently lost his job, a position he had held for twenty-four years. "There are no atheists in fox-holes—and you are in a foxhole right now," she told him. She knew that Rick was fighting for his future. He was looking for answers—and for something that would make sense of the uncertainty he now felt.

Marcia and Rick not only went to church the next day, but now, two years later, they attend weekend and midweek services regularly. They think highly of their pastor and often take advantage of the different classes the church offers on faith-related questions and topics. Marcia recently joined a small group, one filled with women who encourage her as she struggles to believe "as devoutly as I think one who would really call herself a Christian would believe."

Marcia considers herself an active explorer, someone who is working to resolve her questions. But she is not yet ready to fully accept all that Christ taught. "It's not that I don't believe in Jesus," she says, "but I struggle with believing that there's only one path to God. I wonder about things like, if God is all-forgiving, then why won't you go to heaven if you don't believe in Christ? And how could a loving God require Jesus to suffer and die on a cross?"

Still, even though her questions create barriers to her accepting Christ—barriers she has thus far been unable to overcome—Marcia isn't about to give up the quest. For now, attending church fills an important need in her life. "It refocuses me," she explains. "It gets me back on track." She adds that she is "really blessed" to have relationships with so many committed Christians who help her along the way. "I guess God has put me where I belong."

A Profile of Exploring Christ: On the Spiritual Fringe

When you hear the word *explore*, what comes to mind? You might think of a person off discovering new lands, or sailing in uncharted waters—Columbus navigating his three small ships toward San Salvador, for instance, or astronauts blasting off from earth to have a firsthand look at outer space. The word can also suggest investigating or studying something very carefully. We believe "exploring" is a good way of describing those who are in the earliest phase of learning what it means to become a follower of Jesus Christ. They are investigating and studying Christ, and asking questions about the Christian faith.

Those who are Exploring Christ are still on the perimeter of faith, evaluating Christianity's core beliefs and checking out the community of people who embrace those beliefs—but they themselves remain unwilling or unready to fully join in. In general, those within this segment are searching for a *reason* to believe fully in God's existence and Christ's redemptive promise. But their doubts block their progress and prevent them from making meaningful spiritual connections—either with God or with those who believe in him.

Unlike the other segments of a typical congregation, the Exploring Christ segment is composed of two distinct groups of people—those who are *active* explorers and those who are *passive* attenders. The first group (the active explorers) includes those individuals like Marcia who are genuinely seeking to resolve their doubts about the reality and character of Jesus. These are the people we most commonly associate with the descriptor "Exploring Christ." But there is also a second group of people in this segment who are not really "seeking" at all. These are churchgoers who seem content with a shallow spiritual life marked by minimal faith-based beliefs, relationships, and activities. They may have a nominal faith, but they fail to show any signs of active growth. The combination of these two kinds of "explorers" makes the Exploring Christ segment a mixed bag of nonbelievers. While many are actively searching for answers to their spiritual questions, others attend church mostly out of habit or for reasons of social acceptance — and they demonstrate little or no interest in pursuing a relationship with Christ.

The two groups share a common interest, however, in what the church and its leaders might do for them. We learned this after asking everyone taking the survey, including those who would later be identified as members of the Exploring Christ segment, to rank the importance of various things they want their church to deliver for them. When doing so, we gave them six responses to choose from:

"This is critically important."

"This is very important, but not critical."

"This is important."

"This is somewhat important."

"This is somewhat unimportant."

"This is unimportant."

In analyzing the responses, we looked at the things that were designated "critically important" and "very important." Through these combined responses, those in the Exploring Christ segment identified five main things they want from their church and its leaders (chart 2-1).

Two-thirds of the Exploring Christ segment agreed that these areas of assistance are what they hope their church leaders will provide for them. And with only a 2 percent spread in the five responses, we can consider each of them to be of equal importance from the Explorers' point of view.

Those who are in the Exploring Christ segment are clearly interested in Jesus, and they want to understand how they can have a relationship with him. We need to let them know how that works, and we shouldn't shy away from being direct. When it comes to the worship experience they crave, we need to help them understand that worship is not a spectator activity, but something in which they may fully and freely engage. And when it comes to helping them better understand the Bible, we need to teach from Scripture while encouraging them to read it for themselves. We must never back away from boldly teaching straight from the text, as they want and need exactly that.

Notice too that they want to belong. What we have learned is that this desire to belong does not automatically translate into a desire to "help me get connected into a small group or a serving opportunity." Instead, those in this segment want to feel welcomed and they want to know that the church has a place for them — even if they are not so sure about their faith. Pastors can foster this sense of community by acknowledging that there are Explorers in the room during services and events, saying things like, "For those of you just exploring issues of faith ..." Phrases like this help folks know that the church is

The Top Five Things the Exploring Christ Segment Wants from You and Your Church

BENEFITS PROVIDED BY THE CHURCH	Percentage who find the benefit critical or very important
1. Help in developing a personal relationship with Christ	**68%**
2. Compelling worship experiences	**68%**
3. A feeling of belonging	**68%**
4. Help in understanding the Bible in greater depth	**67%**
5. Church leaders who model and consistently reinforce how to grow spiritually	**66%**

CHART 2-1: Based on their rating of nineteen church attributes, these are the five most important factors the Exploring Christ segment wants from the church. Three statements tie as the most important attribute, with 68 percent saying they are critically or very important: (1) help me in developing a personal relationship with Christ; (2) compelling worship services; and (3) a feeling of belonging.

for them too. They sense that they are welcome, and that this is exactly where they belong.

While Marcia, whom you met at the beginning of this chapter, has made progress getting connected at her church, Frank, another active Explorer, is still making his way toward that goal. A fifty-year-old small business owner whose family regularly attends a mainline denominational church, Frank tells us that the thing he most wants from his church is a sense that he belongs. Frank shared with us that his first attempt at small-group involvement was less than satisfactory, and that even the weekend services occasionally present some challenges for him. "People like me who are exploring Christianity don't always have that much in common with the folks who are active in the church, because they are usually several steps ahead of us," he explains. "There are some people who are very good at bringing us in and there are others who are off-putting because we are not where they are. But it's not because we don't *want* to be there, it's just because we're *not* there."

Those who are Exploring Christ are interested in growing, and they are looking to the leaders of the church to show them the way. They are watching the lives of Christian leaders and wondering if they can really believe what they hear preached. To help them sense that pastors are real and relatable, leaders and teachers can share stories from their past, from times earlier in their relationship with Christ. It helps those who are Exploring Christ to hear what it's like when faith started to become important—and to hear leaders talk about their own process of discovery. They are especially interested in knowing if there was a specific time or moment when it "clicked." What triggered that decision? And what happened next?

In considering ways to communicate with people in this initial stage of spiritual growth, it is helpful to keep in mind the Exploring Christ segment's three unique characteristics:

1. They Attend Church Regularly, But Have No Personal Relationship with Christ

It shouldn't surprise us that people who are sincerely trying to determine whether Christianity is truth or fiction also tend to be regular church attenders. Certainly, there are books to read, Christian friends to talk with, and even neighborhood Bible studies to join. But when people want answers to their questions—when they want to understand who Jesus is and what it means to follow him—they turn to the most obvious and direct source of information, the local church. For those who are merely content with showing up each weekend, the motive for attending church is somewhat less clear. Some attend because they want their children to grow up having the "church experience." Others enjoy the music or the feeling of belonging, or they like being part of an organization that is doing some good in their community.

No matter what their motivation might be for attending church, those who are part of the Exploring Christ segment frequently report that they believe in God, but *they are not in a personal relationship with Jesus.* "As a young man, I would not have said I believed in a supreme being," Frank says of his own progress, "but now I am to the point where I do believe in God; I believe in something greater than us. But being a Christ-follower? I'm having trouble with following Jesus as God incarnate. That's still a hard concept for me. I'm not all the way there." It is this lack of a personal relationship with Christ, in fact, that gives identity to this segment and makes them distinct from the other segments on the spiritual continuum.

Let's be clear. Believing in God versus having a personal relationship with Jesus is an important distinction. The vast majority of the people in this segment—74 percent—strongly agree that the God of the Bible is the one true God.[1] Almost one-third of them say that they love God very much (chart 2-2).

---

[1] "The Trinity" is our shorthand for referring to people's agreement with this statement: "I believe the God of the Bible is the one true God—Father, Son, and Holy Spirit."

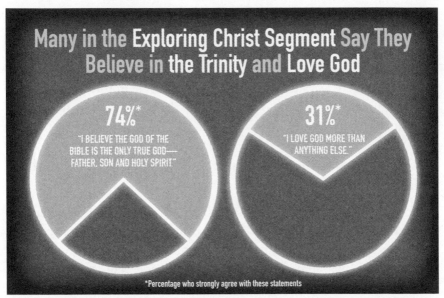

CHART 2-2: Most (74 percent) of the Exploring Christ segment strongly agree with a statement reflecting belief in the Trinity and 31 percent strongly agree that they love God.

Although many of them say that Jesus is not important to their lives, many would also say—and, in fact, believe—that they are Christians. While it may seem reasonable to assume that churches are quite clear about defining Christianity as the practice of believing in and following Jesus, the presence of thousands of people like this in congregations everywhere suggests that this very basic premise is not being effectively communicated.

2. Their Pace of Spiritual Growth Is Sluggish

The sluggish pace of spiritual growth in this segment might seem surprising. We might expect that the spiritual curiosity of those Exploring Christ would at least spur a moderate rate of growth. But the opposite is true (chart 2-3). In fact, people who are Exploring Christ report the slowest rate of spiritual growth of all the segments on the spiritual continuum! Only 18 percent say they are growing rapidly or at a moderate pace compared with 58 percent of the Christ-Centered segment, which represents the most mature believers. If you think about the various segments of the spiritual continuum as cars on a highway, with the percentages marking their growth rates as spiritual speedometers, you could say that the Exploring Christ segment is going eighteen miles an hour. By contrast, the Christ-Centered segment is clipping along at fifty-eight miles

The Pace of Spiritual Growth Accelerates across the Spiritual Continuum

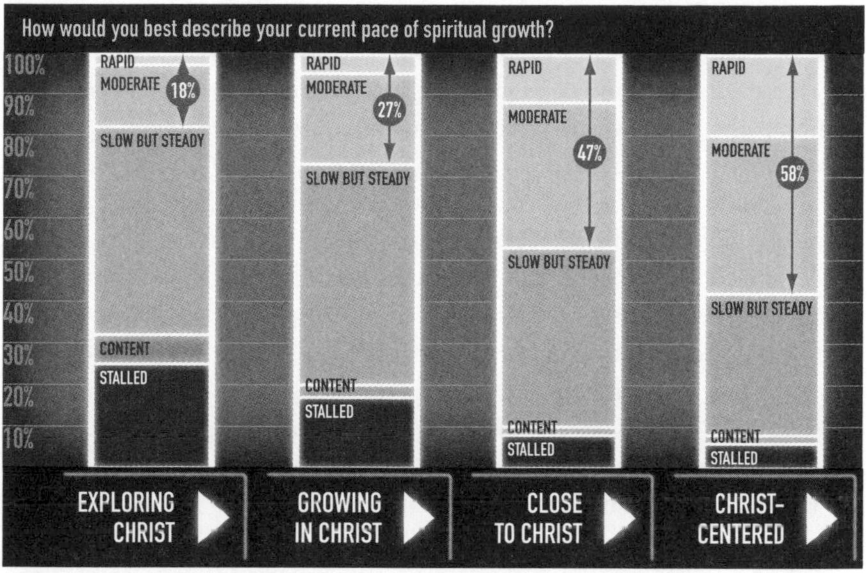

How would you best describe your current pace of spiritual growth?

CHART 2-3: As people advance in spiritual maturity—from Exploring Christ to Christ-Centered—increasing percentages of congregants describe their pace of spiritual growth as either rapid or moderate.

per hour. At these speeds, it takes a long time before those in the Exploring Christ segment cross any significant spiritual mile markers.

3. The Longer They Attend Church, the Less Likely They Are to Become Christ-followers

Just let this sink in for a moment: the *longer* a person Exploring Christ attends a church, the *less* likely they are to follow Christ. Logically, we would assume that the longer someone is exposed to the church, the more likely they will be to eventually cross that line of faith. But this is a great reminder that we aren't simply dealing with predictable human behavior here. Coming to faith in Christ isn't just a matter of convincing people of the truth. It's a work of God's Spirit.

Still, the research and the data are helpful in identifying and better understanding *why* people fail to take the steps necessary to come to faith in Christ. Our research suggests that people in this segment who have attended church for *more than five years* are far more likely than those who have attended church for less than five years to say they are spiritually stalled or content with their spiritual growth (chart 2-4). For them, attending weekend services is more akin to spinning tires on icy roads than actually moving toward a destination.

The diminishing pace of their growth suggests that the likelihood of ever making a decision for Christ *decreases* the longer they attend church.

How can this be? How can people who attend church regularly—where they presumably hear messages about Christ's redemptive promise—be so spiritually apathetic? How can Explorers like Marcia, whose small group is populated with more mature believers, continue to cling to their own skepticism?

We believe that the very nature of the decision they face contributes to their lackadaisical spiritual pace. For them, the decision to accept Christ has no deadline. Unlike the need to vote on Election Day or the redemption of a coupon before its expiration date, long-term members of this segment have often passed by previous opportunities to accept Christ, and they no longer sense any urgency in their quest. The deadline they have set for themselves is indeterminate and vague. Time is not a factor. Many feel like they have all the time in the world to investigate, debate, and ponder theological truths.

But our research suggests that time *is* a factor. Like so many decisions in life, procrastination tends to breed passivity. The longer those who are Explor-

The Longer Those Who Are Exploring Christ Have Attended Church, the Slower Their Spiritual Growth

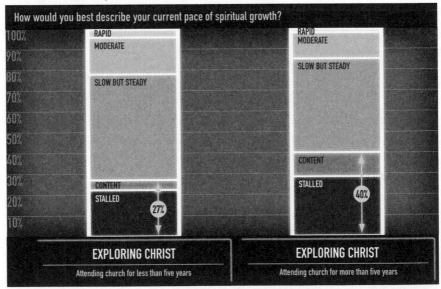

CHART 2-4: In the Exploring Christ segment, those who have attended church for more than five years are much more likely to describe their spiritual growth as stalled (or say they are content with their pace of growth) than those who have attended less than five years. Forty percent of the longer-tenured Exploring Christ churchgoers fall in the stalled or content categories compared with 27 percent of those who are Exploring Christ but have attended church for less than five years.

ing defer their decision to accept Christ, the less likely it is that they will ever make that decision. Those who have attended church for less than five years are often still testing the waters of Christianity. But the majority of those who have attended a church for more than five years—and have not made a decision to follow Christ—are often satisfied with a life marked by limited spiritual momentum. Meanwhile, their spiritual indifference reflects the single most defining characteristic for *everyone* in this segment—a lack of belief in the core claims of Christianity.

There are Explorers in every church who have been hanging around for a very long time. And certainly, we would rather have them attending church instead of staying home. But this fact—that the longer they attend (beyond five years), the less likely it is that they will make a decision to accept Christ—disturbs us greatly. Clearly, we have to challenge our long-standing assumptions and increase our sense of urgency.

Our work as leaders in the church is to help catalyze spiritual movement. If our people are not moving forward, it is up to us to rock their boats—to inspire them to stay open and available to God with meaningful challenges and defined next steps. Might such challenges prompt some of your hangers-on to decide they'd prefer to attend a church more accepting of their complacency? Well, that's not the worst thing that could happen. The *worst* thing would be to let your Explorers continue, year after year, to ignore their urgent need for Christ.

Love of God: A Struggle with Beliefs

There is no more important step in our spiritual journey than choosing to believe that God is real and that his Son Jesus Christ came to earth to give us eternal life. Not only are these beliefs the most crucial, they are among the most difficult for those who are Exploring Christ to accept. In fact, it is the intellectual wrestling with these bedrock beliefs of the Christian faith that best defines the Exploring Christ segment's spiritual experience. Not surprisingly, those who are part of this segment dramatically trail the more mature segments on each of the core Christian beliefs as well as their own sense of "love of God" (chart 2-5).

While 74 percent of Explorers are confident that "the God of the Bible is the one true God," less than half that number (36 percent) believe "nothing I do or have done can earn my salvation." Those in the Exploring Christ segment recognize that God exists. But they are not ready to accept Christ as the path to salvation, nor are they ready to accept the divine authority of the Bible. Even the concept of a "personal" God eludes them.

Sometimes, these beliefs remain out of reach despite a good deal of authentic exploration. Frank, for example, can't get beyond his doubts about the historical details of the Gospel accounts. "For me, it's not so much about what Jesus said," he explains. "It's my concern that maybe the disciples didn't get it exactly right, and maybe if Jesus had written it himself, it might have been written differently. The issue I have is more about believing Scripture word for word."

This is not to suggest that such sticking points will prevail. In the next chapter, you'll meet several individuals who have just put such concerns behind them. And if we are honest, some of the doubts and concerns expressed by those who are Exploring Christ are similar to doubts and questions even more mature followers of Christ might have from time to time. Who among us is unable to relate to the doubts expressed by Jesus' own disciple, Thomas, the classic Exploring Christ character? Even though Thomas had followed Jesus and been an eyewitness to Christ's earthly ministry, he was openly skeptical when the other disciples

Love of God and Agreement with Core Christian Beliefs Are Much Lower for Those Who are Exploring Christ

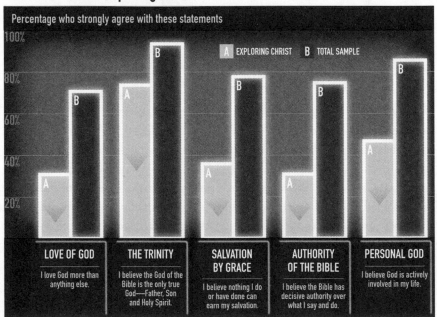

CHART 2-5: For those who are Exploring Christ, willingness to say that they love God and agree with core Christian beliefs is dramatically lower compared with the total sample.

claimed to have seen Jesus after his crucifixion. "Unless I see the nail marks in his hands and put my finger where the nails were, and put my hand into his side," he said, "I will not believe it" (John 20:25).

The data uncovered in the REVEAL survey verifies that those who are Exploring Christ continue to echo his cry. Though we might be tempted to think that twenty-first-century Explorers aren't nearly as concerned about having such proof, the truth is that there are still people who want to be convinced. "Prove it! Show me the evidence! I'll believe it when I see it!" Just like Thomas, they want to meet Jesus face-to-face, to have their doubts erased by an encounter with Christ.

The good news in all of this is that those who are Exploring are taking tentative steps toward the next-best thing. They are trying out a variety of spiritual practices, seeking to encounter Christ in their daily life experience. More than half pray frequently for guidance, and more than one out of five (21 percent) reflect on the meaning of Scripture for their lives at least several times a week. Not surprisingly, these numbers are much lower than the numbers for the church at large (which are 87 percent for prayer and 64 percent for reflection on Scripture). This makes sense when you consider that those who are Exploring Christ are still wrestling intellectually with God's presence in their lives.

No matter how much sense it may make, however, it is still an ever-present source of concern for those of us who love these individuals. For me (Cally), many of my friends and family members fall in the Exploring Christ segment. I have children, siblings, nieces, nephews—even my husband—who are still hanging around the fringes of Christianity. My husband is a structural engineer who designs oil refineries and frequently travels to places like Saudi Arabia, China, and India. He tells me, "I've looked into the eyes of the millions of people who have to be wrong for you to be right." If I ask him, he'll go to church. But like others in this segment, he seems to think he has all the time in the world to figure out whether or not Christianity is truth or fiction.

Whenever I encounter intellectually gifted, highly competent, self-assured people like this, I try to employ what I like to call the hummingbird strategy. For years, to no avail, I tried to attract hummingbirds to my backyard. Then I discovered a secret: to attract hummingbirds, you must place hummingbird feeders out well in advance of their migration. So with early spring's snow still on the ground, I am out positioning feeders all over my yard. For weeks I faithfully replenish the sugar water, without ever seeing a hummingbird. Then—when the birds finally migrate and are at their hungriest—my feeders are ready, refreshed, and waiting for them.

That's the type of approach I believe works best for those who are Exploring Christ. When our lives and our churches become like spiritual hummingbird feeders, they will naturally overflow with evidence of God's goodness, grace, and active presence in our world. And people will see that, and if they are hungry, they will come. But if they aren't hungry for it, they won't come. We must remember that we will never win a person to Christ through an intellectual tug-of-war. But God has a way of transforming people and changing their minds. So when he grabs their attention—and when those who are Exploring become truly hungry for his truth—we need to make sure our feeders of faith are refreshed and waiting.

Love of Others: Not Interested

While the weekend service is likely the most important spiritual influence in the lives of those who are Exploring Christ, only one-third believe that it is necessary to be a member of a local church to grow as a Christian. So, despite regular church attendance, many are relatively uninterested in forming relationships with people who attend the church. This disinterest in joining a faith community shows up in their low participation in small groups and ministry serving. Only 25 percent are involved in community-building church activities like these, compared with 50 percent of all other church attenders. In many cases, for those who are Exploring Christ, the role of the church is merely to provide them with one hour of spiritual content on Sunday that won't significantly impact the secular pathway they pursue the rest of the week (chart 2-6).

The lack of interest this segment shows in forming church-based relationships is reinforced by a relatively low love for others. Less than 30 percent of people in this group strongly agree that they have "tremendous love for people I know and those I don't know." This response, like their responses about love of God, is much lower than that of other segments and may explain why they are relatively uninvolved in church activities or community outreach. Only one out of five people in the Exploring Christ segment serves those in need on a monthly basis, and a similarly low percentage have invited three or more people to church in the past year. These low levels of faith in action mirror the minimal interest this group has in church-based activities and relationships. There are few signs of spiritual momentum in their lives.

It's difficult for us to say with certainty what the specific role of the church should be for those in the Exploring Christ segment. These are individuals

Love of Others and Spiritual Activities with Others Are Much Lower for Those Who Are Exploring Christ

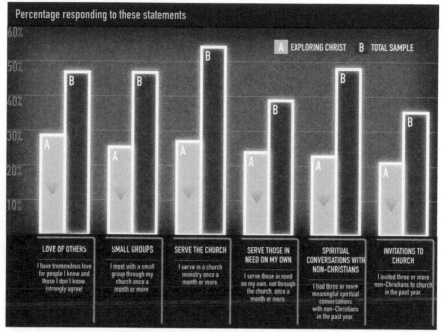

CHART 2-6: For those who are Exploring Christ, willingness to agree that they love others and their participation in spiritual activities that involve others — including serving those in need and evangelism — are much lower compared with the total sample. Their very low participation in church-related activities — small groups and serving — is particularly noteworthy.

who are obviously attending for some reason, but they feel tentative about their involvement — and ambivalent about what they want to do next.

Those of us who serve as leaders in the church may also feel some ambivalence about this segment. We know it is important to give people the space to make their own decisions — a process that may take a different amount of time for each individual. On the other hand, however, we should keep in mind the reality that if people wait too long, they tend to grow apathetic and are less likely to ever accept Christ.

This tension necessitates a delicate balancing act. We need to let those who are Exploring Christ know they are welcome and simultaneously help them see the relevance and urgency of choosing to put their faith in Christ. So at the same time we give them opportunities to explore, we must also give them reasons to believe.

As we work toward this objective, we need to recognize that those in the Exploring Christ segment are often more cautious than curious—characterized less by open-minded inquisitiveness than by doubt, or even fear. Their doubt is often obvious as they struggle with questions about this unseen God and his mysterious promises based on an ancient text that most of them find dense and intimidating.

But their reluctance to enter into a personal relationship with Christ may also be based on fear. While heaven may celebrate when they decide to give their lives to Jesus, there is typically little applause beyond the walls of the church. The skeptical, secular world is a daunting and demanding place, and choosing to follow Christ is never easy. That's why we tend to see so many of those in this segment—like Marcia and Frank—sitting on the fringes of faith for years, some even for a lifetime.

But what if Marcia and Frank overcame their doubts and fears? What if God were to break through and open their eyes to the truth about Jesus? Is it all smooth sailing after that? Hardly. While there is great joy in our lives as Christ-followers, there are still pitfalls and obstacles as well. We're just getting started on our journey across the spiritual continuum. The findings from the REVEAL survey shine a light on both the highs and lows in our lives as believers. Let's find out now what insights that light reveals about the hearts and lives of those who are newest to the faith—the Growing in Christ segment.

A Person Who Is Exploring Christ Is . . .

—On the spiritual fringe

—Investigating but undecided about the claims of Christianity

—Struggling mostly with belief in Christ, not with belief in God

—Attending but not involved in church

—Possibly a long-tenured churchgoer

Stalled in the Rust Belt: A Church That Is Exploring Christ

This church is a hundred years old, tucked away in rural southeastern Pennsylvania. The 350 people in its congregation are largely blue collar, middle age or older, and white. Most have attended the church for more than ten years, yet their REVEAL survey shows that 20 percent of the congregation are still Exploring Christ. Another 44 percent are in the next segment on the spiritual continuum, Growing in Christ. Based on these numbers, you'd think that every Sunday the pastor of this church might talk mostly to people who are actively wrestling with the deep questions about Christianity or charged up about growing their newfound faith. Right?

Wrong. This congregation is spiritually dormant, and the roots of their indifference run deep. Evidence of their spiritual lethargy is found in their core Christian beliefs, which are very weak, and their personal spiritual practices, which are rare. The concept of a personal relationship with Christ, much less the thought of living a life surrendered to God's plan and purposes, is clearly not on their radar.

The pastor, to his credit, is trying to shake things up with more relevant, challenging messages and formats. But it's tough sledding. Dissatisfaction is high, at 29 percent, and many complain that they don't feel like they "belong," which means they are unsettled by the pastor's changes.

Unfortunately this church profile is not uncommon. One out of every five congregations we survey could find themselves within this description – long tenured, spiritually immature, and reticent to change. The pastors of these churches are not surprised by these facts. In many cases, their primary reason for taking the REVEAL survey was, in essence, to confirm their suspicions about their congregation's spiritual apathy.

But going after the truth when you suspect the news isn't good takes guts. How many Christian leaders have the same suspicions but don't want to rattle the spiritual complacency of their people? Many more, we fear, which suggests that the overall percentage of spiritually dormant churches could be much higher than one out of five. A very sobering possibility.

Leading Forward

The primary thing church leaders need to keep in mind about the Exploring Christ segment is that these people are choosing to attend church. They are not individuals far from God who are unwilling to explore issues of faith; rather, they want something from church that they have not found elsewhere in society. So, in many ways, these people are giving us their permission to influence them. Don't ever lose sight of this. They have, on their own, come to the church looking for something — and hoping that we'll deliver the something that they seek.

Not that it is all up to you, of course. As a leader, you are in a role to challenge those who are exploring to take an active role in their search. Assure them that those who seek find (Matthew 7:8), but that the journey requires them to be active participants, engaging their whole heart in the search. "You will seek me and find me when you seek me with all your heart" (Jeremiah 29:13).

Never allow people in this segment to feel comfortable about just showing up to church once a week to receive what you have to offer them. Let them know that passivity is not an option. Help them see that their active spiritual searching is something that can and should occur *throughout* the week.

In addition, help them see that the stakes are high by making it clear that one day they will have to account for their lives. Don't back off from discussing heaven and hell. At the same time, though, make sure they understand that a relationship with Christ is about far more than their eternity. Help them to see what a relationship with Christ can mean to their everyday lives right now — the increased peace, guidance, and basis for hope they will gain as they turn their lives over to Jesus. Again, these people gave you permission to speak into their lives, and our research indicates that they want you to challenge them and show them what steps they should be taking.

Along with your challenges, keep in mind that for those in the Exploring Christ segment, the thought of making a decision to follow Jesus can be fraught with fear. People struggle to believe in a faith that so much of the world sees as scientifically unproven and hard to swallow. They struggle with the risk of ridicule and loss of respect from colleagues, friends, and family outside of the church. In short, those who are Exploring Christ need and deserve our patience, empathy, love, and prayers — plus time to let the Holy Spirit work on their hearts and minds.

Never forget, though, that the priority you offer them may not be open-ended — that too much time can actually be a detriment to their spiritual progress. These folks need places to explore their faith — from classes and events they can attend, to groups where they can process issues further, to invitations to pose their thorniest questions to those with the knowledge to answer. But such support needs to be paired with a challenge. Whenever possible, let Explorers know they're on your radar screen. Inquire about their progress. Suggest specific Scripture that might best address their particular hesitations. Challenge them to read the Bible daily for a certain period of time — and then check in with them to see if they followed through. Read the Bible with them. And if you're afraid that doing these and other challenges might make them think you're a nuisance, get over it. Nothing is more powerful to an individual than your personal interest in his or her spiritual well-being. And nothing is more indicative of high-impact, discipling churches than a "go-for-broke" challenge factor.

CHAPTER 3

Growing in Christ: Getting to Know Those Who Are Open to God

Michael—thirty-two, married, and the father of a toddler daughter and preteen son—has an artistic bent. Trained as a classical trumpet player, he once dreamed of playing for a professional symphony orchestra. When that door closed in his life, he redirected his artistic passions into custom cabinet making.

As a child, Michael had little exposure to any sort of organized religion. He describes his parents as "new age hippies," and growing up, he thought of Jesus as "just a man in history, albeit a highly spiritual or enlightened one, but certainly not God in human form." He was, for the most part, dismissive of Christianity. "Rather than embracing Christ," he says, "I embraced the arguments against him."

Michael began seriously exploring Christianity when he began dating Jen, who—along with her son—regularly attended a church. Jen defended her faith to Michael, challenging him to find a church where he could talk with people and find answers to his questions. So that's exactly what he did. This process of seeking answers to his questions played a pivotal role, not only in his initial decision to accept Christ, but in setting a foundation that would later lead to a sincere commitment to spiritual growth.

Jeff is a single father of three children, all in their twenties, one of whom still lives at home. An experienced finance and marketing executive, Jeff is a no-nonsense, straightforward individual who describes himself as a "fighter," adding, "I have no compunction whatsoever about facing people who are doing the wrong thing and telling them about it." Raised as a Catholic, Jeff had a

Jesuit education all through graduate school, and says that he has long believed in God and has prayed for as long as he can remember. He remembers a trip to Montana at the age of thirteen or fourteen, "sitting on a ledge looking at mountains, listening to the wind in the trees, and thinking, 'There is absolutely no way there was some kind of big bang. This is absolutely *not* the result of some pure accident.'"

In recent years Jeff began to intentionally focus on Christ after he started attending a nondenominational church. "The whole conversation about Jesus," he says, "became much more prevalent and focused for me." Jeff began using his organizational skills to vigorously pursue his own spiritual growth—reading, praying, asking questions, and faithfully attending weekend services. A defining moment in that process came when he was baptized in Lake Michigan—an experience made even more meaningful by the attendance of many family members and close friends. One of his longtime friends, who also happens to be a Presbyterian minister, was there that day to celebrate the baptism. "Before we went into the water, you should have seen him on that beach," Jeff laughs. "He was just ebullient. And he kept repeating, 'Look what God is doing! Look what God is *doing!*'"

Michael and Jeff are two men whose spiritual progress places them squarely within the Growing in Christ segment. While they have different backgrounds, occupations, and family dynamics, they also have much in common. Both are dads, for instance, and both are very articulate when speaking of their newfound relationship with Christ, their dependence on and devotion to their church, and their vision of moving forward in their faith. And, although they do not know one another, both of them were baptized in that same lakeside service on an unseasonably cool Sunday afternoon in August.

In the lives of both men, we find evidence that God was moving them beyond the skepticism and questions that surrounded their exploration of faith into the decisions and practices that characterize authentic belief. Within those decisions and practices, many additional growth opportunities reside—opportunities both Jeff and Michael are now vigorously pursuing.

A Profile of Growing in Christ: Embracing the Church

Growth can be awkward. This is most apparent when we go through adolescence—a stage of life characterized by emotional volatility, physical changes, and social anxiety. Much like teenagers, those in the Growing in Christ segment experience significant intellectual and emotional changes as they adapt their life routines to their newfound beliefs. They may demonstrate adolescent-like insecurity, suggesting that at least some degree of struggle is involved as they absorb the real-life implications of their growing faith.

But despite the struggle — or maybe because of it — those in the Growing in Christ segment are indeed making progress, moving from an *acknowledgment* of God that was largely irrelevant to their daily lives to a *personal relationship* with him that directly impacts their everyday experiences. These newest-to-the-faith believers are typically huge fans of churches that foster the initial steps of spiritual growth. And churches can best respond to that high regard by better understanding the three unique characteristics of this segment.

1. They Represent the Largest Segment on the Spiritual Continuum

The Growing in Christ segment represents 38 percent of the people we surveyed, making it significantly larger than the next-largest segment, the 27 percent of people represented by those who are Close to Christ (chart 3-1).

CHART 3-1: The Growing in Christ segment represents 38 percent of the aggregate REVEAL database. On average, this is the largest segment in most congregations.

This means that in any church gathering, two out of every five congregants fall within the Growing in Christ segment. While there are wide variations in the spiritual profiles of the thousand churches we surveyed, this segment consistently represents more than 30 percent of the church population, often approaching up to 50 percent of those who attend a church.

What are we to make of this statistic? Well, we should begin by recognizing that since the Growing in Christ segment is the largest in a church, it naturally has a greater influence than others. Then the question arises, If church leaders receive the majority of their feedback from this large, but spiritually immature segment of the church, what impact does that have on their decisions? Could it sway them to allocate their resources in a way that serves the largest segment at the expense of others? What might it mean for the ministries of the church if the largest pool of candidates for all volunteer positions, including volunteer leaders, is made up of people who are relatively new to the faith?

These are just a few of the possible questions that church leaders must consider as they recognize that the largest segment in most churches is made up of immature believers in a growing relationship with Christ.

2. They Are the Most Active Participants in Virtually All Church Activities

Those who are Growing in Christ show a significant increase over the Exploring Christ segment in their participation in church activities, including weekend services, small groups, and serving. Although other, more mature believer segments (Close to Christ and Christ-Centered) participate in these activities at higher levels, the shift that occurs when people become part of the Growing in Christ segment is, by far, the most pronounced (see chart 3-2).

Note the increased percentage of those Growing in Christ who serve in a church ministry. The set of bars on the right side of the chart indicate that nearly 50 percent of the people in this segment serve the church at least once a month, almost double the Exploring Christ segment! As one of the less spiritually mature segments, we might expect those Growing in Christ to be a drain on, rather than a contributor to, the resources of the church. After all, aren't these the people who most need the church? Clearly, though, that is not what we find. Half of those in the Growing in Christ segment serve at least once a month — and since they make up the largest segment of people attending most churches, they also make up the highest percentage of church volunteers.

Participation in Church Activities Increases Significantly, Especially in Small Groups and Serving the Church

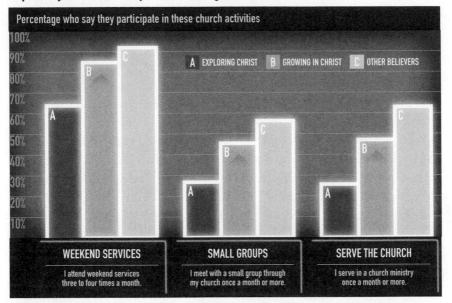

CHART 3-2: The arrows illustrate the rise in participation in church activities for the Growing in Christ segment compared with the Exploring Christ segment. Although other, more mature believers demonstrate still higher participation levels, the increases noted for the Growing in Christ segment are very significant.

3. Their Spiritual Growth Remains Slow But Steady

It can be tempting to assume that when people embrace faith in Christ, their spiritual growth takes off at warp speed. And certainly, we do see a significant shift in the beliefs and spiritual practices of this segment, as well as a high level of engagement with the church. As we have already seen, chart 3-2 depicts this high engagement—85 percent of people in this segment attend church three to four weekends each month, 47 percent participate in a small group at least once a month, and almost 50 percent serve at least once a month. With all of this activity, we might be tempted to assume that spiritual growth is taking place at a corresponding rate.

Unfortunately, we would be wrong. Those who are Growing in Christ actually display significant hesitation when they self-assess their spiritual pace. They are even more likely than those in the Exploring Christ segment to describe their spiritual growth as *slow but steady* (chart 3-3). This relatively modest appraisal of their spiritual growth may reflect a lack of confidence, a feeling of uncertainty. They may be a little intimidated by the journey

The Growing in Christ Segment Is Most Likely to Describe Their Spiritual Growth as "Slow but Steady"

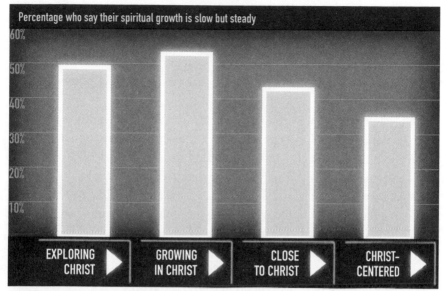

Percentage who say their spiritual growth is slow but steady

| EXPLORING CHRIST | GROWING IN CHRIST | CLOSE TO CHRIST | CHRIST-CENTERED |

CHART 3–3: More than 50 percent of the Growing in Christ segment describe their pace of spiritual growth as "slow but steady," which is the highest percentage for all the segments.

ahead, knowing that a relationship with Christ involves reordering one's entire world and that making these significant changes may require a good deal of time.

How Do They Grow?

What we found with the Growing in Christ segment illustrates one of REVEAL'S most significant findings: *participation in church activities does not necessarily drive spiritual growth.* Again and again, we tested our hypothesis, and this conclusion remained a constant. We repeatedly found that while these new believers are actively engaged in the church and its programs, they are similar to the adolescents we mentioned earlier—eager yet afraid; stepping forward hesitantly, then stepping back again to consider what they've heard and internalize what they've learned. The high level of participation in weekend services, small groups, and serving suggests that they count on the church to be their spiritual coach—the primary source of affirmation, encouragement, and guidance for them as they begin growing in Christ.

A good coach helps his athletes reach their ultimate objective by teaching them what they most need to know, training them, and then putting them into action. A coach provides challenges—and the opportunities and encouragement to take on those challenges. One of the most unexpected things we learned from REVEAL was that those who are Growing in Christ not only desire, but *expect* to be challenged. This is a far cry from previous (and erroneous) assumptions that "baby Christians" want to be coddled or treated with kid gloves.

Jeff, whom we met at the beginning of this chapter, reflects this expectation when he remembers, "I did have the sense, after my baptism, of 'Okay, what now?'" Jeff had felt real excitement building toward the day of his baptism; after achieving that goal, there was now a void to fill in his spiritual life.

Michael too found himself at a place in his spiritual journey where he was looking for direction. He wondered what would come next and cited the church's "Next Steps After Baptism" handout as instrumental in continuing his growth. One of the things on that list was the suggestion that he join a small group—and at the time of his baptism, the church happened to be launching a number of new small groups.

"It was a short-term commitment," he says, "so I went for it—and ended up with a good group of guys who worked well together." In fact, the men in Michael's group experienced such growth that they opted to continue to meet for several months past the date of their original commitment.

Jeff is involved in a small-group Bible study, one made up of men from a number of different churches. In addition, he feels challenged by what he hears in his church's weekend messages. For instance, though he has had a regular practice of praying at the end of each day, he now—following a powerful message focused on being in the presence of God—has made his prayers more of what he calls a "running conversation" with God.

Michael and Jeff are not alone in their desire and openness to direction from the church. In fact, nearly three-quarters of those in the Growing in Christ segment say it is "critical" or "very important" that church leaders *challenge* them to grow and take next steps (chart 3-4).

In other words, those who are Growing in Christ don't want us to beat around the bush. They expect that we will teach them the Bible, challenge them to examine their lives, and encourage them to make whatever changes are necessary to conform to the truth they are hearing. This should not surprise us. Remember that Jesus also challenged those who sought to follow him to count the cost, take up their cross, and give up everything they had (Luke 14:25–33). Talk about a tough challenge! Of course, as we challenge those

The Top Five Things the Growing Christ Segment Wants from You and Your Church

BENEFITS PROVIDED BY THE CHURCH	Percentage who find the benefit critical or very important
1. Help in developing a personal relationship with Christ	83%
2. Help in understanding the Bible in greater depth	82%
3. Church leaders who model and consistently reinforce how to grow spiritually	78%
4. Compelling worship experiences	75%
5. Challenge to grow and take next steps	74%

CHART 3–4: Based on their rating of nineteen church attributes, these are the five most important factors the Growing in Christ segment wants from the church. More than 80 percent say it is critically or very important for the church to help them both develop a personal relationship with Christ and understand the Bible in depth.

who are Growing in Christ, we must also offer them tangible next steps in the growth process—steps that are appropriate for individuals new in their relationships with Christ.

I (Greg) remember processing all of this with our senior pastor, Bill Hybels. Bill considers himself a high-challenge person, always ready to speak the truth and raise the bar when needed, and I've witnessed him make spiritual challenges many times in the twenty-plus years I've known him. But Bill was initially reluctant to "take the gloves off" during every weekend services. He worried that it would be too much for people, especially those early in their spiritual journey. Still, I encouraged him not to back down—that this was what our people needed and wanted—and he responded with various initiatives.

For example, we decided to have a weekend message series called "Read, Relate, and Pray" dealing with the foundational spiritual disciplines of the Christian life. For the first weekend, Bill invited Wayne Cordeiro, senior pastor of New Hope Christian Fellowship in Honolulu, Hawaii, to teach about the value of reading the Bible and to present specific tools that could help people do that. Why did we ask Wayne to teach? Well, of all the churches that have taken the REVEAL survey, New Hope has one of the highest levels of Bible engagement among its people, and we wanted to learn more from them about how they do it.

Bill followed Wayne's message by challenging people to read a portion of Scripture every day, using the guidelines Wayne had presented. Bill also emphasized the importance of taking personal responsibility for this challenge by reminding everyone, "I can't read your Bible for you!" The congregation rose to the challenge and the results have been amazing. When we resurveyed the congregation a year later, we found that the number of people who read their Bible regularly (daily or several times a week) had increased by 18 percent.

We'll be sharing more ideas for helping the entire church take steps of growth in part 3. But first, let's take another look at the Growing in Christ segment, and how they respond to the Great Commandments of loving God and loving others.

Love of God: Becoming a Personal Value

As we might expect, the level of agreement with core Christian beliefs and a corresponding sense of love for God are much stronger among those who are Growing in Christ than they are among those in the Exploring Christ segment (chart 3-5). In fact, 94 percent of people in this group express a firm belief

Love of God and Agreement with Core Christian Beliefs Increase Significantly for the Growing in Christ Segment

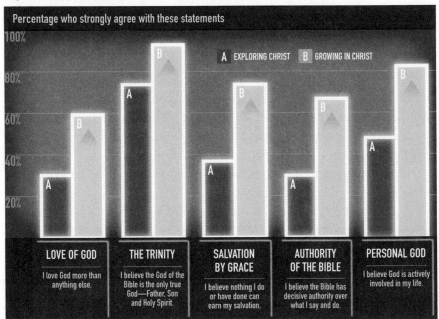

CHART 3-5: The willingness of the Growing in Christ segment to say they love God and agree with the core Christian beliefs is dramatically higher compared with the Exploring Christ segment. Agreement with three statements is two times the level of those Exploring Christ: (1) love of God, (2) salvation by grace, and (3) authority of the Bible.

Personal Spiritual Practices Increase Dramatically and Bible Engagement More Than Doubles

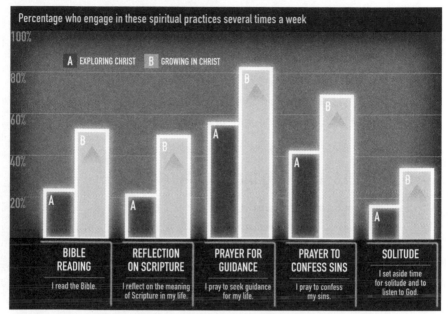

CHART 3–6: The arrows illustrate the significant increase in personal spiritual practices for the Growing in Christ segment compared with the Exploring Christ segment. The rise in both activities related to Bible engagement is especially noteworthy, with 50 percent saying they read the Bible or reflect on Scripture at least several times a week compared with 20 percent of the Exploring Christ segment.

in the Trinity, and 81 percent strongly believe in the existence of a *personal* God who is active in their lives. Those in the Growing in Christ segment are somewhat less sure of their belief in salvation by grace and the authority of the Bible, but their level of certainty on these key beliefs is almost double that of the Exploring Christ segment.

They are also more engaged in personal spiritual practices. Despite some hesitation to believe in the authority of the Bible, half of the people in this segment of the church read and reflect on Scripture several times a week (chart 3-6) — while the other half do not. For example, Jeff begins each day with a devotional based on Scripture, as well as engaging with the Bible reading and discussion that takes place in his small group. On the other hand, Michael is less disciplined in reading the Bible, and Scripture reading is more of an "I-really-need-to-get-started-on-that" practice for him.

Prayer is also an important aspect of spiritual growth, helping those in this segment establish a daily rhythm of conversation with God. Eighty-two percent pray daily or frequently for guidance. Solitude, while it lags behind the other practices, shows some increase as well, as those in this segment grow more and more eager to communicate with God.

Clearly, we see that members of this segment are willing to invest significant personal time, thought, and energy into developing their faith and growing in their relationship with Christ. However, their pursuit of greater spiritual knowledge — and their increasing embrace of the first Great Commandment, to love God — does not always fully translate into action. As we shall see, they are still learning to put their faith into practice by loving others.

Love of Others: Growing but Restrained

Although those who are Growing in Christ reveal an increased understanding of their faith, they still fail to act on what they believe. They are willing students and active participants in church programs, but they are much *less likely* to express their faith outside of the church or among nonbelievers. While they are establishing a spiritual foundation through increased church activities and growing in their personal spiritual practices, they are still less inclined — and even fearful, in some cases — to reach out to others by inviting them to church or serving those in need on their own.

Anne, who became a baptized believer in Christ eight months ago, says that she is only just beginning to feel free to acknowledge her walk with Christ. "I'm in more of a comfort zone now," she says. "I would never really have talked too much about my faith, but now that I'm more secure in it and know where I stand and where I'm pointed, I have much more interest in where other people are. It is just so much more of an interest to me than it was before."

Anne's growth, however, goes well beyond simple curiosity. Recently, she was caught off guard when her brother, who does not attend church, brought up the topic of her new faith in Christ. "He said something to the effect of, 'It's nice to see what you're doing with your church — that you're kind of taking a step out of what we were traditionally raised doing,'" she recalls. "That really caught me off guard, that he would say something like that. And I was like, 'Oh! Okay. Good.'"

And what about inviting her brother to visit her church and experience it for himself? Anne is still thinking about that. "You know, I really need to consider that. I really do."

Serving those in need can also be a bit frightening for those who are Growing in Christ. Consider Mark, a thirty-two-year-old IT project manager who lives with his wife in Wisconsin and makes a daily commute to his job in Chicago. His transition from Exploring Christ to Growing in Christ required a great deal of serious deliberation over a four-year time span, but once he made a decision to follow Christ, he made it a priority to learn how to follow God's direction for his life.

During a recent evening commute Mark came upon a man who seemed to be hungry, standing in front of the Taco Bell at the food court of the train station. "I just felt this nudge — and this is very unlike me — to ask him if he was hungry and if I could get him something," remembers Mark. "But he said, 'No, thank you. I ate earlier.' Then he proceeded to talk to me, which made me extremely uncomfortable. I was thinking, 'Dude, I'll buy you dinner and then you go your way and I'll go my way.' But we ended up talking for several minutes. He said he was an artist and that he wanted me to come by his stand so he could give me some art."

After the conversation had ended and he was on his way home, Mark was enormously relieved. But as he replayed that experience in his thoughts over the next several days, Mark became aware of a stirring in his heart. "I was just overwhelmed by the presence of God. Like this whole opportunity to reflect Christ's compassion came because I took a risk. And it's things like that that just increase my hunger to do more."

Anne and Mark are making progress. They are still growing in their faith. But when we compare where they are at with the more mature believer segments, we see that these new believers are still "learning" and are not yet quite comfortable "doing" the work of a disciple on their own. This is confirmed when we compare the results of the surveys, looking at their self-professed level of love of others and how their spiritual behaviors compare with those of believers in other segments (chart 3-7). Although those who are Growing in Christ show an increased love for others and they are engaging in serving and evangelistic activities at levels significantly higher than those in the Exploring Christ segment, unsurprisingly, the more mature believer segments (light gray) show much higher levels of activity in these areas.

Those who are Growing in Christ have a strong love for God and solid beliefs, but they still have significant potential for spiritual growth. They are growing in their faith, but they still fall short of having the attitude and lifestyle of a more mature believer. Consequently, we need to be patient and encouraging while continuing to challenge them. We need to celebrate their victories, no matter how small or tentative.

Love of Others and Spiritual Activities outside the Church Increase, but Are Significantly Lower Than Those of Other Believer Segments

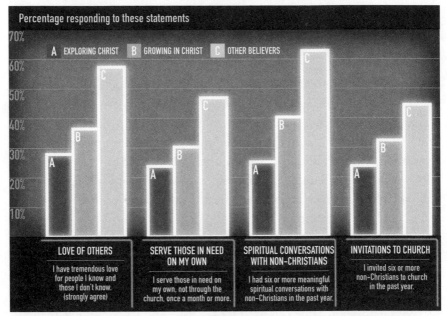

Percentage responding to these statements

A EXPLORING CHRIST   B GROWING IN CHRIST   C OTHER BELIEVERS

LOVE OF OTHERS	SERVE THOSE IN NEED ON MY OWN	SPIRITUAL CONVERSATIONS WITH NON-CHRISTIANS	INVITATIONS TO CHURCH
I have tremendous love for people I know and those I don't know. (strongly agree)	I serve those in need on my own, not through the church, once a month or more.	I had six or more meaningful spiritual conversations with non-Christians in the past year.	I invited six or more non-Christians to church in the past year.

CHART 3-7: The willingness of the Growing in Christ segment to say they love others and their participation in spiritual activities outside the church rise, but the arrows illustrate that they still fall short of the other believers by a wide margin.

The Coaching Role of the Church

As we have seen, the church plays a significant part in helping those Growing in Christ take the steps they need to grow in faith, and it is the coaching role of the church that is most significant for this segment. Those in this segment are eager to grow, but they need encouragement and assistance to overcome their fears and learn how to connect what they are learning with the lifestyle and actions of a committed, mature follower of Christ.

The 1986 movie *Hoosiers* provides a particularly relevant glimpse into the kind of spiritual energy—and insecurity—that characterizes those who are Growing in Christ. The storyline tracks the basketball season of a fictitious little town in Indiana named Hickory. Led by a disciplined but volatile coach (played by actor Gene Hackman), Hickory miraculously advances from winning games against minor rivals to competing for the state championship in Indianapolis. Hickory's wins are captured in a rolling panorama of images that reinforce the small-town heart of this team as we see scenes of lone boys shooting baskets at barnyard hoops. And while their squad clearly doesn't have the size, the speed, or the skills to win the state title, they are driven by a dream born out of those daily barnyard baskets — that if they believe in themselves and their coach, anything is possible.

That dream carries them through … that is, until they get to the big city of Indianapolis. On a pregame visit to the arena at Butler University, these gangly small-town boys react with awe, which leads to dismay and then self-doubt. Soon, it is clear they are terrified at the thought of playing in such a large, intimidating stadium.

In the midst of their overwhelming emotions, their coach walks up to the basketball hoop and pulls out a tape measure. He marks the distance from the rim of the hoop to the floor. "It's ten feet," he says to them. "Just ten feet. No different from the baskets in Hickory."

In many ways, those in the Growing in Christ segment are like the boys from Hickory. They play their hearts out, experiencing small spiritual "wins" as they learn to pray regularly, read their Bibles, and begin participating in small groups and serving in the church. But they begin doing all of this in the safe sanctuary of a "hometown crowd." When they begin living out their new-found faith in the outside world, they are vulnerable to insecurity and doubt. The normal networks of everyday life can be daunting to new believers, who lack confidence in their skills and character, and who frequently waver in their will to follow Christ outside the walls of the church.

But to grow spiritually, that's what they must learn to do. They need their church to encourage them and offer them a reality check. They need a reminder that the same God they worship so passionately on the weekend, and pray to each morning, is also beside them at work, at home, regardless of where they are. They need the assurance that the God of the universe is always with them. When they believe that, the real world won't seem quite so scary.

A Person Who Is Growing in Christ Is …

—On board with core beliefs

—Becoming more comfortable with spiritual practices

—Hesitant to take their faith beyond the walls of the church

—Poised for great spiritual advances and impact

Deep in the Heart of Texas: A Church That Is Growing in Christ

Welcome to Texas, as we visit a rapidly expanding church in an affluent suburb just outside one of the state's largest cities.

The church's growth is reflected in a number of ways, including a beautiful new sanctuary that serves as a magnet for newcomers. The thousand-person weekend attendance is growing as well — although, interestingly, its percentage of those Exploring Christ is low, at only 6 percent. This church is drawing Christians, and a very high percentage (44 percent) fall within the Growing in Christ segment.

Their REVEAL study results demonstrate that these people love their church, which is not surprising since such love is a key characteristic of the Growing in Christ segment. And they clearly respect and admire their senior pastor. But the results also conclude that the congregation's spiritual health is no better than average. Again, this is not surprising, since such a high percentage of the congregation falls in a spiritually less mature segment. But this grates on church leaders, a group of fifteen men and women, predominantly young professionals, who struggle to understand why their people aren't lighting up the spiritual scoreboard. (Those Texans do love their sports.)

Understand that on the surface, lots of things look great — including the fact that almost 70 percent of those who attend are involved in small groups. Again, this is indicative of a congregation marked by a large number of Growing in Christ people who immerse themselves in church activities. Serving in church ministries is only average, but these congregants generally show up and do everything the church asks of them. It is the weak results in evangelism that most catches the staff's attention, though it is an unsurprising finding since their Growing in Christ people are likely insecure about talking about their faith beyond the walls of the church.

In response, church leaders start down the old standby path of more emphasis from the pulpit on reaching the lost and more training to equip believers to share their faith. But in the end, they tap into wisdom beyond their years as they conclude that the lack of such resources is not their biggest problem. After some painfully honest soul-searching, these leaders pause in the midst of their plans and conclude that the biggest obstacle to their congregation's spiritual growth is … them. That's right. The most significant barrier jeopardizing spiritual progress is the church — and specifically, the church's leadership. Their people are no better than spiritually average because their leaders are spiritually average. (Gulp.)

At this point, the group takes a courageous step. They decide their first priority must be to reflect on their own lives and to assess whether the challenge factor in their own hearts is as strong as it should be. They agree to do whatever it takes to build up the collective spiritual strength of their leadership team *before* they launch any new spiritual growth programs for the church at large.

At least a third of the churches we survey are like this church, heavily influenced by a large percentage of Growing in Christ congregants. Their REVEAL results show their spiritual maturity is no better than average. But we believe this particular church reached a way-above-average conclusion: that to spiritually energize a congregation with so many Growing in Christ believers depends, more than anything else, on energizing the spiritual hearts of its leaders. When people love their church, its leaders can sometimes get complacent and lose touch with how essential their own transformation is to the effectiveness of their spiritual leadership. Especially for an "average" church like this one, leadership is key. New believers love their church and they will follow its leaders — whether or not that path leads toward a life of Christ-Centered devotion.

Leading Forward

For many of the church leaders we've talked to, the most surprising finding from our research is that involvement in church activity does not predictably translate into increased levels of spiritual maturity. This insight has several significant leadership implications, but we want to highlight two that are especially important for the Growing in Christ segment: (1) never let the passion to serve eclipse a commitment to personal spiritual disciplines, and (2) don't confuse high levels of service with qualifications for Christian leadership.

1. Never let the passion to serve eclipse a commitment to personal spiritual disciplines. Since those Growing in Christ are very active volunteers, it's easy for leaders to affirm this segment's high levels of serving as a clear measure of their spiritual growth. But leaders must not lose sight of the need to affirm and challenge these individuals in their commitment to personal spiritual disciplines such as prayer and reflecting on Scripture. Spiritual growth is about more than being involved in church activities; among other things, it also requires spending time with God. We talk more about this in chapter 8, but the key here is to make sure the church's message to those Growing in Christ includes a balance between serving and investing in time spent alone with God.

A few years ago, I (Greg) had a friend who, after eighteen months of attending our church as a new believer, thought that what he really needed to do to grow spiritually was to "get involved in as much stuff as possible." I was so discouraged. But then I realized that "get involved" was what he was hearing from the platform. Week after week, he heard the announcements about all the stuff he could "do" in our church. That realization was a wake-up call for me. Once we began doing REVEAL research, I came to understand that we were just living out our own mental model — that more activity leads to more growth. Now, however, we know that is not true.

So pay attention to the unintentional messages you give your congregation — especially those who are Growing in Christ — about what it means to grow spiritually. They are eager to do what you say. So make sure your invitations to serve are balanced with invitations for them to spend time with Jesus, because he loves them for who they are, not because they are serving the church.

As you consider the importance of doing this — and perhaps to convince others that it is necessary, as well — you may want to take another look at chart 3-4 on page 55. Those in the Growing in Christ segment, as compared to those who are Exploring Christ, are looking for some very specific things from their churches. Developing their relationship with Christ continues to be the top need, but that is now followed very closely by the desire to understand the Bible in greater depth. In fact, 82 percent of those in the Growing in Christ segment say that helping them to understand the Bible is a critical or very important thing for a church to provide. People in this segment are hungry for God's Word, so we should evaluate every part of our ministry — including the announcements — based on how well that need is being met.

2. Don't confuse high levels of service with qualifications for Christian leadership. The fact that some people serve a ton in your church does not by itself mean that these individuals are ready for leadership roles — especially ones that require spiritual leadership over a group of people. Their high degree of involvement does not necessarily mean they are mature followers of Christ.

We wish this were not the case. It would be much easier and a lot more convenient to just ask people about their previous serving experience and then place those with the most impressive resumés into leadership. That is how it works in most organizations, and some people in a congregation assume that is how it should also work in the church. They tell us all about what they are involved in and how successful that involvement has been as justification for a leadership position in the church. But we can't let that influence us. Instead, it's vitally important to shift the focus from activities and accomplishments to the condition of the heart. We need to listen between the lines to make sure they are in love with Christ and not just the church. Have they organized their lives so they can spend time with Christ, the one they love, when no one else is watching? It's tempting to settle for a record of service as qualification for leadership — especially when you're trying to find ten or twenty new small group leaders — but resist the temptation.

CHAPTER 4

Close to Christ: Getting to Know Those Who Are on Personal Terms with God

As a practicing attorney in one of America's largest cities, Olivia characterizes her work environment as "a very secular and skeptical world." She explains: "There are lots of difficult times during my day, for instance, when I have to confront situations with opposing counsel." Olivia remembers that her own perspective on faith was once "very cynical." But now, less than two years after accepting Christ, she spends her hour-plus morning commutes reading her Bible. She has also begun giving faith-related books to people she thinks might benefit from them—like a copy of Philip Yancey's *What's So Amazing about Grace?* that she recently passed along to one of her firm's senior partners. She hopes to join a second small group—one in which she can be challenged by members more spiritually mature than herself.

One cold January morning Olivia received an unmistakable prompting that she knew was from God: "Take the Marine to lunch." She immediately knew what this meant. The Marine was one of several homeless people who stood each day on the bridge near her office. Olivia quickly made plans to invite him to lunch, but those plans fell through when she went to find him and discovered he was no longer at his regular place. "I felt very disappointed," Olivia remembers. "I was sure it was a prompting from God, so I kept wondering, where did this guy go?"

When the Marine reappeared on the bridge a few months later, Olivia approached him—and noticed that he was now carrying a Bible! Though he declined her offer to join her for lunch, the two continued to talk each morning.

Olivia began bringing him coffee and asking if he needed anything. One day, pointing to his Bible, she got up the nerve to ask him if he was a Christian. The Marine told Olivia that he was—and had, in fact, recently accepted Christ. After attending a church for several weeks, the pastor had given an altar call and he had gone forward.

Those initial conversations quickly turned to longer discussions about their faith in Christ and eventually led to an ongoing friendship. "We have become close friends and talk just about every day," says Olivia. "He came to my parents' home to celebrate Christmas with my family, and I'm constantly identifying things that God is trying to teach me through this relationship."

A few months after being stationed in Italy while serving as an Air Force munitions and explosives specialist, Mark fell six stories onto a slab of solid concrete. Though his doctors assumed his injuries would prove fatal, Mark miraculously overcame their grim prognoses and survived. "The first doctors who saw me just hoped to make me comfortable as I died," he recalls. Thankfully, God had other plans.

Mark had accepted Christ years earlier, but he had never been a regular church attender. "I would go at Christmas and Easter, but I always told anyone who asked that God could hear me just as well from my barracks room as he could from the base chapel," he says. During the long months in the hospital recovering from his fall Mark remembers that he "spent a lot of time wondering why I survived and trying to understand what happened to me. I went through phases of thanking God for saving me and then berating him for all the pain I suffered every day."

Almost two years after the accident, Mark was transferred to an Air Force base in New Mexico where he met his future wife, Beth. They were soon married. "We periodically told each other we needed to go to church, but we never found one that could give us what we were searching for." A few years later, the couple had a son, Tyler, and things began to change for them. "When he was four, Tyler started asking questions about God that we did not have answers for," recalls Mark. "One of Beth's friends recommended that we attend her church, and it felt like home to us from the very beginning." Within a few years, both Mark and his wife made decisions to follow Christ.

Today, this grateful believer is comfortable sharing his faith and spends time each day in regular spiritual practices while continuing to grow closer to Christ. Reflecting on God's work in his life over the years, Mark acknowledges that he has more peace in his life now than ever before—and that the church has played an important role in that process of growth. He laughs as he recalls how the doctor at the VA, amazed at Mark's progress in recovering from PTSD (Post Traumatic Stress Disorder), just shook his head at him in disbelief asking, "And you're getting all this help ... from your *church*?"

Though their stories are quite different, both Mark and Olivia have a number of characteristics in common — they are eager to be identified as Christians, they are passionate about growing in their faith, and they are willing to take responsibility for their own maturing relationships with Christ. These individuals are representative of believers who have reached one of the most critical stages of spiritual growth: integrating their faith into their lives in a holistic way. Rather than keeping their beliefs and their lifestyle separate, they have begun identifying themselves in a significant and primary way as followers of Christ. But does that mean they feel they have "arrived" in their journey of faith? Not at all. Instead, both of them are focused on continuing to grow. They are growing closer to Christ and learning to demonstrate their love for God and for other people in visible ways.

A Profile of Close to Christ: Building Close Friendships with Jesus

For those in the Close to Christ segment, faith is a deeply personal and significant force that is relevant to their every waking moment. Faith in Christ is no longer defined by an event that happens once or twice a week at church and is only remotely connected to their daily lives. Individuals in this segment are more deeply invested in their faith and are willing to be publicly identified as followers of, and advocates for, Jesus Christ — regardless of whether they are inside or outside the walls of the church.

They are also characterized by an increasing spiritual certainty — a growing confidence in the existence, dependability, and power of God's presence in their lives. "I am constantly prompted by God," says Olivia, "and the more I obey, the more promptings I receive." The initial signs of spiritual transformation that began to appear in the Growing in Christ segment are deepening into consistent practices among people in this segment. They continue to demonstrate their love of God with ongoing, regular communication and through personal spiritual practices. In addition, their increasing love for others shows up most markedly through increased evangelistic activities.

Still, the characteristic that most significantly defines people in this segment is the high degree of *ownership* they take for their spiritual journey.

Unlike those in the previous segment, the faith walk of those who are Close to Christ is *not* dependent on spiritual mentors, dynamic preaching, or compelling Bible studies. While most of them believe that belonging to a church is essential to their ongoing spiritual growth, they take on much of the responsibility for advancing their own relationship with Christ. They walk the talk of being a Christ-follower—using multiple channels to discern God's voice, then leaning on that voice for spiritual guidance, courage, and support. "In the beginning, the church had the greatest impact on my spiritual growth," explains Mark. "But now, both my wife and I are reaching a point where we sit and read the Bible on our own. And we have a child's Bible for our son. The church is guiding us, but we're pushing ourselves."

Not surprisingly, a strong majority of Mark's counterparts in the Close to Christ segment still look to the church for support, but they are also learning to "push themselves" to develop their own personal relationship with Jesus through ongoing dependence on God's grace. In fact, when asked what they most want from their church leaders and churches, four out of five of them say they want encouragement to take personal responsibility for their own spiritual growth (chart 4-1).

The encouragement to take "personal responsibility for spiritual growth" shows up in the top five list for the first time with this group, replacing the desire of previous segments that the church provide "compelling worship expe-

The Top Five Things the Close to Christ Segment Wants from You and Your Church

BENEFITS PROVIDED BY THE CHURCH	Percentage who find the benefit critical or very important
1. Help in understanding the Bible in greater depth	88%
2. Help in developing a personal relationship with Christ	87%
3. Church leaders who model and consistently reinforce how to grow spiritually	84%
4. Challenge to grow and take next steps	82%
5. Encouragement to take personal responsibility for spiritual growth	80%

CHART 4-1: Based on their rating of nineteen church attributes, these are the five most important factors the Close to Christ segment wants from the church. Nearly 90 percent say that it is critically or very important for the church to help them both understand the Bible in depth and develop a personal relationship with Christ.

riences." To be clear, this should not suggest that weekend services are unimportant or irrelevant to those in the Close to Christ segment. It simply means that, relative to other things, those in this segment feel that what happens during a weekly service is less important to them than other factors. To put it simply, they have found other, more personal and meaningful ways to experience God in *addition* to the corporate worship experience.

This desire for encouragement as they begin to take personal responsibility for their own spiritual growth is but one of the ways that the Close to Christ segment reflects a maturing faith. In addition, there are two specific characteristics that also emerge for the first time among these maturing believers.

They Listen to and Talk with God All the Time

The spiritual rudder for those in the Close to Christ segment is their investment in personal spiritual practices. Across the board, this segment is more involved in regular, spiritual practices than both the Exploring Christ and Growing in Christ segments (chart 4-2). Most of them (80 percent or more) read the Bible, reflect on Scripture, pray for guidance, and pray to confess their sins at least several times a week — and, with similar frequency, over half listen to God during quiet times of solitude.

When compared with several of the most common personal spiritual practices, it is interesting to notice that "prayer for guidance" is the most common spiritual practice among all the segments represented in chart 4-2 (done by 93 percent of those in the Close to Christ segment). And although it is also the most common practice for the Exploring Christ and Growing in Christ segments as well, we should carefully note how the prayers of the Close to Christ segment differ in content from the prayers offered up by these other groups.

When members of the Exploring Christ segment talk about prayer as a personal spiritual practice, they often cite such requests as, "If you're there, God, please let me know" or "If you will do this, God, then I will believe." Believers who are members of the Growing in Christ segment, on the other hand, tend to pray about day-to-day issues, turning to God for support as they would to a friend, often intentionally establishing the practice of talking to God each morning or evening, for instance, or making it a habit to pray before every meal. For Christians who are in the Close to Christ segment, however, prayer becomes more of a running dialogue — a conversation with God that they return to throughout their day. These individuals no longer wonder how a person might obey the biblical mandate to "pray without ceasing." In most cases, that's exactly what they are doing.

Personal Spiritual Practices Increase Significantly for the Close to Christ Segment

Percentage who engage in these spiritual practices at least several times a week

A EXPLORING CHRIST   B GROWING IN CHRIST   C CLOSE TO CHRIST

| 100% |
| 80% |
| 60% |
| 40% |
| 20% |

BIBLE READING	REFLECTION ON SCRIPTURE	PRAYER FOR GUIDANCE	PRAYER TO CONFESS SINS	SOLITUDE
I read the Bible.	I reflect on the meaning of Scripture in my life.	I pray to seek guidance for my life.	I pray to confess my sins.	I set aside time for solitude and to listen to God.

CHART 4-2: The arrows illustrate the significant increase in personal spiritual practices for the Close to Christ segment compared with the Growing in Christ segment. The rise in both activities related to Bible engagement is especially significant, with almost 80 percent reporting that they read the Bible and reflect on Scripture at least several times a week.

The distinction between those who are Close to Christ and the prior segments becomes most pronounced when we look more closely at *daily* practices (chart 4-3). On a daily basis, more than half of those who are Close to Christ pray for guidance. Almost half pray to confess sins. This is even more striking in comparison with the other segments, illustrating the increased level of maturity and intimacy exhibited by the Close to Christ segment.

Olivia, the attorney you met at the beginning of the chapter and who has been a Christian for less than two years, shares how this "ceaseless" prayer has manifested itself in her own life: "I keep a prayer list of people and things—and by things I don't mean material things; I mean strength or courage—and every day I pray through that list to myself. Then at various points, I also pray out loud. When I do that, something really strange happens. I almost always end up crying. There aren't tears running down my face, but my eyes are full of water. And it's at those times that I feel 100 percent in sync or that God is right there with me."

Daily Personal Spiritual Practices Are Significantly Greater for the Close to Christ Segment

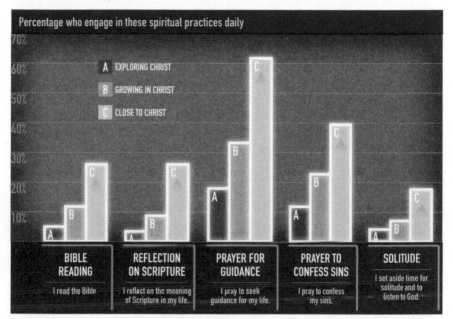

CHART 4-3: The arrows illustrate the dramatic rise in daily personal spiritual practices for the Close to Christ segment compared with the Growing in Christ segment. This indicates an increasingly serious commitment to making the values and teaching of Jesus a central influence in their lives.

Significantly, the Close to Christ segment's frequency of daily engagement in Bible reading, reflection on Scripture, and spending time in solitude is more than twice that of the Growing in Christ segment (chart 4-4). Indeed, one of REVEAL's key discoveries is that personal time devoted to reflecting on Scripture is far and away the most powerful catalyst of spiritual growth, an insight illustrated by the increased frequency of this spiritual practice among those in this segment (we provide more details about this finding in part 2). Almost half of those in this segment indicate that their *pace* of spiritual growth has increased as well, to a moderate or rapid level—a percentage that's nearly double that of the prior segments.

Every time I (Cally) see dramatic increases like those we find illustrated in chart 4-3 and 4-4, I think about my own priorities. We all tend to be very busy. And yet it is a universal truth that we always find time for what really matters to us. Even though it may be difficult, we still manage to make time for the things that we believe absolutely *must* be done. My own priority list changed

Daily Bible Engagement and Solitude for the Close to Christ Segment Are More Than Two Times Greater Than Previous Segments

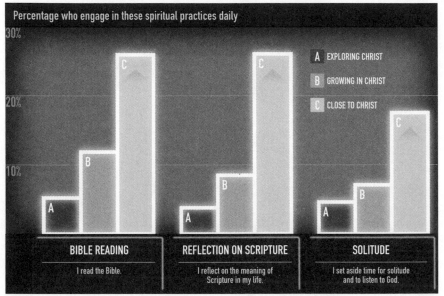

CHART 4-4: The arrows focus on the twofold increase in daily Bible engagement and solitude for the Close to Christ segment compared with the Growing in Christ segment.

dramatically a few years ago when I read a book called *Younger Next Year*. In it, the authors discuss the typical decline in physical condition that most people experience after the age of fifty. But then they make a startling claim. They suggest that this decline is "70 percent optional." Certainly, there are factors like our genetic makeup and other environmental factors that are beyond our control, and these account for the other 30 percent of variables that affect our physical health. Still, though, the authors are adamant that by simply ditching some bad habits and adopting good ones, most of us could arrest many of the natural aches, pains, and disabilities that come with advancing age.

The first good habit they recommend immediately caught my full attention: exercise six days a week, forty-five minutes a day, raising the heart rate up to fat-burning levels. They refer to this as the "new job" for the post-fifty crowd. Exercise. Six days a week. No chitchatting or slacking off. No excuses.

For me, embracing a six-day-a-week, forty-five-minute-a-day exercise routine was a game changer. Exercise went off of my discretionary to-do list and took on the same level of importance as my daily commute to work. If I want to get paid, I'd better show up at work, right? Well, in the same way, if I want to age in a healthy way, I'd better show up at the gym.

Exercise, like so many other things, is a matter of choice. It is a visible reflection of our true priorities. What's most important to us is what ends up getting done. And that's exactly what we find among those who are Close to Christ. Their faith in Christ becomes something of such value to them that they begin putting their relationship with Christ on the short list of highest priorities. What's critical for us to understand in all of this is that the human element—that choice to make Christ a priority—is an essential part of the experience of spiritual growth among those who are Close to Christ. While the Holy Spirit often works to change our hearts and minds in mysterious and powerful ways irrespective of our own efforts, his work of guiding and shaping our lives is enhanced immeasurably when we open our eyes and ears to his influence.

All of this suggests to us that in many ways our own spiritual growth—or lack of it—may also be "70 percent optional." In other words, our level of spiritual development is based in large measure on the choices we make each and every day. Where is Christ as we rank items on our to-do list? How often are we engaging our heart and mind with God's truth by praying and reflecting on Scripture? Six days a week? Forty-five minutes a day? No slacking off and no excuses? That may be a good place to start.

They "Go Public" with Their Faith

Those who are Close to Christ also show an increase in their love for others, most visibly seen by an increased participation in evangelism (chart 4-5). While the Christ-Centered segment demonstrates even higher levels of evangelistic activity, this is where we see a breakthrough as individuals go public with their allegiance to Christ and their advocacy for the core beliefs of the Christian faith.

Interestingly, this breakthrough takes place with *or without* the support of the church—and whether or not the church identifies itself as "seeker friendly." The REVEAL study clearly affirms that regardless of the type of church those in the Close to Christ segment attend, they will share their faith. Their increasing love of Christ motivates their desire to obey his command to reach out to the lost.

Specifically, over half strongly agree that they love others and feel equipped to share their faith. And these feelings of greater love for others combined with evangelistic confidence translate into increased outreach to non-Christians. Over half report having three or more meaningful spiritual conversations with non-Christians in the past year, and nearly a third report six or more such

Those Who Are Close to Christ Express Much Greater Love for Others, More Confidence in Their Ability to Share Their Faith, and Much Higher Levels of Evangelism

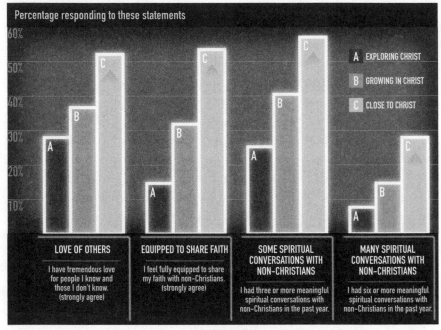

CHART 4-5: Their greater willingness to say they love others combined with increased confidence in their ability to share their faith clearly translates into more evangelistic activities for the Close to Christ segment. However, church leaders will likely find these results disappointing. The bars on the right show that, in the past year, most people in this segment engaged in fewer that six spiritual conversations with non-Christians. On average, that's less than one every two months.

experiences. While these numbers may seem woefully small to pastors who spend their lives inspiring Christ-followers to reach out to the lost, it is nonetheless true that—compared with the prior segments—those who are Close to Christ appear to be getting the message.

Mark, the recovered Air Force specialist, first had a memorable opportunity to share his faith in a suburban elementary school where he now works as a computer specialist. As he sat working on a computer, a group of teachers in the same room began talking about religion. Several shared their opinion that God doesn't really exist. "I sat there thinking, *These people are teaching our children!*" Mark says. "I took it as long as I could, but finally I spoke up and said, 'You guys have got it all wrong. Tell me what your problems are and let me tell you about my faith. I am living proof that God can do anything.'" Mark shared his story with them, and afterwards, one of the teachers told him, "Well, I'm going to reconsider this."

Two unique characteristics first emerge in the spiritual character of those in the Close to Christ segment, and they can be summed up in two words: *personal* and *public*. These are people who invest *personally* through spiritual practices to grow in their faith; and they take their faith *public* through evangelistic efforts, making time to talk about spiritual issues with nonbelievers. They don't flaunt their faith, but they don't hide it either. And while being a follower of Christ doesn't fully define their identity (as is the case with those Christ-Centered believers described in the next chapter), their faith in Christ is on a short list of values that guide their lives. On a personal level, Christ is an important part of who they are.

Love of God: Is a Central Value

There is no question that those who are Close to Christ are committed. They have a solid faith, with more than four out of five expressing strong agreement with core Christian beliefs (chart 4-6). The doubts that we saw expressed by those in the Growing in Christ segment—such as questioning the authority of the Bible—have been largely resolved.

We've already noted that those who are Close to Christ engage in a deeper level of personal spiritual practices. Notice that there is a corresponding increase in the strength of their belief patterns as well. This leads us to ask the question, "Do beliefs and practices work in tandem, or does one lead the other?" Our survey results suggest that, for the most part, beliefs and practices work in tandem with one another. A congregation with strong beliefs typically reports a high level of personal spiritual practices. Likewise, weak beliefs tend to coincide with lower spiritual practices. It is rare to find weak beliefs and strong practices—or vice versa—within the same congregation.

However, as we will see in greater detail in part 2, our research does suggest that there is a slight priority given to beliefs: beliefs tend to lead to practices. A person who doubts the authority of the Bible, for example, is unlikely to read Scripture regularly. Similarly, a person who strongly believes in a personal God is likely to pray often for guidance and encouragement. From this we conclude that a firm foundation in core Christian beliefs is an essential building block to spiritual growth—one that *precedes* a commitment to the personal spiritual practices that are essential to developing a rich personal relationship with Christ. While spiritual growth is obviously more complicated than this simple

Over 80 Percent of the Close to Christ Segment Strongly Agree with Love of God and Core Christian Beliefs

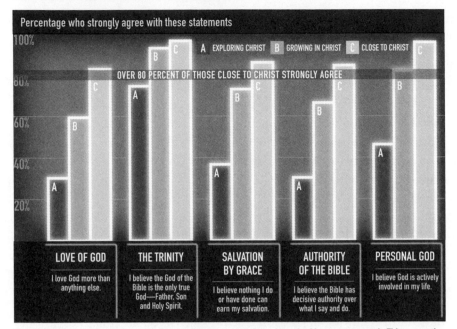

CHART 4-6: Every bar representing the Close to Christ segment rises above the 80 percentage mark. This means the vast majority of people in this segment are firm in their faith-based convictions.

A + B = C formula, our encouragement to churches struggling with both weak beliefs and low participation in spiritual practices is to focus their initial efforts on shoring up beliefs.

Love of Others: The Backbone of the Church

People in this segment are the backbone of the church because they, more than those in any other segment, match what they say about supporting God's work with what they do. In other words, their actions mirror the commitment reflected in their attitudes.

For example, Olivia has organized a volunteer corps of lawyers to meet the legal needs of those served by her church's food pantry. She began this ministry by recruiting a friend in her law firm—then they in turn convinced two more colleagues to join them in this new serving opportunity. A few weeks later, her church put out the call for others in the congregation to do the same, and to date, eighteen attorneys have come alongside more than five hundred people who could otherwise not afford legal representation. And legal counsel is not all these people receive. "It is very central to our ministry that we talk to people about where they are in their spiritual walk," Olivia explains. "We pray with them and we direct them to things at the church that might help in their situations, because often—due to their legal problems—we know the most intimate details of their lives."

Almost half of those who are Close to Christ say that God's work is their number one financial priority, and a slightly higher percentage of them tithe (chart 4-7). More than half say they use their spiritual gifts to serve God, and over 60 percent serve in a church ministry on a regular basis. These behaviors reinforce the observation noted earlier about this segment—that they walk the talk of being a follower of Christ, not only by investing their personal time

Tithing and Serving Attitudes and Behaviors Increase Markedly in the Close to Christ Segment

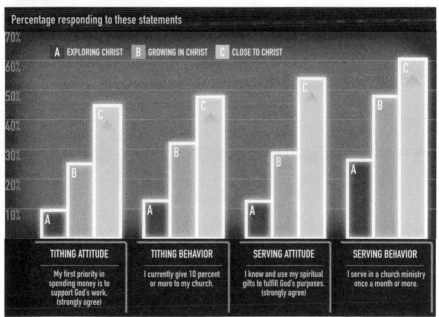

CHART 4-7: These four bars compare attitudes and behaviors related to tithing and serving. The two sets of bars on the left show that almost half of the Close to Christ segment strongly agree that supporting God's work is their top priority; and a similar percentage report giving 10 percent or more to their church. The two sets of bars on the right show the same pattern for an attitude about their intent to use their gifts for God (over 50 percent strongly agree) and their serving behaviors (60 percent serve the church regularly). All four measures are much higher than those for the Growing in Christ segment.

to discern and respond to his voice in their daily lives, but also by providing resources needed to support the local church.

Those who are Close to Christ are clearly devoted to their faith and to their church. In fact, that obvious devotion sparked one of the first questions when we initially presented the idea of the spiritual continuum: With such a high level of spiritual maturity, a strong commitment to personal spiritual practices, and an obvious zeal for evangelism and serving others, how can there even be another segment beyond this? After all, those who are Close to Christ sound like mature Christ-followers — people who know and love God; who serve his purposes inside and outside of organized church activities; who walk the talk of their faith. Is there really another stage of spiritual growth?

We believe there is. While those who are Close to Christ have made the transition from an activity-based faith to a more personal spiritual journey, their responses indicate that they are still largely in the driver's seat, steering the direction of their lives. While Jesus influences their decisions and actions, there are several other values that compete and contribute to the choices they make. They are close to Christ. They are intimate with him. They have begun the process of spiritual transformation. But there are still many areas in which they need to grow. In fact, many of them consciously choose to emulate those we have identified as Christ-Centered, the next and final segment of the spiritual continuum. These are the individuals who let Jesus drive. They gladly experience the journey he determines for them — sitting beside him in the passenger seat.

A Person Who Is Close to Christ Is ...

—Making their relationship with Jesus part of their everyday life

—Confident in God's presence and power

—Connecting daily with God through personal spiritual practices

—Beginning to show signs of spiritual transformation

—The backbone of the church

North and South: Two Churches Who Are Close to Christ

Ninety miles outside of Minnesota's Twin Cities is a 140-year-old church with weekend attendance of three hundred, and yet it shares the same challenge facing a thirty-year-old church with weekend attendance of a thousand in San Antonio, Texas. In each of these churches, both members of the same mainline denomination, the Close to Christ segment represents 33 percent of the congregation, much higher than the average. That level of spiritual maturity is exciting—and testifies, no doubt, to some very effective leadership.

Their challenge? Both churches also share high levels of dissatisfaction within their congregations—24 percent in Minnesota and 30 percent in Texas. Moreover, members of both congregations identify the same thing as the cause of their unhappiness: lack of in-depth Bible teaching.

Just as they share a similar challenge, the two churches offer us consistent insight. Because—whether inadvertently or intentionally—these churches have communicated to their people that, no matter where they are on their spiritual journey, the role of the church is to be their central source of spiritual expertise and experience. As a result, even as people mature in their beliefs and embrace personal spiritual practices as part of their daily routines, their expectation is that it will be the church, not their own initiative, that will feed their spiritual hunger.

These churches probably did not mean to communicate that message to their maturing Christ-followers. But the reality is that most ministry activities—like weekend services and small groups—are typically targeted toward those large majorities of attenders in the earlier stages of spiritual development. Consequently, if churches don't clearly create the expectation that maturing believers ultimately need to take responsibility for their own spiritual growth, they can wind up with maturing Close to Christ people who, not surprisingly, aren't happy. When the church fails to meet their expectations, they become dissatisfied.

This profile is not unusual. It is, in fact, fairly common to find mature congregations who are deeply committed and engaged in growing their own relationship with Christ through personal spiritual practices, but who still expect the church to continue to be their primary spiritual teacher/director.

The solution to this dilemma could be complex, involving the reallocation of church resources toward in-depth Bible classes and networks for spiritual mentoring. In fact, efforts in that direction are now underway in several REVEAL study churches, as evidenced by new equipping strategies like having a weekend series dedicated to personal spiritual practices or the addition of supplemental classes in areas including evangelism and serving.

But the solution also might be as simple, and as tough, as helping adolescents leave the family nest. Parents love their maturing children, just as a church loves its maturing Christ-followers. But there is a point when it's time for the maturing children to go and make their own mark on the world. Good parents take responsibility for helping their maturing children figure out that path: communicating their need to take on personal responsibility, helping them take their first steps in that direction, and assisting them in measuring their progress.

The REVEAL research shows that our churches don't always do those things as well as good parents might.

Leading Forward

Members of our congregations within the Close to Christ segment are going to share their faith. In fact, most of them are not only eager to do so; they are incapable of doing otherwise. That's the great news.

The not-so-great news is that our churches sometimes miss the opportunity to foster this worthy passion. We forfeit the chance to assist in the process of making these men and women effective witnesses for Jesus. They have a strong desire to reach out to those far from God, but they sometimes lack the guidance or confidence that would help them to be even more effective in doing so.

What if we could make a connection between the internal desire generated by the Close to Christ segment's increasing love of Christ and their desire to obey his command to reach out to the lost, with help and support from the local church? Sparks would fly!

As these folks begin to go public with their faith, it is critical that they know the church is supporting them. As a church leader, you can assist them by providing training opportunities that help them to comfortably share their story of coming to faith in Christ. You can also provide them with examples of how you personally are investing in the lives of people far from God. Share your victories and disappointments. I (Greg) have always benefited from Bill Hybels's willingness to share such stories — not only of the people he has led to Christ, but of the people far from God whom he continues to love and pray for after ten, twenty, or even thirty years of effort. After attending our church for over twenty years, I never get tired of hearing Bill's stories, and every time he shares from his own experience I am motivated to be even bolder in reaching out to others.

We know this segment is self-motivated about their spiritual growth and we need to let them take increasing ownership, but in the area of personal evangelism we believe the church does have an important role to play. Most people are initially scared to share their faith. They have willing hearts but are afraid they may say the wrong things at the wrong times. They understand that the stakes are very high. So encouraging evangelism is an important role the church can play in their lives.

Another important role for church leaders and pastors, as referenced early in this chapter (see p. 68, chart 4-1), is to step up to the stated needs of those in the Close to Christ segment. Their REVEAL surveys have made those needs very clear. A desire to understand the Bible is now at the top of their list, and the intensity of that desire has also grown, now cited by 88 percent of survey respondents as "critical" or "very important." The desire for church leaders who model and reinforce how to grow has increased in intensity too, as has the desire to be challenged. In fact, their extremely high levels of expressed desire in support of each of these stated needs leaves no room for any doubt about what they're asking of their churches. Do you sense the urgency of their spiritual hunger?

These folks may be gracious to the max. They may appear mild mannered on the surface. But beneath that exterior are individuals who passionately desire a deeper experience of God. Take this as enthusiastic permission to teach them all that Christ commanded, challenge them to conform all aspects of their life to Christ's life and teaching — and show them the way by the example you set. Those in the Close to Christ segment are not looking for average messages, simple next steps, and a safe way of living. They are looking to feed a fire deep in their souls.

It is clear from the responses of those Close to Christ that they are ready to be weaned. They no longer want you to feed them everything they need. Their faith is very personal and they are taking ownership for their ongoing development. This is cause for celebration.

We suspect, though, that some leaders may not feel, initially, that this is good news. They might think it means their people don't need them anymore. That is not the case. They just need their leaders in different ways, like teenagers need something very different from their parents than do toddlers or grade-school kids. So help them learn to feed themselves. Encourage them to do so in ways that build their strength and nourish their endurance. And watch them grow more than they (or you) might ever have anticipated – right into the midst of the Christ-Centered segment you will meet in the next chapter.

CHAPTER 5

Christ-Centered: Getting to Know Those Who Are Surrendered to God

When rumors of layoffs began swirling through the Christian college where Megan worked, a coworker turned to her for counsel. "She was obviously very fearful," Megan remembers, "so she came into my office to talk and to pray." After six years as director of career services, Megan was known for her deep devotion to Christ. And she loved her work, building her department while enjoying personal interaction with hundreds of students as they prepared to launch their own careers.

Megan didn't suspect that the layoffs would directly affect her own position: she was simply praying out of concern for her friend. "Then, all of a sudden, I just stopped in the middle of the prayer and opened my eyes," she says. "Right there in the office that I loved, in this school that I loved, in a job that I loved, I said to God, 'Bring it on.'"

Her friend sat up in surprise, but Megan continued her prayer, "Bring it on, God. Whatever you have that is going to make me more like you and make my life glorify you more, bring it on." Less than twenty-four hours after that prayer, Megan's boss informed her that her job had been eliminated.

Megan would be the first to tell you that you cannot pray without trusting that God knows what is best for your life. And she readily acknowledges that she spent a year grieving the loss of a job that she loved. Recently, though, she began a new job, working for a vocational college in the Chicago suburbs. "It's very, very different from my old position," she says, "but I find I am enjoying going to work every day. And this whole thing was just another way to open the door to God. To say, 'You know what? I'm going to step aside, God. Do whatever you want to with my life.'"

In his twenty-six years of employment with a large urban bank, Richard has had an impressive career. Now fifty-three, he serves as a vice president and senior portfolio manager, earning a living that provides a comfortable, upper-middle-class suburban lifestyle for him and his wife; their daughter, age fifteen; and two sons, eighteen and twenty.

Richard began attending church in 1998, responding to what he describes as his call from God: "Enough foolishness; it's time to come home." In doing so, he reclaimed the foundation of faith his family had provided during his childhood. "Thank God for the blessing of my parents and the upbringing that I had," he says. "Even though I had drifted away from the faith, some of that was still with me."

Now, as a father, he wanted to provide a similar foundation for his three young children. In his interactions with them, Richard found that the parental guidance he offered often brought his own less-than-perfect behaviors to mind — things he now was sorry he had done. "I remember thinking, 'I guess I'm glad I'm feeling remorseful about that and I want to straighten that out.' And I thought that maybe part of my role now was to see to it that I contributed what I could to putting my children on a better path, a more eternally directed path."

Richard's own journey to Christ required him to confront an unhealthy mindset that had developed alongside his marketplace success — a consuming preoccupation with the things that money could buy. He found himself constantly influenced by thoughts like, "It's mine, and if it's not mine, I'm going to do what I can to make it mine. If you're going to throw an addition on your house, I'm going to throw a bigger addition on my house. Join the club. Buy the boat. I just got consumed with all of that."

Eventually, Richard reached a point where his eyes were opened to his faulty definition of success, and he began to trust in Christ. "In some measure, that was my cry of surrender," he reflects. "It was 'Lord, help me; there has got to be another way. This is crazy — and I don't want this for me anymore. I don't want this for my children whom you've blessed me with and asked me to shepherd and steward along.' So it's like I was either going to go nuts, which was sort of happening, or come to my senses. And coming to my senses meant coming to Jesus. It meant doing life God's way."

Both Megan and Richard have surrendered their lives to Jesus — not only in their vocational pursuits, but in other areas of their life as well. And with that mindset of surrender in place, they represent the defining characteristic of the Christ-Centered segment.

What Does It Mean to Be "Surrendered"?

We typically associate the word *surrender* with defeat—giving up or giving in to the demands of others. Surrendering involves yielding to the power of another, like surrendering to an opponent in an athletic competition or to an opposing army in a war. Such conflicts basically boil down to struggles over control, whether it's control over who owns the most properties on a Monopoly game board or who operates the largest number of oil wells in the Persian Gulf. These battles for control end when a decision is made—when one side yields control to another.

The word *surrendered*, therefore, is an appropriate description of the Christ-Centered segment—of believers who have yielded control of their lives to Jesus. That, of course, begs the question: *What controlled their lives before they surrendered them fully to Christ?* If surrender is about "giving up," what did they walk away *from* in order to walk *toward* Jesus? Everything and anything that defines our contemporary human condition—the brokenness and temptations that plague the human heart, from the desire for power or money to the love of comfort or food or alcohol. The struggle to submit our lives wholeheartedly to Christ is not easy or simple, which is why Bill Hybels, the senior pastor at Willow Creek, believes that this spiritual chasm—between those who are Close to Christ and those who are Christ-Centered—is perhaps the most difficult line to cross. It involves giving up the things that matter most to us, surrendering them to God.

Christ-Centered believers emerge from a battle between two sets of values—the secular values that define personal identity, happiness, security, and success for much of the world, and the spiritual values of selfless love and dedication to others that characterize a life centered on Jesus. In every other segment of the spiritual continuum, the values scale tips in favor of the secular. Even those who are Close to Christ have worldly aspirations that constantly compete with Jesus to influence the direction of their lives. But the men and women who make up the Christ-Centered segment have, in large part, relinquished those secular values and worldly aspirations and yielded that control over to Christ.

The sacrifice this lifestyle requires is magnified by the *daily* nature of their commitment. More than a one-time decision, those who live the Christ-Centered life regularly face their struggles and must choose each day to follow Jesus rather than giving in to the pull of the secular world. They learn by habitual practice to deny themselves, pick up their cross, and follow Christ. But like those who battle to overcome physical addictions, the addictions of the human heart don't fade overnight. The roots of our desire for recognition, wealth, power, and pleasure are buried deep in our souls. They claw at our hearts and don't easily give way.

The grip of physical addictions — to drugs, alcohol, even food — can offer us a helpful context in which to better understand our own spiritual struggles. Spiritual growth can be seen as a progressive *release* from addiction — in this case, from the magnet of a self-serving, self-absorbed lifestyle. Though the root of this addiction is severed through the grace of God, the ongoing drag of worldly temptations requires constant vigilance.

How does the pull of a culture dominated by self-centered values impact our ability to be like Jesus? Not surprisingly, each segment in the spiritual continuum reflects a different level of concern. Those who are Exploring Christ demonstrate little concern, and are sometimes in denial that there's any need to question mainstream, worldly values. Those Growing in Christ worship and honor Jesus, but they tend to segregate their lives into spiritual and secular dimensions. They confine much of their spiritual activities to the church, letting the secular world continue to dictate their life direction and daily decisions. Those Close to Christ acknowledge and lean on God's voice and the personal presence of Jesus to help guide their daily lives, but worldly temptations continue to influence aspects of their behavior.

Those who are Christ-Centered, however, are much like a recovering addict seeking sustainability through support groups. They know their weaknesses. They acknowledge their dependence upon Christ. They humbly confess, "My name is _____, and I am a fallen creature. I surrender myself to you, Jesus." There are no denials. No attempts to shift the blame. And there is no ongoing guilt either. They have come to honestly recognize that left to themselves, the lure of the world is irresistible. They can only escape its pull through the power of the gospel of Christ.

Such a comparison may seem a bit exaggerated. We are not suggesting that Christ-Centered individuals have arrived and are no longer in need of growth. But it is the reality of a surrendered life that defines them and frees them to respond to the call of God. The choice to fully surrender to Jesus all that we hold dear is not just a one-time event — it is an ongoing process, a lifestyle of daily surrenders that define our character. And that's what makes it so difficult.

Difficulty was certainly at the core of my (Cally's) initial experience of surrender. It happened in 1993. My life was going great. I had a terrific career at a Fortune 50 company, two children with my husband of fifteen years, and a house in the suburbs. It was picture perfect.

Then ... the phone rang. There had been an accident. My eleven-year-old son had been hit by a car as he was riding his bike home from the grocery store. At the hospital we were told that he had a severe closed-head injury, and there were three possible outcomes, all equally likely: He could die. He could survive, but be brain-dead. Or he could survive, but be significantly disabled.

So we started a waiting game, watching his head pressures increase as the brain began to swell in response to the injury. We were told that if the swelling surpassed the volume of the skull, he would die. Those pressures, which are normally in the zero-to-ten range, rose into the thirties, then the forties. Three days into our watch he had emergency brain surgery to slow the swelling. But the pressures kept rising—past the forties, the fifties, into the seventies. His blood pressure dropped and his pupils became unresponsive, a sign of brain stem death. I was told that, according to the monitors, he was now dead.

All seemed lost. Human solutions had been exhausted. My world was shattered. I could no longer pretend that I was in control over anything in my life. The doctors could not save my son. God was all I had left. So I sat down on the orange carpet outside the waiting room and prayed in utter desperation and grief, "Lord, I know you do miracles. *Now* would be a very good time."

Today, my son (who has been seizure-free since 1997) is a college graduate, healthy, happy, married, and a new father. To meet him you'd never suspect what happened to him years ago.

But that's not the point of this story. In that moment on the orange carpet I learned firsthand that all the human trappings of parental protection, medical solutions, and worldly security are an illusion. It takes just a phone call to strip them away. Through this experience, God taught me to stop putting my faith in the things of this world and to depend fully on Christ. My son's recovery was, admittedly, a long journey—sometimes filled with so much pain I didn't think I could bear it. But that moment on the orange carpet was the first of many choices I would make—and continue to make each day—to surrender my dependence on an untrustworthy world for reliance on an unfailing Jesus.

A Profile of Christ-Centered: Undeniably Transformed

The true north for these believers is Jesus Christ. A moral compass defined by a deep and abiding love for God guides their daily lives. They are genuinely submitted to the guiding authority of God's Word. Christ is their life, their source of spiritual nourishment, and their central purpose is to be a living example of his values and commandments. Are there ever any chinks in the spiritual armor? Of course. At times the spiritual behaviors of this segment can seem pretty anemic when compared to the skyrocketing spiritual passions and levels of activity seen in other segments. Having great love for Christ and a rapidly growing willingness to serve him do not always translate into robust spiritual activities.

The Christ-Centered segment has three unique characteristics.

1. They Are Christ's Workforce

The people in this segment represent the most active hands and feet of Jesus on the planet. They do everything—serve the church, care for the poor, tithe, and evangelize—and they demonstrate all of these spiritual behaviors, not just one or two of them, in greater proportion than any other segment (chart 5-1).

Sue is a Korean-American woman who has translated the difficulties of her own life into a lifestyle of compassion. After years spent working three jobs to eke out a living for herself and her daughter, she looks back on those difficult times with a recognition that God used that season to help her grow: "It was the darkest time of my life. God was the only one I could depend on. I cried

The Christ-Centered Segment Serves the Church, Serves Those in Need, Evangelizes and Tithes More than Any Other Segment

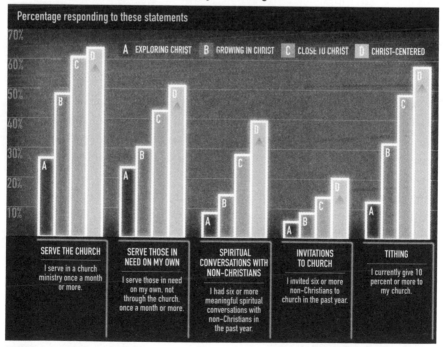

CHART 5-1: Across the board, the Christ-Centered segment demonstrates higher levels of all faith-based activities, from serving in a church ministry to inviting people to church to tithing.

out to him in prayers and he heard my prayers. He walked me through my trials and showed me life isn't all about having things, it's about God and the people he deeply cares about."

Sue cares about them as well. Not only does she volunteer in her church's prayer and guest services ministries, she recently agreed to serve as a pastor on call, a ministry requiring ongoing, four-hour weekday commitments. "I had been telling myself it was not possible. Maybe someday, when I work part-time. Then I realized, 'What are you talking about, when you work part-time? That's not going to happen. Probably I'll have to work until I'm seventy years old to make ends meet. My serving time is right now.' So I began to knock on the door. If it's what God wants me to do, then the door will be opened. If it's not, then I'll be fine."

Sue made her application, completed her interviews, and arranged to serve during the only time she could come up with—using half a vacation day from her job as a municipal accounts payable clerk for each of her serving sessions. Her church welcomed her into the ministry, and Sue says she can't wait to start her training. "I am so grateful," she says. "I can remind those I serve that just like God was there with me, God is there with them when they are going through tough times."

2. Their Love for God Exceeds That of Every Other Segment

Researchers like to focus on top-box responses because the top box—the strongest response—is the best gauge for understanding real differences among groups of people. And it's this top-box lens that illuminates the dramatic increase in spiritual attitudes for the Christ-Centered segment. Their "very strong" agreement with statements describing their love of God soars compared with the responses of other segments (chart 5-2). Almost 80 percent, for instance, very strongly agree that they love God more than anything, a percentage that is roughly double that of the Close to Christ segment.

These "very strongly agree" responses for other spiritual attitudes—relating to sharing faith, contributing financial resources, and using spiritual gifts— are also significantly higher than all other segments along the continuum.

3. They Have Two Big Spiritual Gaps Between What They Say and What They Do

The behaviors of those in the Christ-Centered segment do not always align with their impressive Christ-Centered attitudes. While their spiritual behav-

Spiritual Attitudes Increase Substantially for the Christ-Centered Segment

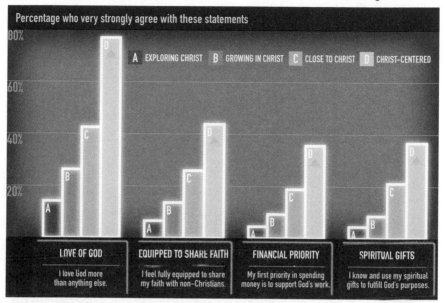

CHART 5-2: Agreement with spiritual attitude statements surges forward at the highest level (very strongly agree) in the Christ-Centered segment. The leap in their willingness to say they love God (shown in the first set of bars on the left) compared with the Close to Christ segment is particularly noteworthy.

iors are demonstrably higher than other segments (chart 5-1), they don't seem proportionally consistent with their extraordinary increase in spiritual attitudes (chart 5-2).

In order to compare an emotional measure (how much someone believes in supporting God's work) with a related behavior (whether or not he or she tithes), we created a level playing field by measuring everything starting at 1.0. The following charts illustrate how, in three specific areas, spiritual attitudes compare to spiritual behaviors across the spiritual continuum.

The Stewardship Gap. There is a big gap between attitudes expressed about financial stewardship and the behavior of tithing. The Christ-Centered segment strongly agrees that giving money to God's work is their number one financial priority, but their actual tithing falls far short (chart 5-3).

You may think this shortfall could be explained by the donations Christ-followers make to Christian organizations outside of the church — that if their church contributions and donations to these organizations were added together, they might well reach ten-percent-of-income levels. While that could be a factor, when we tested this hypothesis with our own congregation, the

There Is a Gap between Their Willingness to Give Money to God's Work and Tithing in the Christ-Centered Segment

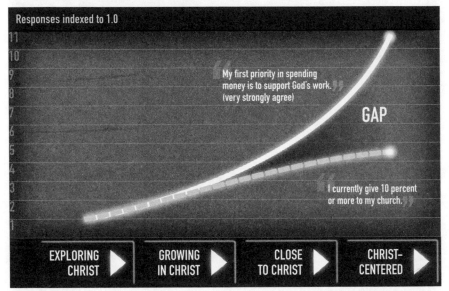

CHART 5-3: There is a mismatch between what people in the Christ-Centered segment say they believe about giving ("my first financial priority is to support God's work") and what they actually do. On a relative basis, the percentage of those in the Christ-Centered segment that express a desire to support God's work is eleven times greater compared with the Exploring Christ segment. But their actual behavior (the percentage who give 10 percent or more to the church) is only four times greater.

results did not support this explanation. Other anecdotal evidence suggests that this gap could be due in part to financial hardship, and that as a person's economic circumstances improve, the size of the disparity in this comparison may diminish. For instance, Megan, the college counselor you read about at the beginning of the chapter, reports that while she has tithed at various times in her life, she is not doing so now—opting instead to reduce her substantial debt. These explanations may have some validity, but all we can report conclusively is that the Christ-Centered segment's tithing to the church lags behind this segment's desire to financially support God's work—and by a considerable margin.

The Serving Gap. There is also a significant gap between attitudes about spiritual gifts and the decision to use those gifts to serve others. The Christ-Centered segment believes in using their spiritual gifts for God's purposes. But the increase they report in their attitudes doesn't always translate to serving those in need—either through the church or on their own (chart 5-4).

There Is a Gap between Willingness to Use Spiritual Gifts and Actual Serving Behaviors in the Christ-Centered Segment

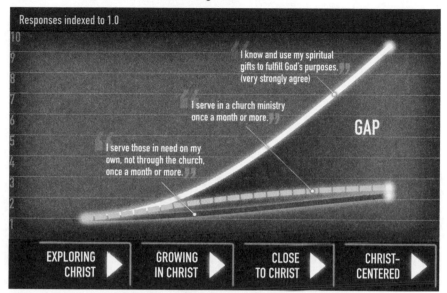

Responses indexed to 1.0

I know and use my spiritual gifts to fulfill God's purposes. (very strongly agree)

I serve in a church ministry once a month or more.

I serve those in need on my own, not through the church, once a month or more.

GAP

| EXPLORING CHRIST ▶ | GROWING IN CHRIST ▶ | CLOSE TO CHRIST ▶ | CHRIST-CENTERED ▶ |

CHART 5-4: There is a mismatch between what people in the Christ-Centered segment say about serving ("I know and use my spiritual gifts to fulfill God's purposes") and their actual serving behaviors. On a relative basis, the percentage of those in the Christ-Centered segment that want to use their gifts for God is nine times greater compared with the Exploring Christ segment. But their actual behavior (the percentage who serve those in need or serve the church at least monthly) is only two times greater.

No Evangelism Gap. Interestingly, the Christ-Centered segment does not show a gap in the area of evangelism. In other words, their evangelistic behaviors match their evangelistic attitudes. What they *do* matches what they *say* when it comes to sharing their faith with others. In fact, we find that evangelistic activity rises in direct proportion with people's confidence in their ability to evangelize (chart 5-5). As we discussed in chapter 4, this means that if we equip people to evangelize, they will enthusiastically respond. This is true for all segments.

Richard, Megan, and Sue share their faith on a regular basis—and all of them are well-acquainted with their pastors' counsel to constantly be "testing doors," checking to see whether a person might be open to a spiritual conversation. "You just don't know," says Richard. "I've been surprised so many times when I felt a nudge by the Spirit to test a door and my reaction was, 'You've got to be kidding me; there is not a chance this person will respond.' And then it comes again and I'll say to God, 'Okay, I'll *show* you there is no way!' And I tap on whatever the door is and it opens and I can't believe this is happening.'"

There Is No Gap for Any Segment — Including Christ-Centered — between Attitudes and Behaviors about Evangelism

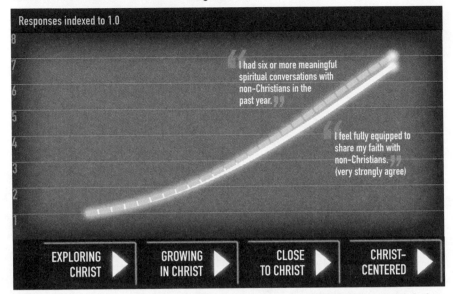

Responses indexed to 1.0

> I had six or more meaningful spiritual conversations with non-Christians in the past year.

> I feel fully equipped to share my faith with non-Christians.
> (very strongly agree)

EXPLORING CHRIST

GROWING IN CHRIST

CLOSE TO CHRIST

CHRIST-CENTERED

CHART 5-5: Comparing what people say about feeling equipped to share their faith with their evangelistic behaviors (having meaningful spiritual conversations) shows that every segment matches a growing level of evangelistic confidence with actions. In other words, the Christ-Centered percentage expressing confidence in their ability to share their faith with non-Christians is seven times greater than that of the Exploring Christ segment. And their actual behavior (the percentage who have had more than six meaningful spiritual conversations with non-Christians in the past year) is seven times greater.

Often, conversations like the one Richard is talking about have profound meaning for both people involved. When Megan was thirty, her mother was diagnosed with a brain tumor — a condition that ended her life just two months later. Alone with Megan in the hospital room about a week before she died, her mother removed her oxygen mask and said, "I'm afraid." When Megan asked what she was afraid of, her mother answered, "That I won't get there. That I won't get to heaven."

"I had dreamed of this moment for years," Megan says, "to help usher this woman I loved more than anyone in the world into the presence of God; that she would know him. I just said, 'Mom' — and it came out of me like I say it every day and it was the most natural thing — I said, 'Mom, do you believe that Jesus Christ is the Son of God, that he died for your sins? Do you love him with all your heart?' She said 'Yes,' and I said, 'Then you're already there, Mom. This room is filled with angels rejoicing in the fact that you know Jesus, and you don't have to be afraid. He's waiting for you.'"

4. What the Christ-Centered "Gaps" Mean for the Church

There are two different ways to view the evident gaps in the spiritual behaviors of the Christ-Centered segment, and they largely depend on your own perspective. Is the sky outside partly cloudy or partly sunny? For some, the gaps between attitude and behaviors found in the Christ-Centered segment may be a great disappointment. Across the board, their attitudes seem to reflect a love for Jesus. But you might wonder, "Where's the beef?" Where is the behavioral evidence that Christ-Centered people are leading transformed lives in response to their love for Christ?

On the other hand, the Christ-Centered segment can also represent an incredible opportunity for spiritual impact. These are passionate believers with faith in the truth about God and the gospel of Christ. They are students of the Word who tune in daily for God's guidance and direction. The gaps between their spiritual attitudes and behaviors may simply reflect a lack of teaching in a specific area, or they may be underchallenged. Perhaps they lack the support they really need to close this gap, and that support is not yet a priority for their church. After more than five years of spiritual-growth research with thousands of congregants, we believe that lack of support from the church is a strong possibility—thus representing a great opportunity for the church.

This opportunity becomes clearer when we review what the Christ-Centered segment wants from the church. They want the exact same things (chart 5-6) as the Close to Christ segment wants—although Christ-Centered people want it with even more intensity. Those who are in this segment are hungry for God, and they want to lean on their church for support in their ongoing spiritual development.

While these needs are quite similar to the Close to Christ segment, the difference in intensity supports our view that the two segments are distinct in a very significant way. The Close to Christ segment sees Christ as vital to their everyday life. They depend on him and seek his guidance throughout their day. They view Jesus as their friend—someone who cares for them and helps them navigate life. But the Christ-Centered segment takes that perspective one step further—and begins seeing Jesus in a radically new way. Rather than expecting Jesus to be there for the sole purpose of helping *them* with *their* lives, they respond to his call to sacrifice and lay down their lives to serve *Jesus* and advance *his* mission in the world. He is not here for our personal needs. We exist for *him*—to know, love, obey, serve, and be with him forever.

The rich young ruler in Matthew 19 provides us with a pertinent example. Here was a person who did everything the law required. He did all the

The Top Five Things the Christ-Centered Segment Wants from You and Your Church

BENEFITS PROVIDED BY THE CHURCH	Percentage who find the benefit critical or very important
1. Help in understanding the Bible in greater depth	90%
2. Help in developing a personal relationship with Christ	89%
3. Church leaders who model and consistently reinforce how to grow spiritually	87%
4. Challenge to grow and take next steps	84%
5. Encouragement to take personal responsibility for spiritual growth	84%

CHART 5-6: Based on their rating of nineteen church attributes, these are the five most important factors the Christ-Centered segment wants from the church. Similar to the Close to Christ segment, almost 90 percent say that it is critically or very important that the church helps them both understand the Bible in depth and develop a personal relationship with Christ. Being challenged and encouraged to take personal responsibility for their spiritual growth is also vital to this segment.

right things. But he came up short in one area—he was unwilling to sacrifice everything he had to follow Jesus. He wanted something *from* Jesus, but was unwilling to turn over *to* Jesus the one thing that was the most important to him: his wealth and possessions. But those who have a Christ-Centered heart recognize that they gain everything by laying down their own lives and their own agendas to serve Christ. They embrace the cross, denying their own selfish desires each and every day, and follow Jesus. And they seek to love him with all their heart, soul, mind, and strength.

Some churches, like the one that is profiled in this chapter, are actively facilitating this type of growth. But our study also reveals that most churches are still operating with an infrastructure that is primarily geared to challenge and support the earlier segments of spiritual development. In part 2, which is devoted to unpacking the catalysts of spiritual growth, we suggest that going to weekend services, participating in small groups, and volunteering in church ministries *are* significant drivers for spiritual growth at the earliest stages. Many churches have dedicated enormous resources to these activities. However, we believe the church may be undersupporting, underresourcing, and underchallenging those in the Christ-Centered segment—people who, if inspired and equipped, would be most likely to make a difference in the world for Jesus.

It is our point of view—admittedly from a glass-half-full, partly-sunny-sky perspective—that the Christ-Centered segment may simply be underchallenged. And we are cautiously optimistic that there are specific ways church leaders can apply these insights to prosper the cause of Christ.

Love of God: Willing to Risk Everything

"Are you willing to risk everything that's important in your life for Jesus Christ?" Fifty percent of the Christ-Centered segment not only agreed that yes, they were willing, but they "very strongly" agreed. Their top-box response, along with their very strong response to love of God, distinguishes those in the Christ-Centered segment from those in every other segment on the spiritual continuum (chart 5-7).

Megan is a real-life example of what this response means. "I have not always been very consistent with attending church, with tithing, with serving," she says. "No excuse. That's just the truth. What I have been consistent with is loving Christ—with reaching out to him, with prayer, and with being

Love of God and Willingness to Risk Everything for Christ Increase Substantially for the Christ-Centered Segment

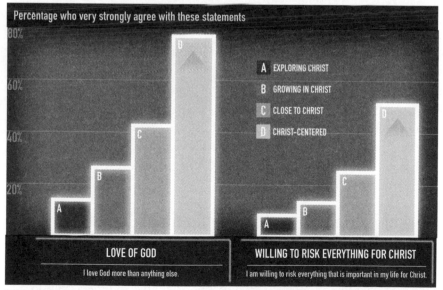

CHART 5-7: This chart illustrates the dramatic rise in the Christ-Centered segment's response to two statements about love of God and their willingness to risk everything important in life for Christ. In both cases, the percentage of Christ-Centered people who very strongly agree with these statements is virtually twice the level of any other segment.

Daily Personal Spiritual Practices Increase Even More Dramatically for the Christ-Centered Segment

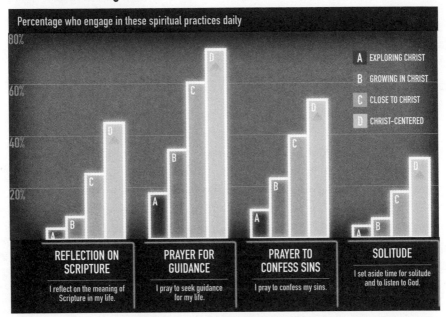

CHART 5-8: The significant rise in the percentage of people participating in spiritual practices every day was noted earlier for the Close to Christ segment. Those percentages increase to even higher levels in the Christ-Centered segment. Note that 30 percent of Christ-Centered people experience each one of these four practices on a daily basis.

as real with him as I am capable of. I tell him thank you regularly. I get away to be alone with him. I sing to him. I argue with him. I cry and cry and cry to him. I write to him. I laugh with him. I tell him I love him."

Those who are in the Christ-Centered segment typically back up their sense of commitment and devotion to Christ with a daily devotion to personal spiritual practices. The number who spend time in daily reflection on the Scriptures is almost double the Close to Christ percentage (chart 5-8).

Love of Others: On the Brink of Spiritual Greatness

Those in the Christ-Centered segment believe they have hearts that have been transformed by their love of God, but the gap between their professed love of God and their love of others is often perplexing. Love of others trails love of God for all segments, but the gap is the *widest* among those who claim they are most devoted to Christ—the Christ-Centered segment (chart 5-9).

Love of Others Trails Love of God, Especially for the Christ-Centered Segment

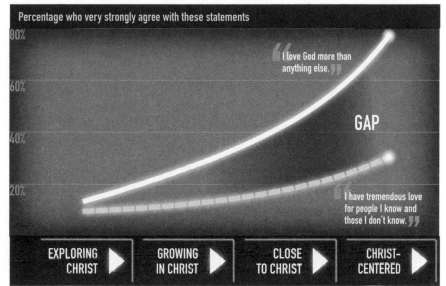

Percentage who very strongly agree with these statements

80%

60%

40%

20%

I love God more than anything else.

GAP

I have tremendous love for people I know and those I don't know.

| EXPLORING CHRIST ▶ | GROWING IN CHRIST ▶ | CLOSE TO CHRIST ▶ | CHRIST-CENTERED ▶ |

CHART 5-9: Note that the gap between the percentage who very strongly agree they love God and the percentage who very strongly agree they love others widens progressively across the spiritual continuum. The widest gap by far exists in the Christ-Centered segment.

This finding is disappointing, but it is also consistent with earlier observations we have noted about the gaps between spiritual behaviors, like serving and tithing, and spiritual attitudes. When questions focus on evaluating their personal relationship with God and their willingness to serve Christ, Christ-Centered responses are sky-high. However, their spiritual behaviors — which still are the highest across the spiritual continuum — lag far behind what we might expect from such strong professions of commitment to Christ.

Consider this discrepancy in particular. While the percentage of Christ-Centered people who have more than six meaningful spiritual conversations with non-Christians is the highest of all other segments, it's still *only* 40 percent. And only 20 percent of those in the Christ-Centered segment have invited six or more people to church in the last year. In other words, more than half of those who feel they are Christ-Centered have fewer than six spiritual conversations with non-Christians in a year — and 80 percent of them invite fewer than one person to church every two months.

Once again, we conclude that those in the Christ-Centered segment are under-challenged — not about loving God, but about loving others. They have the potential of doing truly magnificent things for Christ. They are not unwilling. They are simply uninspired and unmotivated. They may get the highest marks for spiritual attitude and performance. But despite the high scores, they are still not living up to their God-given potential.

This may be the most significant finding to come out of the whole body of REVEAL research. Nothing else we have found represents such a tremendous opportunity for the kingdom.

Spiritual Leadership Requires Constant Challenge

Earlier in this chapter, we cited the example of the rich young ruler, and how he was willing to do everything except surrender himself to Christ — the one thing that would have made all the difference. What would have happened, do you think, if the rich young ruler had said yes to Jesus? If he had been more like Matthew and Zacchaeus, who were wealthy and yet obeyed Jesus and rearranged everything to follow him. What might God have done through this young man's life? How many people would have been blessed as he distributed his wealth to the poor?

In light of the four segments on REVEAL's spiritual continuum, perhaps the rich young ruler was stuck, unwilling to fully surrender his life to Christ. He did not yet understand that "people's lives are not their own" (Jeremiah 10:23). He had someone (Jesus) who actually challenged him to take the final step. But the sad truth is that in many of our churches, those who are Close to Christ don't have anyone challenging them to take that final step. We let them remain comfortable having Jesus as their friend, helping them live their lives, but never learning to fully surrender to his leading. Leaders especially must model a life of surrender to their congregations. We need to demonstrate that we take the prompting of the Spirit and the call of the gospel seriously. And we must challenge others to follow our lead, as together, we spur one another on to love and good deeds for the sake of Jesus.

A Person Who Is Christ-Centered Is . . .

—Christ's greatest workforce

—Head over heels in love with God

—Tithing, serving, and evangelizing more than anyone else

—Underchallenged by the church

—On the brink of spiritual greatness

Loving Jesus in the Smokies: A Christ-Centered Church

Located in a small town nestled in the tree-covered mountains of far western North Carolina is a church that fairly glows with spiritual vitality. Founded in 1977, this nondenominational church met in a founding family's basement before moving to a larger venue in an old dry-cleaner's building. Now the church's thirty-four-acre campus is home to seven hundred members — which is especially noteworthy when you consider that this number represents half of the town's official population.

But then *noteworthy* is a word that applies quite often to this church. The pages of its REVEAL survey are filled with up arrows, which means the congregants' spiritual attitudes and behavior measurements are off the charts. These people are in love with God, and this church serves as the hub for their extraordinary outpouring of Spirit-led energy and service.

The photos posted on the church's website depict people of all ages — interacting, learning, and obviously enjoying one another's company. But are their leaders satisfied and complacent? Absolutely not. Their senior pastor is humble about their success, pointing out that their survey results indicate some 17 percent of the church's congregants are "dissatisfied." Actually, this percentage is right in line with most of the churches we survey, but this pastor takes that result as a challenge, saying he will work to do a better job of bringing some of the longer-tenured people along with his vision of where the church is heading.

We wish him well. But the fact is that the spiritual force pouring out of this church is already astounding. Forty-three percent of the congregation are Christ-Centered, and their influence is everywhere. Nearly two-thirds of the congregation tithe; almost half meet monthly with spiritual mentors; two-thirds are in small groups; and one-third reflects on Scripture daily. Almost 40 percent serve those in need monthly, through the church, and the same percentage had meaningful spiritual conversations with more than six non-Christians in the past year. (All of these percentages are more than 50 percent higher than what takes place in most other churches.)

According to the survey results — and reflective of the spiritual vitality of its people — every corner of this church buzzes with Christ-Centered activities, conversations, and attitudes of prayerful surrender to the purposes they feel God has designated for them.

And the best news is that this church is not unique. It is not a one-of-a-kind congregation. In fact, at least one of every ten churches taking the REVEAL survey posts similar high-energy results — results generated by best practices that they are eager to share. In part 3, we'll learn more from those churches, like this stunning North Carolina role model, that seem to breathe the Spirit of God into everything they do. Stay tuned.

Leading Forward

So practically, how do we lead and support those in the Christ-Centered segment? How do we challenge them to put their extraordinary potential to work on behalf of the kingdom?

First, as with the other segments, it is important that they know we value them and are committed to their ongoing development. Around Willow, we periodically talk in our weekend services about the gap between someone who is Close to Christ and someone who is completely surrendered to Christ. One of the ways we illustrate the difference between these two heart conditions is by sharing the stories we've heard from people in our congregation — Christ-Centered people who are living their lives out of a place of true surrender to God. Recently, for instance, we shared the story of a couple who had radically simplified their lifestyle so they could devote more of their time and financial resources to help those in need. They did without new cars. They stayed in a smaller house, even as their family grew. The husband served as leader of our church's Habitat for Humanity efforts and had personally led the construction efforts for more than a hundred homes. All of this was motivated out of their deep love for Christ and a belief that "this is what God has made us for." This couple sensed that God was calling them to this lifestyle, so — as people whose lives were surrendered — their choice was not difficult to make.

By sharing this story, we provided the entire congregation with a glimpse of what this level of spiritual maturity looks like — and assured them that such an objective truly is reachable. But just as importantly, we affirmed all our Christ-Centered congregation members, making it clear that we value and admire their commitment to Jesus. In a world where such decisions are typically misunderstood, scoffed at, or worse, such an endorsement of their countercultural commitment to Christ can be heartening and reassuring.

Second, we need to continually challenge the people in this segment to constantly be in a process of *re*surrender: To make it part of a daily discipline that includes handing over to Jesus anything that has control of their lives. To make more and more of themselves available to him. To follow that up with a priority-altering prayer, "God, what do you want from me today? Whom can I serve? Whom can I love?" Then we need to strongly encourage people in this segment to follow God's promptings. As leaders, we need to foster our ability to help others discern the voice of God, because it is their deepest desire to follow him.

Third, we need to willingly release them from serving exclusively in an official ministry of our church. Too often a pastor's worldview is too limited. We think that good ministry can only flow from something that is authored by the church and its staff. But as individuals who are Christ-Centered practice the discipline of resurrender and listen to the promptings of the Spirit, odds are that they will increasingly be led to serve *outside* of an official church ministry. We should not only encourage this but also celebrate it. Seventy-four percent of Christ-Centered people say it is "critical" or "very important" to them that their church "empowers me to go out *on my own* to make a significant impact in the lives of others" (emphasis added). Jesus did not ask the disciples to stay in the synagogue; he sent them out into the world, two by two, to make a difference in it. Don't be concerned that these Christ-Centered folks will *stop* serving in the church when they *start* serving in the community.

Remember Sue, the woman who arranged to use her vacation days to volunteer as a pastor on call? A few years before she volunteered for that position, she says she felt prompted by God to become a chaplain at a local hospital. "God gave me the desire," Sue says. "Still I wonder why; still I don't know. Why a hospital? Why sick people?"

As Sue shares just a few of her experiences, however, the answer becomes clear. Take her visit to a young man with a brain injury, on just her second day as a chaplain. After talking with him about his life, she asked if he would like her to pray for him. "He said yes and I was very nervous," Sue remembers. "But I put my hand on his head and began to pray for his healing. When I opened my eyes, I saw tears running down from his eyes. And he said, 'I never had anybody pray for me in my whole life.' That really broke my heart. I began to cry, too." You may recall reading that Sue is involved in her church's prayer ministry. Now you also know that it was her community service experience that led her to that ministry in the church.

While still a hospital chaplain, Sue talked with a very ill elderly woman who told

Sue, "I don't know whether I am going to be in heaven, but I want to." Sue says, "That gave me a chance, so I was able to tell her the whole Genesis to Revelation story, and then after that, I asked, 'Are you willing to accept Christ as your Savior?' She said yes, so she repeated the salvation prayer after me. The joy in my heart — I was so energized! And I saw the light; her face cleared up. And she said, 'I can't wait to see God. I can't wait to go to heaven.'"

Think what these and scores of other hospital patients would have missed if Sue's church had discouraged her volunteer work in the community. One caveat: Over the past few years, as this value has become more significant in our church, we hear members ask whether their service to their neighbor "counts." And that just begs the question, "Counts for what?" Too often, their response is something like, "Counts toward my membership commitment to be serving in the church." Yikes! That is an example of how a church process that does good for some can be twisted, unintentionally, to do harm. Our churches should always celebrate God-prompted service to others, and we need to understand that this is especially important to those among us who are Christ-Centered.

PART 2

Spiritual Movement

The Catalysts of Spiritual Growth

Can you name a key turning point in your life? Perhaps it was a choice you made in your youth—who to befriend, what school to attend, who to date. A turning point is a big decision, or one that seems inconsequential at the time but ultimately has a dramatic impact on your future.

I (Cally) experienced such a turning point in eighth grade. I enjoyed my first Spanish class so much that I decided to pursue additional foreign language courses. That decision, in turn, triggered later decisions, including my choice of college and a career path. It was through my career that I met my husband—and that relationship led to decisions about where to live and how many children to have. Each of these choices has shaped my life in profound ways, yet in one sense they were all born out of my middle school interest in learning other languages!

Your life, too, has been shaped by a series of decisions. Those decisions may have been driven by passions that began in your youth. Or perhaps a seemingly mundane choice—like whether to attend an event, stay on vacation an extra day, or volunteer with a local charity—led to previously unconsidered possibilities.

Of course, such decisions aren't always positive or proactive. Sometimes they are reactive choices we make because we're facing circumstances beyond our control—like losing a job or dealing with a medical crisis. But whether we're charting our future or figuring out how to respond to unexpected or unwelcome circumstances, our life is the product of a series of choices, decisions we make each and every day.

Certainly, some of our decisions are reversible (think about how often college students change their majors), but most of them are inescapable—life inevitably brings unexpected opportunities and challenges beyond our control. Some of us relish these moments of change; others are paralyzed by them. But whether we approach decision making with joy or terror, we can't avoid it. Life requires *movement*.

Not surprisingly, our spiritual growth is also impacted by our decisions. This does not diminish the necessity of the abiding presence and work of the Holy Spirit who initiates our growth and is always working to draw us closer to God. It is simply an acknowledgment that human choice plays a crucial role, in partnership with the Holy Spirit, in readying our hearts for spiritual growth. Certain decisions lead to spiritual "turning points"—like the decision to believe the good news that God came to earth in the person of Jesus Christ for the purpose of redeeming the world.

As vital as this decision is to spiritual growth, it is hardly the last decision a person makes along his or her spiritual journey. In fact, each and every day we make many choices that determine our spiritual progress—choosing, for instance, whether or not to pray, to open our Bibles, or to risk spiritual conversations with neighbors or coworkers.

For most of my life, I (Greg) have tried my best to discern and follow the Holy Spirit's leading. I remember one morning when I woke up early to do some writing. My neverending, constantly growing to-do list had made this increasingly difficult for me. Unwilling to sacrifice family time to write, there I was up in the early hours of the morning, anxious to make some progress. I was feeling the lack of sleep and struggling with worry over some looming deadlines. And none of this was helping me to think clearly or creatively.

As hard as I tried to focus on my work, though, my mind kept returning to the story of King Solomon. Lately, I had been studying the life of Solomon with my eight-year-old son, so the story was fresh on my mind. I kept thinking about how Solomon's wisdom came not from his own striving but as a gift from God. And as I sat there thinking, feeling the tension and stress of deadlines and responsibilities looming over me, the Holy Spirit kept that word *striving* in front of me. I began to understand that's exactly what I had been doing—focusing all my efforts on getting things done and depending on myself rather than seeking God's direction. So I made the decision to turn off the computer and spend time with God to fully listen to what he was trying to tell me. I spent the next forty-five minutes listing all the ways I'd been trying to live my life without God's help. I confessed that I had lost my way, that I needed to stop striving and just receive God's assistance in all areas of my life.

Decisions like this—ones that we make every day in response to the Holy Spirit—are crucial. But which faith-based decisions matter most? The REVEAL research has identified twenty-five decisions that are critical to helping people stay on a path toward full devotion to Christ. We call these deci-

The Catalysts of Spiritual Growth • 107

sions the "catalysts" of spiritual growth, because they lead to some type of spiritual change.

The role of the church is to help people make the choices that will open their hearts to God so they can become fully committed disciples. The REVEAL research offers church leaders fact-based insights about the twenty-five decisions that are most catalytic in helping people do exactly that.

Decisions That Catalyze Spiritual Growth

As spiritual growth takes place, people move from one segment to the next across the spiritual continuum. As we have seen, the characteristics for each segment are distinct, ranging from people with very little faith connection (Exploring Christ) to people deeply devoted to Jesus (Christ-Centered). These four segments exist in every one of the congregations that participated in the REVEAL survey, which means that every church is a collection of people who are spiritually heterogeneous. They may have similar characteristics or live in the same community, but they are at very different stages of spiritual maturity.

However, knowing *which* segment people belong to is not as important as understanding what needs to happen for these people to move across the spiritual continuum. That's why the twenty-five decisions that catalyze spiritual growth is truly the heart of the REVEAL survey. And it's why we called this book *Move*, because we want to help *move* people toward God.

To better understand these catalysts, we've divided them into four categories:

- *Spiritual Beliefs and Attitudes*, which are core Christian beliefs such as salvation by grace and the authority of Scripture.
- *Organized Church Activities*, including the most common onsite activities like weekend worship services and serving in a ministry.
- *Personal Spiritual Practices*, which are the disciplines including prayer and reflection on Scripture that are involved in growing a person's faith.
- *Spiritual Activities with Others*, including evangelism and serving those in need, which happen largely outside the organized church.

We evaluated the impact of these spiritual catalysts by highlighting those that are most influential in the three *movements* of spiritual growth, movements that take place as people advance from one segment on the spiritual continuum to the next (chart 6-1). By focusing on these three forward shifts, we can better understand the decisions people need to make.

Spiritual Growth Occurs in Three Movements Across the Spiritual Continuum

Exploring Christ

Growing in Christ

Close to Christ

Christ-Centered

MOVEMENT 1

MOVEMENT 2

MOVEMENT 3

CHART 6-1: People progress across the spiritual continuum in three movements: Movement 1, early spiritual growth; Movement 2, intermediate spiritual growth; Movement 3, advanced spiritual growth.

So how do the three movements relate to the four segments on the spiritual continuum?

Movement 1: The Earliest Stage of Spiritual Growth. As people move from the Exploring Christ to the Growing in Christ segment, they gain their initial understanding of the Christian faith and accept that Jesus Christ offers the only path to salvation.

Movement 2: The Intermediate Stage of Spiritual Growth. As those in the Growing in Christ segment become more active in their personal spiritual practices and experiences, they progress to a more intimate relationship and grow Close to Christ.

Movement 3: The More Advanced Stage of Spiritual Growth. In this movement, believers shift from a daily awareness of Christ's presence and involvement (a Close to Christ relationship) to a redefinition of their identity, based on their relationship with Jesus (a Christ-Centered relationship).

To further understand how each of the three spiritual movements reflects a different stage of development in a person's relationship with Christ, it's helpful to think about them in the context of how human relationships develop. Movement 1, for example, resembles the early growth of a friendship—a relationship that progresses when an acquaintance becomes a regular lunch companion, for instance. Similarly, in this early movement of spiritual growth, a person gets to know Jesus within the familiar context of church activities.

Movement 2 represents a casual relationship that advances from being defined by the boundaries of a shared setting (like work or school) or shared activities (sports or a hobby) to a personal friendship characterized by frequent communication about the daily issues of life. This relational shift occurs when someone you'd call for a racquetball game becomes someone you'd call in a crisis, which is an apt metaphor for the stage of spiritual growth in which people become more involved with Christ through their personal spiritual practices.

Movement 3 portrays the relational shift from one that is personal to one that is intimate— from being the sounding board when your friend is in crisis to fully sharing your life with him or her. This takes place when you align your identity with another through marriage, for example, or possibly a long-term business partnership in which decisions, big and small, are made collaboratively. The commitment to such a relationship becomes fully integrated with daily life, which is exactly what happens when Christ defines a person's identity in the most advanced stage of spiritual growth.

In both human and spiritual terms, the nature of our relationship shifts across a continuum, from one based on common interests to one based on sharing life's joys and triumphs as well as its heartaches and defeats. On the spiritual side, each of these shifts is facilitated by decisions people make that take them from a relationship with Christ that is largely irrelevant to one that is central to everything they do.

In what follows, we'll unpack each of the four categories in which these crucial decisions reside: spiritual beliefs and attitudes, organized church activities, personal spiritual practices, and spiritual activities with others.

Category 1: Spiritual Beliefs and Attitudes

Beliefs and attitudes reflect what we accept as true or real. Beliefs always require some level of trust—a measure of faith. For example, we believe the world is round even though most of us have not been in space to see that for ourselves. Christian spiritual beliefs are no different. Although there is substantial corroborating historical and archeological evidence to support the beliefs of the Christian faith, it is less a matter of believing in irrefutable data, and more about accepting that the relationship God offers us in Jesus Christ is possible and desirable.

The REVEAL survey measures the spiritual beliefs and attitudes of people by asking them to express their agreement with various core spiritual values (chart 6-2).

On this chart, the belief statements listed under each movement indicate that strong agreement with those beliefs is catalytic to growth in that movement. For example, the decision to believe in salvation by grace is a fundamental catalyst that moves people from the Exploring Christ segment to the Growing in Christ segment. The responses to the following questions can help us better understand how this works.

What does it mean that spiritual beliefs and attitudes are spiritual catalysts?

As we pointed out earlier, a catalyst makes change happen. In the category of spiritual beliefs, this is demonstrated by the increasing intensity of a person's agreement with a belief statement. For example, belief in salvation by grace ("I believe nothing I do or have done can earn my salvation") is highly *predictive* within Movement 1. Since we consistently find more people who "very strongly agree" with belief in salvation by grace in the second segment (Growing in Christ) than we do in the first segment (Exploring Christ), we can conclude that the decision to accept this belief is a catalyst that influences the movement of people *from* Exploring Christ to Growing in Christ.

Is the order of the statements significant?

Yes, the statements are ranked, top to bottom, by the degree to which they influence movement. For example, in this category of spiritual beliefs and attitudes, belief in salvation by grace is the most significant catalyst for Movement 1. Belief in the authority of the Bible is an important catalyst in this movement as well, but not as significant as the four statements that precede it.

Where do these statements come from?

The eight belief and attitude statements that appear (frequently more than once) on chart 6-2 are based on significant and recurring biblical themes. While there are many other potential beliefs and attitudes that the Bible suggests are helpful for our spiritual growth, these statements have consistently emerged in ongoing research of America's spiritual culture as those that best describe and define a

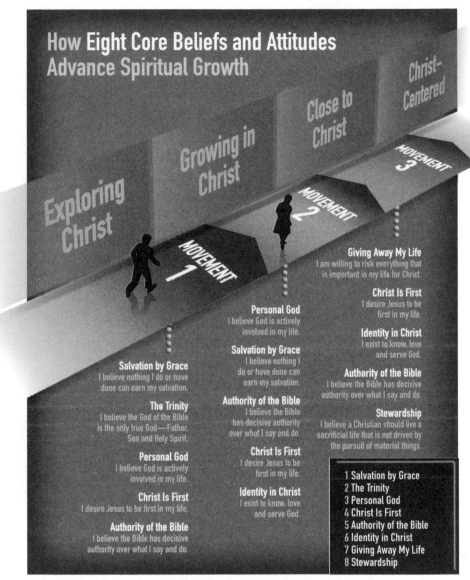

CHART 6–2: The spiritual beliefs and attitudes that are most influential to spiritual growth are listed under each movement in order of importance. Note that the catalyst of greatest impact shifts from belief in salvation by grace in Movement 1, to statements reflecting a more personal and deeper relationship with God in Movements 2 and 3.

person's spiritual condition. (For more detail, see "What Are the Spiritual Belief and Attitude Statements and Where Do They Come From?" page 124, 267).

These insights about spiritual beliefs and attitudes have definite implications for church leaders. No, we can't flip a switch and *make* a person move from disbelief to belief. However, the following observations may help those who lead local churches more fully appreciate what's at stake in the invisible and hard-to-define world of spiritual convictions.

Observation 1: Weak Beliefs Inhibit Spiritual Growth

Has anyone in your congregation ever responded to your explanation of a spiritual belief with something like, "Yeah. You know, I think I can pretty much accept that"? What that person may have intended as an encouraging response might actually feel fairly *dis*couraging. Because if people don't *fully* buy into these eight core Christian beliefs and attitude statements, they will not grow into followers of Christ. To truly grow, a person cannot be half-heartedly convinced that these statements are true. If the beliefs and spiritual attitudes of the people in your congregation are weak, it is virtually certain that their personal connection with God is also weak.

Observation 2: People Do Not Buy into These Beliefs All at Once

Beliefs are typically embraced one at a time. In fact, a progressive order exists — one that makes sense and tells a powerful story about how faith in Christ develops. First, people become convinced of the fundamental truths of salvation by grace and the Trinity (Movement 1). Next, we find that they affirm a personal God — a God who is "actively involved in my life" (Movement 2). This belief in God's omnipresence leads to a strong desire for "Jesus to be first in my life" and a humble, heartfelt willingness to "risk everything that is important in my life for Jesus Christ" (Movement 3). This progression provides a window into how spiritual transformation works, something that we have seen repeated time after time as we have examined the responses of thousands of God's people.

We intentionally began our discussion of spiritual catalysts with beliefs and attitudes because this is where the spiritual journey begins. Just as other relationships in our lives grow as people prove themselves trustworthy, our relationship with Christ begins with a decision to trust his promise and character. How do we come to these decisions? In addition to the supernatural work of the Holy Spirit in our lives, we can also say that the church — the body of Christ — typically plays a central role in shaping our first impressions of faith and introducing us to core Christian beliefs. That is the focus of the next category, organized church activities.

Category 2: Organized Church Activities

The church is the most significant organized influence on spiritual growth, so participation in church activities naturally emerges as an important catalytic factor. Our latest findings about the role of the church confirm the conclusions we reached back when our research tapped into only a handful of churches: *The catalytic power of the church is limited primarily to the first two movements of spiritual growth* (chart 6-3). Moreover, the activity that commands most of the church's resources — weekend services — shows up as only moderately important beyond Movement 1.[1]

When we apply our context of human relationships to these findings, it makes perfect sense that organized activities become less important. The closer you are to someone — the more likely you are to depend on them to process your life issues — the less important organized settings tend to be. While you may have formed the relationship in a structured experience — in the workplace, perhaps, or at a neighborhood gathering — that setting is typically a springboard for the relationship, not something required to sustain it. Organizations create a natural proximity for people with shared interests, but as relationships become more personal, people create their own settings and experiences to meet and communicate. The central role of the organization declines.

Many will argue that a church is different — that the large gathering of the body of Christ in a physical setting is foundational to spiritual growth, regardless of spiritual maturity. We would agree that it's important to be discerning about this finding in light of biblical teaching on the important role of the local church (Ephesians 3:10; Hebrews 10:24–25). We would nuance this by suggesting that it's the *organized* activities of the church that diminish (but never disappear) in importance. The *organic* contribution of the church to spiritual development continues to be strong across all movements.

Organic refers to growth that occurs naturally. Organic vegetables, for example, are grown without the assistance of artificial environments or manufactured nutrients, so without much human assistance beyond the planting of the garden itself. In a similar way, the church plants a spiritual garden, providing organized settings that allow natural growth to occur. Beyond providing the setting for worship and spiritual enrichment through weekend services, the church also provides a setting where spiritual relationships and skills can

---

[1] It's important to note that this finding comes from a database with a large percentage of churches (43 percent) that do not consider themselves seeker targeted or seeker friendly.

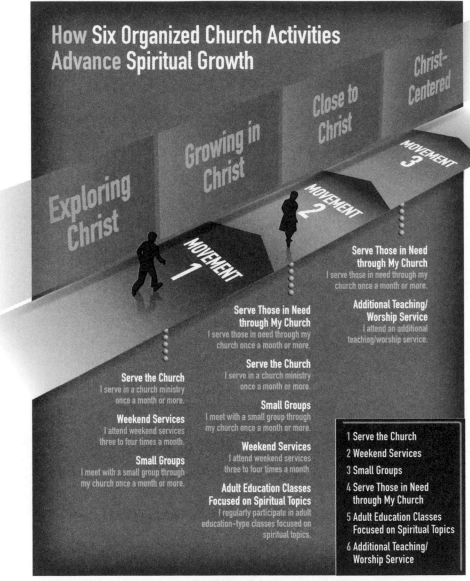

How Six Organized Church Activities Advance Spiritual Growth

Exploring Christ

Growing in Christ

Close to Christ

Christ-Centered

MOVEMENT 1

MOVEMENT 2

MOVEMENT 3

Serve the Church
I serve in a church ministry once a month or more.

Weekend Services
I attend weekend services three to four times a month.

Small Groups
I meet with a small group through my church once a month or more.

Serve Those in Need through My Church
I serve those in need through my church once a month or more.

Serve the Church
I serve in a church ministry once a month or more.

Small Groups
I meet with a small group through my church once a month or more.

Weekend Services
I attend weekend services three to four times a month.

Adult Education Classes Focused on Spiritual Topics
I regularly participate in adult education-type classes focused on spiritual topics.

Serve Those in Need through My Church
I serve those in need through my church once a month or more.

Additional Teaching/ Worship Service
I attend an additional teaching/worship service.

1 Serve the Church

2 Weekend Services

3 Small Groups

4 Serve Those in Need through My Church

5 Adult Education Classes Focused on Spiritual Topics

6 Additional Teaching/ Worship Service

CHART 6–3: The church activities that are most influential to spiritual growth are listed under each movement in order of importance. Note that the act of serving, either within a church ministry or serving those in need, has the greatest impact on spiritual growth in all three movements.

develop. For example, spiritual friendships and mentor relationships blossom as an outcome of small groups and serving experiences, and remain important spiritual lifelines long after participants have moved on to other activities. Similarly, participation in church classes about how to access and interpret

Scripture set the stage for increased personal spiritual practices years after the classes themselves have ended.

The REVEAL findings shed light on the following three key implications for church leaders as they seek to facilitate both organized *and* organic growth.

Implication 1: Weekend Services Most Benefit Those in the Earlier Segments

Note that weekend attendance and satisfaction with weekend services *do not decline* as people mature spiritually, but they do plateau. What does this mean? Using a golfing metaphor, we might describe the role of weekend services as a "driver" of spiritual growth for those in the earlier stages. Likewise, we could describe those same services as a "putter" for those closing in on spiritual maturity. While the driver hits the ball the longest distance, the putter remains very useful in finishing the hole. Likewise, weekend services are the big driver at the earlier stages of spiritual growth, but they are far less likely to prompt significant in-depth spiritual insight for those who are farther along in faith.

Occasionally, we come across an exception to this trend. For example, there is a small, spiritually thriving church in Danville, Virginia, that offers weekend services where people report 80 percent satisfaction — across all segments of the continuum. This is not an accident, but the direct result of the senior pastor's adherence to two important strategies for creating high-impact services for new believers and mature Christ-followers alike.

The first strategy is to continuously revisit the basics with fresh efforts to engage everyone, including the most mature. He does this by having intentional times of direct interaction with God, through response times of prayer and solitude, which are woven throughout the service. His second strategy is this — to go "rogue" if the Holy Spirit whispers about a special need stirring in the congregation. He is at ease dealing with an out-of-the-ordinary experience from the Sunday platform.

Recently, this pastor had a growing sense that the congregation was dealing with increasing levels of spiritual warfare. So he followed that leading by offering a special midweek in-depth teaching on this area of theology. The result? Fully one-third of the congregation showed up, affirming the pastor's discernment that many of his people were confused or struggling with this issue. In doing so, he provided all of us with a great example of how to respond outside of normal, regular church activities — which, in turn, leads us directly to our second observation.

Implication 2: Other Church Activities Serve Distinct Purposes

Virtually all churches in our survey offer three activities for congregants: weekend services, small groups (or some other type of limited-size connection opportunity), and serving activities. A number of churches also offer additional worship or educational experiences, which can be spiritually catalytic, especially for more mature believers. Not surprisingly, "adult education classes on spiritual topics" popped up as a significant catalyst in Movement 2. And "additional teaching/worship services," which were typically midweek services, also appeared as a catalytic church activity in Movement 3 (approximately 40 percent of the churches surveyed provide "additional teaching/worship services").

Consistent with the Virginia church's success, these results suggest that a broader portfolio of offerings may serve the mission of spiritual growth more effectively than a rigid concentration of church resources into weekend services and small groups. And that spiritual spontaneity, staying open to sensing the needs of your people and demonstrating the flexibility to do something irregular or unusual, seems to better serve a church's more mature Christians.

Implication 3: Serving Is the Most Catalytic Experience Offered by the Church

We'd also like you to notice (in chart 6-3) that the top-ranked factors in all three movements start with the word *serve*. This is a consistent finding, but one that should not surprise us since our progress in the spiritual life is defined by increasing likeness to Jesus Christ ("For even the Son of Man came not to be served but to serve others," Matthew 20:28 NLT). When we serve as his hands and feet, whether within a church ministry or outside the church, we grow to be more like Jesus. Interestingly, serving experiences appear to be even more significant to spiritual development than organized small groups, although small groups do show up as catalysts in the first two movements. Also note that serving those in need (as opposed to serving in a church ministry) tops the list of catalysts for Movements 2 and 3.

The implication for church leaders is that we must encourage people to serve — in *any* capacity, in *whatever* valid opportunity their gifts and interests lead them to. Serving should be a high priority for our churches, since such experiences appear to be more conducive to spiritual growth than blockbuster weekend services.

Category 3: Personal Spiritual Practices

Personal spiritual practices are very powerful catalysts. Consistent with the teaching of the Scriptures and the spiritual formation traditions of the church, the REVEAL study confirms the incredible impact of personal spiritual practices on accelerating growth. Why are personal spiritual practices so important? Because, in the absence of seeing or hearing God through our sensory capabilities, they are the primary channels he uses to communicate love and guidance to us. We access and respond to God through reflecting on Scripture, praying, engaging in solitude, and other practices. Apart from these personal spiritual practices, our ability to listen to God is mostly limited to whatever we pick up through intermediaries—the pastor at a weekend service, for instance, or the author of a Christian book.

The depth of our relationship with Christ, like the depth of human relationships, develops with increasingly frequent and intimate communication. Consider the difference between relationships characterized by a casual hand wave across a parking lot and the interaction between people who can complete each other's sentences. That's the difference between a relationship with Christ characterized by passive weekend church attendance and a relationship alert and responsive to his divine promptings.

As our data and analysis has become more comprehensive and enriched through the participation of additional churches, we continue to see this pattern emerge: personal spiritual practices are the secret to a fully engaged Christ-Centered identity. If we could recommend only one spiritual growth pathway for people to follow, personal spiritual practices would be it. Recognizing the essential nature of these particular catalysts to deepening a relationship with Christ, here are two key implications to help church leaders determine the best way to inspire and equip their people to embrace them.

Implication 1: Reflection on Scripture Is the Most Powerful Spiritual Practice for Every Segment

We would love to print the header above this paragraph across the top of the program for every church leadership training event in the country. Reflection on Scripture is, by far, the most influential personal spiritual practice for every segment and *across all three movements* (chart 6-4).

And that's only part of the story. Because when we statistically compare the responses of those who take the REVEAL survey, of all the personal spiritual practices, we find that Reflection on Scripture is much more influential

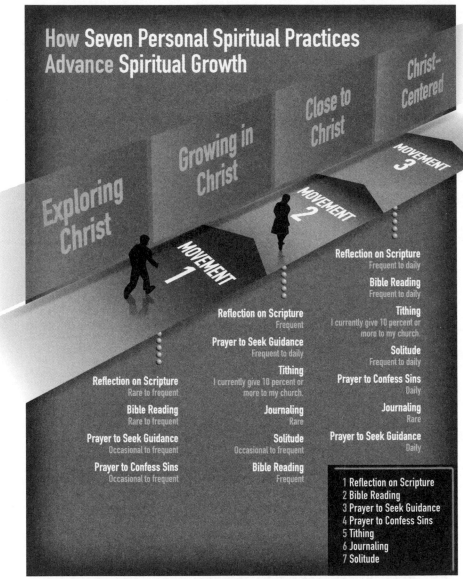

How Seven Personal Spiritual Practices
Advance Spiritual Growth

Christ-Centered

Close to Christ

Growing in Christ

Exploring Christ

MOVEMENT 3

MOVEMENT 2

MOVEMENT 1

Reflection on Scripture
Frequent to daily

Bible Reading
Frequent to daily

Tithing
I currently give 10 percent or more to my church.

Solitude
Frequent to daily

Prayer to Confess Sins
Daily

Journaling
Rare

Prayer to Seek Guidance
Daily

Reflection on Scripture
Frequent

Prayer to Seek Guidance
Frequent to daily

Tithing
I currently give 10 percent or more to my church.

Journaling
Rare

Solitude
Occasional to frequent

Bible Reading
Frequent

Reflection on Scripture
Rare to frequent

Bible Reading
Rare to frequent

Prayer to Seek Guidance
Occasional to frequent

Prayer to Confess Sins
Occasional to frequent

1 Reflection on Scripture
2 Bible Reading
3 Prayer to Seek Guidance
4 Prayer to Confess Sins
5 Tithing
6 Journaling
7 Solitude

CHART 6-4: Seven personal practices emerge as powerful catalysts of spiritual growth across the spiritual continuum. It is noteworthy that reflecting on Scripture "for meaning in my life" is the spiritual practice of greatest influence in all three movements.

than any other practice by a significant margin. In fact, for the most advanced segments—Close to Christ and Christ-Centered—it's *twice* as catalytic as any other factor on the list. This means it has twice the power of any other spiritual practice to accelerate growth in spiritually mature people.

What does all this mean for church leaders? Clearly, we must do much more than simply suggest that our congregants get into their Bibles on a regular basis. We need to teach this as a *necessity*. Insist on it. Follow up. Challenge our congregations to reflect on the Scriptures week after week.

Such efforts can sometimes prove frustrating though. Since personal spiritual practices typically occur outside of the mainstream of church activities, they are harder for church leaders to track and oversee. But the power of being immersed in the Bible is undeniable. We know that reading and reflecting on the Scriptures is critical to spiritual growth, and the REVEAL results confirm that there may be nothing more important we can do with our time and effort than encouraging and equipping our people in this practice.

Implication 2: Every Congregation Needs Consistent, Intentional Encouragement to Communicate with God on a Daily Basis

In all our interactions with the hundreds of churches who process their own REVEAL results, this area of ministry generates the most attention. For whatever reason, many REVEAL churches have discovered that consistent, daily communication with God is an area of spiritual deficiency among their congregants. The good news is that churches have responded in multiple ways to address this issue. For example, a number of churches have begun handing out weekly Scripture reading lists to help people prepare for the following weekend's message. And many are experimenting with incorporating extended response times for prayer and solitude during their services.

Admittedly, it's tough to get people to open a regular time slot for spiritual practices in the midst of busy schedules and leisure options like surfing the Internet and watching television. And, unfortunately, failure is inevitable. Everyone fails to keep to their spiritual practices at some point, which is why church leaders have to be vigilant teachers and role models when it comes to these essential spiritual growth habits. People need to understand — and be consistently reminded — that our Creator invites us to communicate and dialogue with him so that we can be changed by his presence. The REVEAL results remind us that there's nothing more wonderful and amazing than this invitation.

Category 4: Spiritual Activities with Others

We've all heard—and probably used—the phrase, "Practice makes perfect." And while I (Cally) may not be able to claim much in the way of perfection, I do know what it means to practice. As a child, I practiced for countless hours before walking on stage for dance recitals or competing in tennis tournaments. Later, in the marketplace, I prepared for presentations by memorizing key message points and practicing my delivery so that my inevitable nerves wouldn't derail the outcome.

In spiritual growth, practice also prepares us for "performance." Personal spiritual practices prepare our hearts and minds for the public experiences of faith reflected in this final category—spiritual activities with others, which are activities that largely occur outside the church. These may take place in informal networks of spiritual friendships and confidants. They might include some element of evangelistic outreach. Or they may involve serving those in need "on my own," through an organization like Habitat for Humanity or simply by helping a neighbor who is going through a crisis (chart 6-5).

The power of this category of catalysts lies in their relational dynamics. Because they involve our interactions with others and are more public in nature, they also involve some level of risk for most people—like the risk of going public with your faith through evangelism or exposing spiritual shortfalls to a mentor. Building faith privately through personal spiritual practices or within the confines of the church are relatively safe roads to travel for many people when compared to the public displays of faith involved in these catalysts. But taking a risk is essential to building faith, and we observe an increasing willingness to do exactly that in the catalysts that emerge across the three movements.

What follows are three key implications for church leaders that highlight the significance of these more "public" catalysts for spiritual growth.

Implication 1: Spiritual Community Is a Critical Catalyst of Spiritual Growth

Spiritual community shows up as a growth catalyst in all three movements, though the specific form of that community shifts as people grow in faith from more casual friendships to mentor relationships, relationships that typically involve greater accountability and intimacy. The importance of spiritual friendships as a catalyst also coincides with involvement in a small group (chart 6-3), which is not surprising. We can reasonably assume that for many people, spiritual friendships begin within some type of organized church activity.

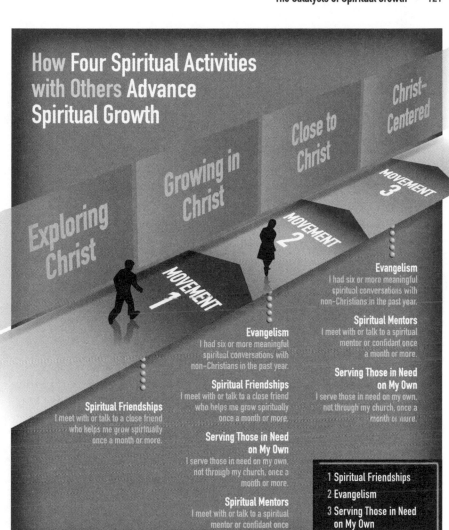

How Four Spiritual Activities with Others Advance Spiritual Growth

Exploring Christ

Growing in Christ

Close to Christ

Christ-Centered

MOVEMENT 1

MOVEMENT 2

MOVEMENT 3

Movement 1:

Spiritual Friendships
I meet with or talk to a close friend who helps me grow spiritually once a month or more.

Movement 2:

Evangelism
I had six or more meaningful spiritual conversations with non-Christians in the past year.

Spiritual Friendships
I meet with or talk to a close friend who helps me grow spiritually once a month or more.

Serving Those in Need on My Own
I serve those in need on my own, not through my church, once a month or more.

Spiritual Mentors
I meet with or talk to a spiritual mentor or confidant once a month or more.

Movement 3:

Evangelism
I had six or more meaningful spiritual conversations with non-Christians in the past year.

Spiritual Mentors
I meet with or talk to a spiritual mentor or confidant once a month or more.

Serving Those in Need on My Own
I serve those in need on my own, not through my church, once a month or more.

1 Spiritual Friendships
2 Evangelism
3 Serving Those in Need on My Own
4 Spiritual Mentors

CHART 6-5: Spiritual relationships outside the organized setting of the church are catalytic influences as people mature spiritually. In particular, evangelistic outreach through meaningful faith-based conversations with non-Christians has a significant impact on the growth of more mature believers in Movements 2 and 3.

Implication 2: Evangelism Is the Most Powerful Public Catalyst for Movements 2 and 3

There is a natural human tendency to delay the public introduction of a new relationship to friends and family until that relationship is on firm footing. Christ-followers appear to mirror this reluctance when it comes to speaking about their faith with nonbelievers. This helps to explain why evangelistic activities lag for those in the less mature segments.

But it is clear that evangelism becomes a powerful catalyst for those who are more mature in their faith. Again, this is not surprising. If we apply our analogy of human relationships once more, the experience of introducing someone you care about into a relationship with Christ is akin to feeling the glow of approval from friends and family over your choice of a date or a friend. That approval reinforces the relationship in multiple ways as family and friends include him or her in their conversations, gatherings, and events.

We would say that evangelism is both a "cause" and an "effect" of spiritual growth. Evangelism is certainly an output—an effect—of a growing heart for Christ. But we would also argue that the practice of evangelism (defined as "having six or more meaningful conversations with non-Christians in a year") is also a *cause* of spiritual growth—a catalytic experience that, in itself, grows the heart of the Christ-follower.

Implication 3: Fear of Going Public Marks This "Final Frontier" of Spiritual Growth

What is it that makes you nervous? What do you fear? Whenever this question is posed to people, the responses invariably include the fear of public speaking. It is estimated that 95 percent of people experience anxiety when engaged in such activity, a percentage higher than the number who fear dying! As comedian Jerry Seinfeld has noted, "The average person at a funeral would rather be in the casket than delivering the eulogy."

Most people are hesitant to speak "publicly" about Christ. "What will these people think? How will they react?" This fear may help to explain why evangelistic activities are difficult, even for the Christ-Centered segment. (Revisit chapter 5 for more detail, but as a reminder, only 20 percent of this most mature segment invited more than six people to church and 40 percent had more than six meaningful conversations with nonbelievers in the past year.) Such activities are the "final frontier" of a maturing relationship—and signal an enormous step of faith.

As a pastor or church leader, you are expected to raise faith-related issues, even in your non-church-related conversations. But for the typical member of your church, talking about Christ takes great courage—regardless of whether that person is a sympathetic believing friend or a skeptical spouse or coworker. Church leaders should be careful not to underestimate the power of these fears. Evangelism is not an activity that can be pushed or forced upon people.

Rejection, disapproval, or ridicule can jeopardize the growth of fragile seeds of faith. We need to celebrate the small victories — like the early conversations with spiritual friends and the experiences of serving those in need through the church. We also need to encourage and equip people for outreach efforts — when their own relationship with Christ is on solid footing.

But we're getting ahead of ourselves. We began this chapter with the observation that spiritual growth is strongly influenced by many decisions we make. We've reviewed twenty-five spiritual catalysts, which — based on our research — are the key decisions that open people up to God and help them collaborate with the work of the Holy Spirit (chart 6-6).

The Twenty-Five Spiritual Growth Catalysts

Eight Spiritual Beliefs and Attitudes

Salvation by Grace
The Trinity
Personal God
Christ is First
Authority of the Bible
Identity In Christ
Giving Away My Life
Stewardship

Six Church Activities

Serve the Church
Weekend Services
Small Groups
Serve Those in Need through My Church
Adult Education Classes Focused on Spiritual Topics
Additional Teaching/Worship Service

Seven Personal Spiritual Practices

Reflection on Scripture
Bible Reading
Prayer to Seek Guidance
Prayer to Confess Sins
Tithing
Journaling
Solitude

Four Spiritual Activities with Others

Spiritual Friendships
Evangelism
Spiritual Mentors
Serving Those in Need on My Own

CHART 6-6: These twenty-five factors emerged as the most influential catalysts of spiritual growth.

But twenty-five is a big number. And while each one is important and necessary in some way, wouldn't it be great to know which of these decisions are the *most* critical? Wouldn't you rather focus on a smaller, more manageable number of spiritual catalysts? That's where we'll turn next—to identifying the most important five catalysts in each of the three movements. Then we'll narrow things down even further. To a single spiritual catalyst—the one decision that towers above the rest to help people grow into Christ-Centered disciples.

What Are the Spiritual Belief and Attitude Statements and Where Do They Come From?

The purpose of our research is to uncover insights about what advances spiritual growth and what gets in the way. Our working definition of spiritual growth is based on Christ's teaching about the greatest commandment—to love God and to love others (Matthew 22:36–40). In order to assess where people are spiritually, we used statements about spiritual beliefs and attitudes and asked them to describe how strongly they agreed with those statements. Here are the statements we used:

Salvation by Grace: I believe nothing I do or have done can earn my salvation (Ephesians 2:8–9).

The Trinity: I believe the God of the Bible is the one true God—Father, Son, and Holy Spirit (2 Corinthians 13:14).

Personal God: I believe God is actively involved in my life (Psalm 121).

Christ Is First: I desire Jesus to be first in my life (Matthew 6:33).

Authority of the Bible: I believe the Bible has decisive authority over what I say and do (2 Timothy 3:16–17).

Identity in Christ: I exist to know, love, and serve God (John 1:12–13).

Stewardship: I believe a Christian should live a sacrificial life that is not driven by pursuit of material things (1 Timothy 6:17–19).

Giving Away My Life: I am willing to risk everything that is important in my life for Jesus Christ (Romans 12:1–2).

Giving Away My Faith: I pray for non-Christians to accept Jesus Christ as their Lord and Savior (Ephesians 6:19–20).

Giving Away My Time: I give away my time to serve and help others in my community (Colossians 3:17).

Giving Away My Money: My first priority in spending is to support God's work (2 Corinthians 8:7).

These statements are based on Scripture and derived from the *Christian Life Profile Assessment Tool* created by Randy Frazee, senior minister of Oak Hills Community Church in San Antonio, Texas. Dozens of church leaders, theologians, and others engaged in a rigorous process of biblical inquiry to find the core, repeatable characteristics of a follower of Christ. The statements were then tested and refined in multiple forums, including *The Spiritual State of the Union*, an ongoing benchmark of the "spiritual temperature" in America, sponsored by The University of Pennsylvania and The Gallup Organization. Among the experts contributing to this comprehensive effort were Dallas Willard, J. I. Packer, and Larry Crabb. The thoroughness of this approach, as well as the caliber of people engaged in the process, prompted us to adopt these statements for use in our research.

CHAPTER 7

Movement 1: From Exploring Christ to Growing in Christ

H elp me develop a personal relationship with Christ."

This statement reflects the number one desire collectively expressed by the 250,000-plus congregants in the REVEAL database. Of the eighteen *church* attributes we measure, "Help me develop a personal relationship with Christ" consistently ranks at the top of the list. In addition, it almost always appears among the top five priorities people assign to their church, meaning most people want their churches to *do more* to help them develop a personal relationship with Christ. This is true regardless of the size of the church or the denominational affiliation—Lutheran, Episcopal, Presbyterian, Methodist, Baptist, Reformed, as well as other nondenominational and evangelical churches.

One of the churches that participated in the REVEAL survey, an 850-member church located just outside of Denver, Colorado, found that their people loved the church and respected their senior pastor. But they were also clear that they wanted help developing their relationship with Jesus. After talking through the findings of the survey with the leadership team of the church, one of the pastors asked us a very natural question.

"How do I do this? I know they want help, but what does that mean?"

His question made us pause. This was a veteran church leader, and we had just covered forty-five pages of REVEAL results that affirmed a strong spiritual momentum for his church. His question seemed pretty basic, and it made us wonder if in the midst of all our statistical data, we were distracting pastors from what they most needed to know—that helping people grow spiritually is primarily dependent on the steps we take to help them *strengthen their personal relationship with Jesus.*

Those first spiritual growth steps start right here—in Movement 1. Before we dig into those things most helpful in moving people from the Exploring Christ into the Growing in Christ segment, let's revisit the basic objective we're trying to achieve.

One Essential Fact about Spiritual Growth

All of our findings are derived from one essential fact: that spiritual growth—defined as an increase in love of God and for others—is not a product of growing participation in church activities or changes in lifestyle or the result of our natural aging process. Rather, spiritual growth advances in lockstep with a *growing personal relationship with Christ*. The goal of spiritual formation is spiritual maturity, "attaining to the whole measure of the fullness of Christ" (Ephesians 4:13) and becoming conformed to the image of Christ (Romans 8:29). People grow spiritually as they grow in their relationship with Christ.

Like the pastor from Colorado, you too may be sitting there wondering: "Well, what does that mean? How do I help my people grow in their relationship with Christ?" Our answer to him and to you reflects the heart of our work: "It depends." What people need in order to grow closer to Christ depends on where *they are now* in their relationship with him. The goal of the next three chapters is to define and explain that "It depends" answer in terms of each particular segment. We'll see that what people need differs for each segment on the spiritual growth continuum.

Thirteen Catalysts That Lead to Accepting Christ

In chapter 6, we set the stage for this discussion by covering the twenty-five catalysts that are most influential to spiritual growth. Thirteen of these were the most significant contributors to Movement 1. It is noteworthy that the thirteen catalysts most influential in Movement 1 (chart 7-1) include factors from all four categories covered in chapter 6. This means that even at the earliest point of spiritual development people benefit from things like personal spiritual practices and spiritual friendships.

Not surprisingly, though, when the goal is to convince someone that Christ is the Son of God and they have a real need for the salvation Christ offers, the category of Spiritual Beliefs and Attitudes includes the largest number of these direct-contributor catalysts. All thirteen, however, represent decisions that people typically need to make in order to move from skeptic to believer.

The Most Influential Catalysts for Movement 1

Moving from Exploring Christ to Growing in Christ

Spiritual Beliefs and Attitudes
Salvation by Grace
The Trinity
Personal God
Christ Is First
Authority of the Bible

Church Activities
Serve the Church
Weekend Services
Small Groups

Personal Spiritual Practices
Reflection on Scripture (rare to frequent)
Bible Reading (rare to frequent)
Prayer to Seek Guidance (occasional to frequent)
Prayer to Confess Sins

Spiritual Activities with Others
Spiritual Friendships

CHART 7-1: From the twenty-five most influential spiritual growth catalysts, thirteen emerge as most significant in Movement 1 when people first become believers. A number of core beliefs appear on this list because accepting the doctrine of the Christian faith is critical at this stage.

In my (Cally's) early days on staff at Willow Creek one of my responsibilities, as the church's communications director, was to oversee the writing and distribution of press releases — documents designed both to influence opinion and motivate action. In the business world, these media "pitches" might involve financial results, a product release, or an upcoming event. But at Willow they typically had to do with special guest speakers or events — or an occasional church milestone, like the launch of a regional campus.

No matter what the subject matter, I was always aware of the dual objectives we hoped these releases would achieve: to *influence* people to view the church in a positive light and to *motivate* them to experience Willow Creek through its services and ministries.

We've used the words *catalysts* and *decisions* interchangeably to describe the factors that influence spiritual growth. Like the press releases I once wrote, these catalysts have the ability to *influence* change in people's thoughts and *motivate* them to action. They impact people's attitudes (how they think/feel) and spiritual behaviors (what they do). Catalysts (or decisions) influence people to grow in their love of God and others — and to act upon that change of heart. These factors won't *make* change happen, of course, any more than a press release will control the opinions or actions of those who read them. Instead, they stimulate and inspire minds, hearts, and actions to shift in favor of Jesus.

So, if it helps to clarify and simplify what these catalysts represent, you can think of them as spiritual press releases—those factors most likely to stir people's hearts and encourage them to think and act differently in response to their growing faith. As we have studied the list of catalysts for Movement 1, we believe they hold two very important insights for church leaders:

Insight 1: **The church is indispensable.** In Movement 1, the church is crucial and sets the stage for growth.

Insight 2: **The church's most important job is to build trust in Christ.** In Movement 1, the top-priority goal for the church is to convince those far from God that the core Christian beliefs are trustworthy.

Insight 1: The Church Is Indispensable

Our first insight relates directly to the one essential fact about spiritual growth— that it's all about *growing a personal relationship with Christ.* In human terms, personal relationships begin when we meet someone, often at a place that the two of us have in common—a school, an office, a social setting. Similarly, the church is typically the place where people first meet Christ, and the significance of this introductory experience sets the stage for everything that follows.

Beyond its obvious role as a spiritual gathering venue, the church is also the primary *source* for virtually all of the thirteen factors most helpful in advancing from spiritual doubt to belief in Christ. For example, early spiritual friendships are critical, and those relationships often begin in small groups. Initial experiences with prayer and the Bible are also important, and the church is where faith-explorers, who might otherwise rarely or never pray or open a Bible, will likely find the inspiration and training to do so.

No other setting provides as many indispensable elements to early spiritual growth. But the church's greatest contribution in Movement 1 is its role as teacher, encourager, and persuader of core Christian beliefs. And it's in this critical role we find the second insight—that fundamental to a person's decision to believe in Christ is *an increasing trust in the central teachings and values of the Christian faith.*

Insight 2: The Church's Most Important Job Is to Build Trust in Christ

Trust is a vital element in all relationships, and convincing a skeptic to trust in a God who is invisible, inaudible, and abstract is no easy task. In fact, apart from the grace of God, it's impossible! But that doesn't detract from the purpose and mission of the church: to proclaim the truth about God and model the love of God in a way that *draws people near* so they can hear and experience the good news about Jesus.

Essentially, today's church serves as a spiritual matchmaker: it provides a meeting place, an idea of the "next steps," and the foundational teaching that ultimately leads people to trust in core Christian beliefs. Absent the contribution of the local church, the majority of people who are Exploring Christ end up staying right where they are—separated from God, now and for all eternity.

Evidence of the church's unique role in Movement 1 is most apparent in rising levels of participation in church activities. In fact, participation in weekend services, small groups, and serving increases at a higher rate for those who move from Exploring Christ to Growing in Christ than for any other movements across the spiritual continuum (chart 7-2).

These rising participation levels suggest that, for those who don't yet trust Jesus, the church provides them with an opportunity to get to know him better. That opportunity also appears to influence their attitudes and beliefs, as we observe a similar pattern of increasing agreement with core Christian beliefs (chart 7-3).

Participation in Church Activities Increases Significantly in Movement 1

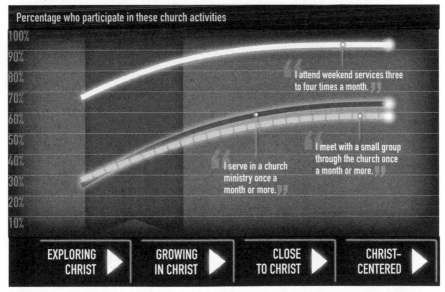

CHART 7–2: As people advance from nonbeliever to new believer, their participation in church activities, such as attending weekend services and small groups, rises to higher levels.

Building Beliefs Is Crucial for Movement 1

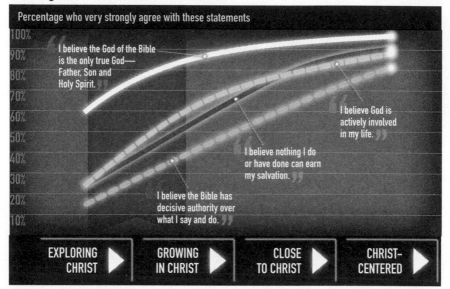

Percentage who very strongly agree with these statements

100%
90%
80%
70%
60%
50%
40%
30%
20%
10%

"I believe the God of the Bible is the only true God—Father, Son and Holy Spirit."

"I believe God is actively involved in my life."

"I believe nothing I do or have done can earn my salvation."

"I believe the Bible has decisive authority over what I say and do."

EXPLORING CHRIST ▷ GROWING IN CHRIST ▷ CLOSE TO CHRIST ▷ CHRIST-CENTERED ▷

CHART 7-3: People are increasingly willing to express strong agreement with core Christian beliefs at this early stage of spiritual growth. It is within this movement from Exploring Christ to Growing in Christ that the doctrinal foundation of the Christian faith becomes firmly established.

When we see agreement with beliefs like salvation by grace and the Trinity increasing so dramatically in Movement 1—and we see this happen in concert with increasing church involvement—we can draw two key conclusions. First, that overall trust in Christ is growing and the foundation for deepening a relationship with him is being established. And second, that the church is a significant source of support for this increasing trust.

These conclusions are especially encouraging for those who exercise leadership in the church. Yes, the church plays a significant role in leading people to trust in Christ and take initial steps to grow in their faith. But—keeping in mind the questions raised by the Colorado pastor—we realize that our conclusions might also be misleading. For example, does all of this mean that we should focus *exclusively* on making sure Exploring Christ congregants understand and agree with those five beliefs most catalytic for Movement 1?

Not necessarily. Each and every one of the thirteen catalysts on chart 7-2 represent decisions that are significant for early spiritual growth. That list, however, does not designate which decisions are, in fact, the most important. If our church is only able to focus on a few, the list of thirteen catalysts doesn't tell us which of the thirteen will have the greatest potential to transform lives.

The Five Most Influential Catalysts for Movement 1

That's where we turn now—to a ranking of the most significant catalysts for spiritual growth as people transition through Movement 1. As we rank these top five catalysts, we can also take note of how much *more important* one catalyst is, as compared to another. Our goal is to identify the handful of catalysts that show the greatest evidence of change in the spiritual life—the ones that are particularly crucial for those in your congregation who are still living apart from a personal relationship with Jesus.

We have all heard the advice to eat a balanced diet—that overindulging or depriving ourselves of any primary food group is unhealthy. As the top five catalysts for Movement 1 demonstrate, we also need a balanced *spiritual* diet. The five most important catalysts for those who are Exploring Christ include:

- Belief in salvation by grace (I believe nothing I do or have done can earn my salvation)
- Belief in the Trinity (I believe the God of the Bible is the one true God—Father, Son, and Holy Spirit)
- Serving the church (at least once a month)
- Praying for guidance frequently (at least several times a week)
- Reflecting frequently on the meaning of Scripture (how does it impact my life?)

This "balanced diet" for those who are in the process of coming to know Christ includes catalysts from three different categories of spiritual experiences (chart 7-4). Interestingly, even though core Christian beliefs are critical for those who are just beginning a spiritual journey, only two of those beliefs—salvation by grace and the Trinity—appear on this high-priority list. Catalysts from other categories prove to have more spiritual impact for those approaching Movement 1 than the other belief statements (like belief in the authority of the Bible). Serving the church on a regular basis and two spiritual practices—prayer to seek guidance and reflection on Scripture—round out the list of five top catalysts.

These five most significant, highest-impact spiritual growth catalysts for Movement 1, ranked by level of importance, represent the decisions that most commonly move someone sitting on the sidelines of faith into a relationship with Jesus Christ.

The ranking is both relevant and important; it tells us that belief in salvation by grace is typically the catalyst with the greatest spiritual growth impact for Movement 1. In other words, if you, as a church leader, could emphasize

The Top Five Spiritual Catalysts for Movement 1

Christ-Centered

Close to Christ

Growing in Christ

Exploring Christ

MOVEMENT 1

MOVEMENT 2

MOVEMENT 3

Salvation by Grace SPIRITUAL BELIEF
I believe nothing I do or have done can earn my salvation.

The Trinity SPIRITUAL BELIEF
I believe the God of the Bible is the only true God—Father, Son and Holy Spirit.

Serve the Church CHURCH ACTIVITY
I serve in a church ministry once a month or more.

Prayer to Seek Guidance SPIRITUAL PRACTICE
I pray to seek guidance for my life.
(occasional to frequent)

Reflection on Scripture SPIRITUAL PRACTICE
I reflect on Scripture for meaning in my life.
(rare to frequent)

CHART 7-4: The top five spiritual catalysts are listed in order of importance for Movement 1. These five factors represent the combination of catalysts that are most predictive of movement from Exploring Christ to Growing in Christ.

only one thing to those in Movement 1, salvation by grace would be your target.

Still, we need to remember that a belief in salvation by grace, while ranking as the most important catalyst for this Movement, is not alone in having a significant effect on spiritual transformation. It is only 10 percent more influential than the second catalyst, belief in the Trinity. The importance of each catalyst that follows falls by a similar percentage (roughly 10 percent), so that by the time we get to the fifth entry on the list—reflection on Scripture—it has just over 40 percent less influence than the highest-ranked catalyst, belief in salvation by grace. This relatively narrow spread from the top to the bottom means that all five of these catalysts share fairly similar levels of spiritual impact. No single catalyst stands head and shoulders above the rest.

It might even help to picture these catalysts as stopping points on a spiritual road map for a person moving from Exploring Christ to Growing in Christ. Imagine that you are planning a car trip from San Francisco to Boston. Making the trip in one day is not feasible, so you need to plan some stops along the way. Pulling out a map, you see the distribution of cities across the country. While most of them might generally fall on the path toward your destination, without actual mileage markers it is difficult to chart the most efficient route.

So it is with the journey that people take as they travel from Exploring Christ to Growing in Christ. The initial thirteen catalysts are all generally on the way to where you want to go, but which ones make the most sense as stops along the way? Which ones line up best to take you to your destination most efficiently? Traveling from San Francisco to Boston, you could go by way of Phoenix, Dallas, and Washington, DC. But perhaps Denver, Chicago, and Buffalo would be a more efficient path. (We Midwesterners would suggest you think twice about this second route if traveling in January.) Similarly, the five top catalysts aren't indicating the *only* path for spiritual growth, simply what our research suggests is the most common and helpful spiritual pathway from Exploring Christ to Growing in Christ.

At this point, some may wonder: "Shouldn't I just teach things according to the importance that Scripture gives them, and let God take it from there?" We would never suggest that pastors and church leaders ignore or minimize the importance of God's Word. Nor would we suggest that church leaders simply let survey results dictate how much importance should be given to teaching essential doctrines of the Christian faith. However, we are suggesting that a better understanding of the proven and practical spiritual impact of these doctrinal truths, as demonstrated by the results of the REVEAL survey, can inspire and inform the teaching in our churches.

Because belief in salvation by grace is at the top of the list, it does not make the other beliefs *less* important. It simply suggests that this particular catalyst will take those who are Exploring Christ the farthest distance toward the goal of Growing in Christ and provide the greatest spiritual impact at this stage of spiritual growth. It is unlikely, however, to take them all the way to their destination. For that, they'll need to make plenty of additional stops—stops like belief in the Trinity and serving at the church. While typically not as powerful in their impact as belief in salvation by grace, they are — in combination with that belief — far more likely to create the spiritual momentum required to traverse Movement 1.

How the Church Can Help

Now that we understand the five spiritual catalysts that can have the greatest impact in Movement 1, we can better answer the question raised by our Denver pastor at the beginning of this chapter. He wanted to know what the people needed in order to develop their relationship with Christ. Hopefully, you now have a better understanding of which specific catalysts would be most helpful for him to focus on to facilitate growth for those in Movement 1. But we still haven't yet addressed the second part of his question: "*How* do I help them?"

Part 3 of *Move* is dedicated to answering that question by describing what the top REVEAL churches — those most effective in achieving spiritual growth among their people — have to share on this subject. As a prelude to the insight they offer, however, we will close with a "How do I help them?" suggestion that relates specifically to Movement 1 — an idea that has emerged from the experiences of hundreds of REVEAL churches.

When it comes to introducing newcomers to faith, *The Purpose-Driven Church* model enjoys a phenomenal success record. We highlight it here, not because of its widespread popularity, but because we are struck by its consistent spiritual impact — especially for facilitating movement between the Exploring Christ and Growing in Christ segments. In our interaction with the healthiest REVEAL churches, we found that a significant majority provides an orientation program or a series of classes patterned along the lines of the baseball diamond ministry framework taught in Rick Warren's *The Purpose-Driven Church* (see "A Purpose Driven Approach for Movement 1," page 136).

A great example of one of these churches is a large, flourishing church located on the Texas-Mexico border. Its senior pastor gives high praise to the Purpose-Driven model, saying it boils down the complexity of church leadership to the basics, which he likes to describe as "doing church for dummies." This pastor has spent countless hours studying and revising the original Purpose-Driven framework so it would better fit his multicultural congregation, but — like most of the pastors we talked to — he still follows the book's basic steps: teach the vision and beliefs of the church; provide opportunities to connect with others and serve the church; and introduce the fundamentals of personal spiritual practices. Despite the pressing demands of his rapidly grow-ing congregation of three thousand, this pastor continues to personally teach the first class on church vision—a foundation he considers vitally important.

The Purpose-Driven model offers a rare hand-in-glove fit between the five most significant catalysts for spiritual growth in Movement 1 and a logical, structured church program. If your church doesn't have something similar in place, it's worth considering—especially for churches that attract people in the Exploring Christ segment, whether they are actively exploring or complacently just attending. In either case, this simple formula for addressing the needs in Movement 1 (vision/beliefs + serving and community connection opportuni-ties + basic spiritual practices) offers the potential to accelerate spiritual growth.

Once such a structure is in place, those early in their spiritual journeys will now have a plan and process to support their next steps. One by one (or if God is gracious, dozens by dozens), those formerly Exploring Christ will be presented with the gospel and be called and discipled into a personal relation-ship with Jesus.

Will we then share high fives and consider our mission accomplished? Hardly. Following the growth we are likely to experience with those who are Exploring Christ, we can anticipate the next stage of spiritual growth—Movement 2—in which the Growing in Christ segment advances to a more intimate Close to Christ relationship. This next Movement presents an enor-mous challenge—and opportunity—for the church, because the Growing in Christ segment is by far the largest group in most congregations. Once we have identified the highest-impact spiritual stops for new believers to make as they continue to navigate their road map of faith, church leaders can better decide how to allocate time and resources with greater clarity and focus. And then look forward to additional high fives as the members of this largest congrega-tional segment within the church grow closer and closer to Christ.

A Purpose-Driven Approach for Movement 1

Church leaders young and old are familiar with the best-selling purpose-driven books written by Pastor Rick Warren of Saddleback Church in Lake Forest, California. *The Purpose-Driven Life,* which has sold over thirty million copies since it was published in 2002, captures the thematic spirit of this influential movement in its first sentence: "It's not about you." For individuals, the message is to search for God's purpose in their lives. For pastors, the message is to search for and fulfill God's purpose for their churches.

The source for the ministry model embraced by many of the most spiritually vital REVEAL churches is *The Purpose-Driven Church,* published seven years earlier, in 1995. It uses a baseball diamond image to demonstrate four key purposes and four sequential classes that can help direct a person's path toward a Christ-Centered life:

• Class 101: Membership covers church vision, purpose, and affiliations as well as Christian beliefs and sacraments like baptism and communion.

• Class 201: Maturity introduces personal spiritual practices through four basic Christian habits: time in God's Word, prayer, tithing, and fellowship.

• Class 301: Ministry helps people discover their spiritual gifts and connects them into serving opportunities.

• Class 401: Mission trains people to share their faith and encourages them to discover "God's mission for my life."

Although the REVEAL churches may or may not follow this sequence precisely, the influence of the purpose-driven concepts is very much in evidence. A church may offer three membership orientation classes or as many as fifteen classes that take newcomers deeply into the Bible, but thriving churches offer a clear set of next steps for first-time visitors. These pathways typically bear a strong resemblance to the purpose-driven model.

It's not the individual classes themselves that are particularly unique; it's the connect-the-dots flow of ministry activities that spiritually growing congregations find most helpful. And it's worth noting that the logical progression of the 101–401 stepping-stones provides an intriguing fit with the five most influential spiritual catalysts for Movement 1 (chart 7-4, page 132).

CHAPTER 8

Movement 2: From Growing in Christ to Close to Christ

By most standards, this mainline, denominational church radiated success. With three weekend services (two traditional and one contemporary) drawing an average of more than eight hundred people, as well as live Internet streaming and weekly TV and radio coverage, they were effectively reaching a wide audience in their community. The church's affluent and well-educated congregation was faithful in their support for the church, with stellar attendance rates and a high regard for their leaders. They enjoyed a handsome facility, with special areas for everything from private prayer meetings to weekly basketball games. And the senior pastor, who had been with his denomination for more than thirty years and had led the church for the past six, was highly respected—serving as a frequent consultant to churches throughout the nation.

On this day, however, the pastor was troubled and concerned about the spiritual profile we had just presented to him, the REVEAL survey results for his church. The report painted a disappointing picture—a congregation that had grown content with being spiritually "average."

Despite the fact that 60 percent of the congregation reported attending the church for more than ten years (with an average frequency of three to four services each month), nearly half of the church population remained in the Growing in Christ segment. Beliefs and spiritual practices were average in comparison with the results of other churches, but any evidence of outreach beyond an occasional church-sponsored activity was nil. The level of evangelism was well below the REVEAL database norm,[1] as was their level of spiritual community.[2]

---

[1] Only 13 percent reported having more than six spiritual conversations with non-Christians in the last year, compared with a 22 percent average.

[2] Less than 30 percent were in small groups compared with a 50 percent average.

In a moment of frustration, this pastor mused aloud, "Sometimes I think I'm leading more of a social club than a faith community." The results of the survey seemed to back up his concerns. The congregation showed lukewarm attitudes reflecting their love of God and others, including an obvious reluctance to give away time or money to faith-based initiatives. There were irregular patterns of participation in ministry activities beyond the weekend services. Page after page of REVEAL results confirmed that growing in a personal relationship with Christ was *not* a motivating desire in the lives of these people.

To the pastor's great credit, he did not remain discouraged for very long. He had undertaken the survey out of a desire to move his people from a mere recognition that Jesus Christ is the Son of God into a strong and growing personal relationship with their Savior. His burning question as he sat looking at the survey results was simple: "How do I make them *want* it?"

It's a question every church leader asks at some point.

The challenge we are talking about here is one of the most difficult we see in our work with churches: How can we inspire people with long-standing, superficial spiritual attitudes and behaviors to want more from their faith than a Sunday service and their names on the membership roll? Many church leaders struggle with this same dilemma, wondering how they can uproot those who are Growing in Christ from settling for the comfort of the status quo—while simultaneously motivating them to hunger for a personal relationship that is Close to Christ.

This is why we consider Movement 2—the movement from an intellectual acceptance of Christ to a relationship characterized by interaction and intimacy—to be the most dramatic shift on the spiritual continuum. Within this movement faith travels from the head to the heart, and the word *personal* begins to describe how people relate to Jesus in their daily lives. No longer abstract, distant, or theoretical, Christ becomes, instead, a real person—someone they depend upon for guidance, wisdom, and encouragement in the course of everyday events.

It might help to visualize believers in the midst of Movement 2 leaving church after a Sunday service, walking with Jesus beside them as they continue, at least tentatively, the conversation they began with him during the worship experience. They drive out of the church parking lot with Christ in the passenger seat. And their conversation with him continues from time to time throughout the week—until they walk into church *together* the following weekend. The key dynamic created by this movement is that their relationship with Christ is set free from organized church activities and becomes, instead, a central force that influences the believer's life choices and direction.

In fact, we could sum up the spiritual change of heart taking place in this movement with the phrase, "Jesus has left the building." Not that Jesus is ever simply present in a building, of course. But the key idea is that he goes wherever a believer goes, alongside them as they move from the awkward, knowledge-gathering stage of Growing in Christ to a lifestyle of greater dependence and trust, a one-on-one relationship that we call Close to Christ.

Movement 2 is a dramatic and important shift as believers mature, but it is also one that many churches unintentionally neglect. Why? We wonder whether at least part of the answer might lie in this movement's similarity to the family dynamic of the middle child.

Much has been written about the impact of birth order on a person's psychological development and eventual life accomplishments. Various theories suggest that those who are firstborn are more assertive and confident, due to the nature of being "first" to assume new responsibilities and take new steps, like attending kindergarten. Those who are the "babies" are rumored to be more self-involved and less inclined to take risks, since they tend to benefit from the love and caretaking of siblings as well as parents.

Those who are in the middle, however, are said to be somewhat forgotten — even ignored at times. There is little new ground for them to take since the firstborn precedes them. And because babies demand a disproportionate share of parental attention, the middle child is said to be regularly forgotten or dismissed, not needing the special consideration of younger siblings.

Regardless of whether or not the birth order dynamic is true in families, we believe something like this is at work in most churches. Believers who are going through the transition in Movement 2 may suffer to some extent from an experience similar to the "middle child" syndrome. Church leaders have historically devoted much of their focus to the two ends of the spiritual spectrum — those who are struggling to believe in Christ (Movement 1) and those who actively embrace their faith and devotedly serve their church (Movement 3). Movement 2 believers seem to be lost in the middle (perhaps ignored or even forgotten) due to the attention that those who are less mature — and more mature — demand from church leaders in their respective stages of spiritual growth. Consider, once again, that almost 40 percent of most congregations fall into this Growing in Christ segment. Why aren't more believers growing in faith and maturing to the next stage of spiritual development?

While it may not be true in every church, church leaders will want to carefully consider whether or not this middle-child syndrome may be at play in their own congregations. If that proves to be the case, additional time and resources must be diverted to help those caught in the middle — those who have accepted Christ but still keep him at a distance, not allowing him to shape and influence their daily lives.

We believe that the efforts of pastors and church leaders will be most productive if they seek to guide new believers toward the catalysts that are most influential in Movement 2.

Twenty Catalysts Lead to a Personal Relationship with Christ

Of the twenty-five catalysts reviewed in chapter 7, twenty are particularly relevant to Movement 2 (chart 8-1). Twenty catalysts may feel like a long laundry list of things that need to happen so that a relationship with Christ can become truly personal, but we believe that speaks to the complexity and demanding nature of this very significant spiritual shift. These catalysts represent the decisions people typically need to make so that their individual relationships with Christ can advance from a conceptual one, defined by an intellectual acceptance of beliefs, to a deeply personal relationship defined by daily connection and interaction.

Recall from the last chapter the most influential catalysts for Movement 1. What are the differences between the catalysts that are key to helping a person believe in Christ and those most helpful in moving him or her into a relationship with Christ as a central personal value? When we compare the two lists of catalysts (one for Movement 1; the other for Movement 2), we uncover three important insights:

Insight 1: Confidence Is Crucial. In Movement 2, accepting certain core theological beliefs builds confidence in the existence of a personal God (one who is "actively involved in my life").

Insight 2: Personal Spiritual Practices Are Key. In Movement 2, increasing the frequency of spiritual practices opens the door to a personal relationship with Christ.

Insight 3: Going Public Is Catalytic. In Movement 2, as they grow bolder in their faith, people begin to "go public" and engage in outreach experiences that catalyze growth.

Let's take a moment to unpack each of these differences—and their particular relevance to Movement 2.

Insight 1: Confidence Is Crucial

You may recall that in Movement 1, people are most commonly grappling with core theological concepts like the Trinity and salvation by grace. Those two beliefs were the top two most influential catalysts of the entire twenty-five

The Most Influential Catalysts for Movement 2

Spiritual Beliefs and Attitudes

Personal God
Salvation by Grace
Authority of the Bible
Christ Is First
Identity in Christ

Church Activities

Serve Those in Need through My Church
Serve the Church
Small Groups
Weekend Services
Adult Education Classes Focused on Spiritual Topics

Personal Spiritual Practices

Reflection on Scripture (frequent)
Prayer to Seek Guidance (frequent to daily)
Tithing
Journaling (rarely)
Solitude (occasional to frequent)
Bible Reading (frequent)

Spiritual Activities with Others

Evangelism
Spiritual Friendships
Serving Those in Need on My Own
Spiritual Mentors

CHART 8-1: From the twenty-five most influential spiritual growth catalysts, twenty emerge as most significant in Movement 2 when people begin to invest in their relationship with Christ outside of the organized church setting. Not surprisingly, a number of personal spiritual practices are critical at this stage.

in Movement 1 — two dominos that must fall for early spiritual movement to occur.

In Movement 2, that core base of beliefs broadens. Belief in a personal God tops the list of spiritual beliefs that are most helpful in generating spiritual growth. Belief in the Trinity disappears, replaced by a spiritual attitude we call "identity in Christ" ("I exist to know, love, and serve God") (chart 8-2).

These shifts signal the change of heart that defines this spiritually maturing movement. At this point, believers have already accepted the fundamentals of Christian theology, including the above-mentioned belief in the Trinity. They are now embracing their faith at a deeper, more heartfelt level. Knowledge of God is being translated into heartfelt love and a growing desire to communicate and walk with Christ throughout the week. This is demonstrated most clearly by the appearance of "identity in Christ" as a catalyst for this movement. People are beginning to allow their relationship with Jesus to

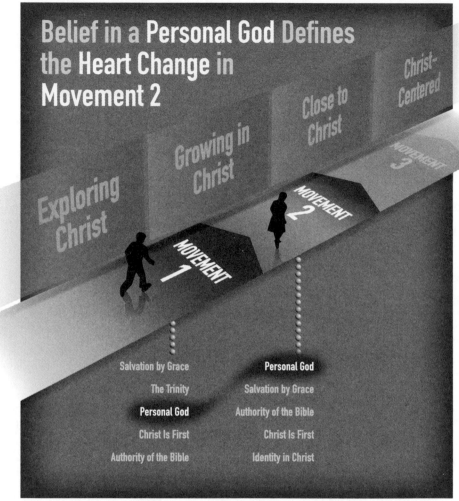

Belief in a **Personal God** Defines the **Heart Change** in Movement 2

Christ-Centered

Close to Christ

Growing in Christ

Exploring Christ

MOVEMENT 3

MOVEMENT 2

MOVEMENT 1

Salvation by Grace	Personal God
The Trinity	Salvation by Grace
Personal God	Authority of the Bible
Christ Is First	Christ Is First
Authority of the Bible	Identity in Christ

CHART 8-2: Belief in a Personal God ("I believe God is actively involved in my life") rises to the most important spiritual belief catalyst in Movement 2 compared with third-most-important in Movement 1.

define their own identity—which is a big step beyond simply believing that Christ is the Son of God.

Two beliefs and one spiritual attitude show up on the lists of the most influential catalysts for both Movement 1 and Movement 2—salvation by grace, authority of the Bible, and "Christ is first" ("I desire Jesus to be first in my life"). The fact that they appear in both movements means that these catalysts *began* to take hold in Movement 1. But *increasing agreement* with these statements is highly influential in continuing to grow and mature as a Christ-follower.

Deepening conviction—or strengthening one's agreement—with certain fundamental Christian beliefs and attitudes occurs as people wrestle with increasingly demanding spiritual concepts. Certainly, few would disagree that having a deep conviction about salvation by grace and a firm belief in the authority of the Bible seem to be prerequisites for a Close to Christ relationship—much as basic musical scales are prerequisite for playing Chopin. Why, then, does belief in the Trinity[3] fall off our list of catalysts for Movement 2? Not because it's insignificant or unimportant, but rather because conviction regarding the Trinity peaks at such a high level in Movement 1 that the possibility for increased conviction is limited. Said another way, doubts about the Trinity are essentially erased in Movement 1, while doubts about other core beliefs remain. As people mature in faith, however, these doubts are also very likely to diminish—or disappear altogether.

We believe this increasing conviction—or diminishing doubt—in spiritual beliefs is a direct result of the activity addressed in our second insight—that, in Movement 2, increasingly frequent personal spiritual practices open the door to a more intimate relationship with Christ. Just as increasing interaction with people tends to build our trust in their character and values, increasing interaction with Christ builds up our faith.

Insight 2: Personal Spiritual Practices Are Key

In Movement 2, the frequency and intensity of communication with God increases significantly (chart 8-3). We should not only reflect on the importance of the behaviors themselves, however, but on the underlying change in personal values those behaviors represent. There is almost always a cost involved in changing behavior patterns—a cost in personal time and focus. There are only twenty-four hours in a day, and whether a person is eighteen or eighty, those hours can quickly fill to the point of overflowing. The choice to dedicate some of this limited time to spiritual reflection through prayer, Bible study, or journaling—rather than the multitude of other options available—is a noteworthy mark of increasing maturity.

Just as Movement 1 is primarily about building trust in Christ through acceptance of foundational beliefs, Movement 2 is all about growing a personal relationship with Christ through increasingly frequent communication—communication that is achieved through personal spiritual practices.

---

3. "The Trinity," is our shorthand for referring to people's agreement with this statement: "I believe the God of the Bible is the one true God—Father, Son, and Holy Spirit."

Personal Spiritual Practices Increase in Movement 2

Percentage who engage in these spiritual practices daily

80%

70%

60%

50%

40%

30%

20%

10%

" I pray to seek guidance for my life. "

" I pray to confess my sins. "

" I reflect on the meaning of Scripture in my life. "

" I read the Bible. "

| EXPLORING CHRIST ▶ | GROWING IN CHRIST ▶ | CLOSE TO CHRIST ▶ | CHRIST- CENTERED ▶ |

CHART 8-3: The steep increases (highlighted) in the percentage of people reporting daily spiritual practices shows that establishing a regular routine of spiritual disciplines is a significant influence to movement from Growing in Christ to Close to Christ.

These first two stepping-stones of relationship development create a natural path toward our final insight: that "going public" through outreach experiences catalyzes growth. In our human relationships, we typically don't introduce people to close friends and family until we're fairly certain of the relationship. That is also the case when it comes to our relationship with Christ. Going public through any type of outreach activity requires a level of spiritual maturity that begins to emerge in Movement 2.

Insight 3: "Going Public" Is Catalytic

In Movement 2, believers begin to acquire the courage of conviction required to live out their faith in public. As a result, we see solid advances in outreach, particularly in activities related to serving those in need and having spiritual conversations with non-Christians (chart 8-4).

In this area, the role of the church is very clear. Serving those in need through the church is *the most influential church activity* among the twenty key catalysts for Movement 2. And the second-most-influential activity is serving the church. If we consider these two facts in light of the budding evangelistic confidence that emerges in this movement, it appears that the church's role is

Outreach Activities Increase in Movement 2

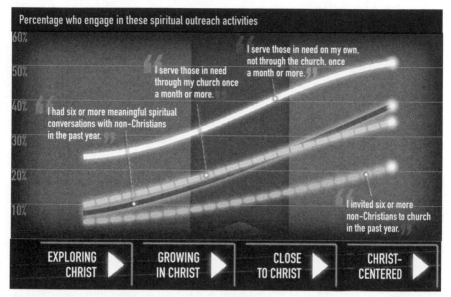

Percentage who engage in these spiritual outreach activities

60%

50%

40%

30%

20%

10%

I serve those in need on my own, not through the church, once a month or more.

I serve those in need through my church once a month or more.

I had six or more meaningful spiritual conversations with non-Christians in the past year.

I invited six or more non-Christians to church in the past year.

| EXPLORING CHRIST ▶ | GROWING IN CHRIST ▶ | CLOSE TO CHRIST ▶ | CHRIST-CENTERED ▶ |

CHART 8-4: Regular outreach activities, such as inviting people to church and serving those in need, become more commonplace as people advance from new believer status (Growing in Christ) to a more personal relationship with Jesus in the Close to Christ segment.

shifting from being a teacher of Christian beliefs (Movement 1) to being an equipper of spiritual activities (Movement 2).

In the spirit of our earlier catchphrase "Jesus has left the building," we would suggest that the role of the church in this phase is to build up the spiritual skills and the confidence of those who are Growing in Christ so they can take their faith with them when they walk out the church door. Only after people have left the building, after all, will they engage in personal spiritual practices that help them build confidence in their faith. Outside church is also where they'll carry out spontaneous acts of service and have meaningful spiritual conversations with friends and family.

In essence, the church needs to encourage its people to take the most logical first faith-steps outside of the church, much as parents must encourage youngsters to welcome the first day of kindergarten. The world is a big place and we would miss a lot if we never left the family nest. Similarly, staying in the comfort zone of church pews and church-related activities will ultimately stifle the growth of our personal relationship with Christ. For that growth to continue, maturing Christians need to live out their faith beyond the walls of the church. And as church leaders, we need to help them do that.

Increasing commitment to outreach activities wraps up our review of the twenty catalysts for Movement 2, demonstrating that the full range of relationship-building experiences is now in place. Those experiencing Movement 2 are establishing trust in Christ's character through increasingly solid beliefs. They're keeping communication lines open through personal spiritual practices, which are becoming part of their regular rhythm of life. And they're going public with their faith, living it out through increased outreach activities.

And that's what should happen, according to the examples of discipleship we see modeled for us in the Scriptures. The earliest disciples began their journey of discipleship with a step of faith, trusting Christ and taking him at his word (Mark 1:17). They continued to grow by listening and learning, spending personal time with their rabbi and teacher (Mark 4:10–11, 34). Eventually, they were given opportunities to take their faith public and practice what they had learned and experienced as followers of Christ by serving and sharing the message of Jesus with others (Mark 6:7, 12).

This is what we hope to see in a growing, healthy church. But let's circle back to the pastor who was frustrated about his social-club congregation. His long-tenured people have been Growing in Christ *for years*. There's no way he can simultaneously tackle all twenty catalysts with equal effectiveness. But he might be able to advocate a few.

So which five catalysts have proven — time after time — to be the most likely to get this pastor and his congregation, as well as countless others in similar circumstances, out of the starting gate?

The Five Most Influential Spiritual Catalysts for Movement 2

The top five catalysts for Movement 2 are dramatically different from those we found in Movement 1 which focused on the *fundamentals* of faith: accepting core beliefs (the Trinity and salvation by grace) and taking the first, early steps in spiritual practices and serving the church (chart 8-5). Movement 2 expands on this by emphasizing the importance of putting those fundamentals into *practice* by:

- Believing in a personal God (I believe that God is actively involved in my life)
- Praying to seek guidance daily (instead of frequently)
- Reflecting on Scripture frequently
- Having six or more meaningful spiritual conversations with non-Christians in a year (approximately one every two months)
- Tithing (giving ten percent or more to the church)

The Top Five Spiritual Catalysts for Movement 2

Christ-Centered

Close to Christ

Growing in Christ

Exploring Christ

MOVEMENT 2

MOVEMENT 1

MOVEMENT 3

Personal God SPIRITUAL RELIEF
I believe God is actively involved in my life.

Prayer to Seek Guidance SPIRITUAL PRACTICE
I pray to seek guidance for my life.
(frequent to daily)

Reflection on Scripture SPIRITUAL PRACTICE
I reflect on Scripture for meaning in my life.
(frequently)

Evangelism SPIRITUAL ACTIVITY WITH OTHERS
I had six or more meaningful spiritual conversations with others in the past year.

Tithing SPIRITUAL PRACTICE
I currently give 10 percent or more to my church.

CHART 8–5: The top five spiritual catalysts are listed in order of importance for Movement 2. These five factors represent the combination of catalysts that best predict movement from Growing in Christ to Close to Christ.

These five highest-impact spiritual growth catalysts for Movement 2 (chart 8-5) represent the most common decisions and actions of those who are growing in their personal relationship with Christ and becoming Close to Christ.

Movements 1 and 2 show similarities between two of their top five catalysts—prayer to seek guidance and reflection on Scripture. There is a notable difference, however, between the two movements in the *frequency* of the practice. In Movement 2, these spiritual practices occur more often.

It might be helpful to think about the role of each of the five catalysts and their relationship to one another as something of an international travel plan. My (Cally's) husband's job requires him to travel all over the world. And whenever the trip is to Europe or the Middle East, he is typically routed through one of three cities—London, Amsterdam, or Frankfurt.

Just as these three European cities are the most frequent gateways to my husband's travel destination, the top three catalysts serve as high-impact gateways to spiritual growth within Movement 2. This means that any one of these three catalysts will have a more significant impact on spiritual growth for those who are Growing in Christ *than any other catalyst will have,* just as travel through any one of the three cities will position my husband to more efficiently move to his final destination.

And like the three cities, which are clustered together geographically, the three top catalysts are clustered together in a similar arrangement according to their level of influence. Where London is typically the most efficient stop on the international travel plan, belief in a personal God is the most commonly influential catalyst for Movement 2. But it's only about ten percent more influential than prayer to seek guidance, which is, itself, only ten percent stronger than reflection on Scripture. "Travel" through any of these three catalysts is always a good part of a smart spiritual growth plan, and the effectiveness of choosing one over the others is marginal at best. It all depends on the specific details of where you want to go.

To take the international travel analogy one step further: just as any one of these three European cities will bring you most of the way to your final destination (at least if you are traveling from the States), experience with any of the top three catalysts will cover much more spiritual "distance" than four or five. On average, evangelism (#4) and tithing (#5) have only about half the influence of any of the top three catalysts. While they still are more influential to Movement 2's spiritual growth than the remaining fifteen listed in chart 8-1, evangelism and tithing have significantly *less* impact than any of the top three.

You may be wondering at this point: *Why does any of this matter?* Well, recently we spoke with a pastor of discipleship at a new church plant in San Diego. She was frustrated by her congregants' lack of interest in engaging Scripture on their own. "I know how important it is for new believers to start reading the Bible for themselves," she said, "but I just can't get them motivated to do it."

This was a pastor who already embraced the importance of Bible engagement in spiritual growth. She just wasn't sure *how* to best engage people in taking personal responsibility for growing in that spiritual practice. Our response, based on the results of our study, was to suggest that she point her people to "belief in a personal God," the catalyst that sits atop the list of most important catalysts for those in this movement. We suggested that it's tough to convince people to spend time communicating with someone if they aren't even convinced that person can hear or respond to them. We reminded her that just because people have accepted the truth of God's existence and Christ's promise of salvation, it doesn't mean they completely understand that Christ's presence is alive and active in their lives.

So how do we help people in our churches learn to hear and recognize the voice of God? As leaders, we need to help people learn to turn off the noise and tune into God's voice. It's not easy, to be sure, and there are helpful resources that can aid you in teaching your congregation how to do that. But this is the key to Movement 2—and to growing a *personal* relationship with Christ.

The fact that our relationship with God can be personal is the hub of truth around which this entire movement turns. And people will *want* that only if and when they believe it is possible.

How the Church Can Help

We began this chapter by sharing the frustration of a pastor who asked what he could do to make his congregation *want* a personal relationship with Christ. At one level, we must confess that it is impossible to make people want this. Only the Holy Spirit can change and renew the heart with genuine love and desire for God. But that doesn't diminish the *very* significant responsibilities pastors and shepherds have in the spiritual transformation process. The pastor we introduced you to at the start of this chapter recognized these responsibilities. He wasn't content to shrug his shoulders and wish things could be different. In fact, in his quest to find the answer to his question, he called together other leaders within his denomination, some of whom were dealing with similar problems in their churches. They traveled from several states to spend a full day discussing strategies and desired outcomes, plotting their courses, and praying together.

To encourage these pastors and others like them, we'd like to close this chapter with the story of one church, Fox River Christian Church in Waukesha, Wisconsin, that helped its congregation shift from having a majority of people Growing in Christ to one with a significantly higher percentage of people who are Close to Christ. In other words, based on their REVEAL results, this church activated Movement 2.

Attendance at Fox River Christian Church had grown from a few hundred to over two thousand congregants in ten years. It was one of the first churches to take the REVEAL survey when it became available in the fall of 2008. One year later, it was also one of the first churches to take the survey a *second* time. When we saw the results from the second survey, we were encouraged. In just twelve months, these statistically meaningful changes occurred:

- Small group participation increased from one-third to more than one-half of the congregation.
- Daily Bible reading increased from 16 to 30 percent, increasing in all four segments across the spiritual continuum.
- Daily reflection on Scripture increased from 18 percent to 24 percent overall.
- Satisfaction with the church's role in spiritual growth increased significantly, especially for the Close to Christ segment, where it moved from 49 to 67 percent.
- In the Growing in Christ segment, the percentage of stalled people declined from 16 percent to 7 percent; the percentage of dissatisfied declined from 15 to 10 percent.
- The Close to Christ segment rose from 21 to 24 percent of the church profile.

Based on the consistently positive pattern of these changes, we were convinced that something dramatic had happened at Fox River Christian. Sure enough, senior pastor Guy Conn and his leadership team had taken significant steps to react to the first survey.

After seeing the initial results, Guy was "disappointed, but not surprised." The church had been drawing a high percentage of people who were actively Exploring Christ, so their spiritual profile was relatively immature, with over 60 percent in the Exploring Christ and Growing in Christ segments combined. But even given the spiritual immaturity and inexperience reflected in their congregation, church leaders were struck by the markedly low percentages of people engaging in personal spiritual practices, particularly related to the Bible.

They tackled the challenge of encouraging and equipping people to engage with Scripture through the use of an integrated strategy that involved the weekend services, the small-group system, and their church building. First, they kicked off a series of beginner Bible classes during the week, taught almost exclusively by the senior pastor. Congregants were encouraged to use the lessons taught in the Bible classes in their small groups, and the church building was made available throughout the week to provide convenient locations for small groups to meet. The church even provided low-cost childcare options several nights a week to accommodate parents of young children.

The Bible classes were a hit, and small-group participation soared. Then Guy launched a weekend series challenging the entire congregation to read the New Testament in seventy-two days. The church provided a small-group curriculum that complemented the series.

But this was more than a one-shot deal. The church now has an ongoing commitment to connecting congregants to classes and small groups that help them experience spiritual practices. Weekend services complement the Bible classes and small groups through study materials that unpack the weekend teaching. And the church continues to open the building during the week to provide easy, family-friendly locations for getting together.

The spiritual growth results speak for themselves—and attendance has not suffered. In fact, the Fox River Christian congregation grew 12 percent during this time period. The most important change, however, has little to do with the church's numbers. The greatest change during this process has been in the initiative of the leadership team. They made the difficult decision to focus all of the tangible and intangible assets of the church on one objective—building the competence and confidence of their spiritually immature congregation in their ability to read and reflect on Scripture.

Are we saying that their classes and programs *made* spiritual growth happen? Once again, we want to clearly say "No." But we believe that these changes opened the door for the Holy Spirit to do the work that only God's Spirit can do. A pastor who leads one of the most spiritually vital churches among those we surveyed told us, "When human intentionality combines with the power of the Holy Spirit, that's when transformation happens." We agree. The combination of intentionality, focus, discipline, and a commitment to growing disciples has opened the door for the Holy Spirit to work—and for spiritual growth to happen—at Fox River Christian.

The challenge to grow disciples, however, is far from over at this church—in fact, it's possible that their greatest challenges lie ahead. What happens when these hungry new believers embrace the pathway of personal responsibility for their own spiritual growth? Once their aptitude for personal spiritual practices is firmly established, and their early efforts to serve others and talk about their faith bear fruit, what then?

Then they will be knocking at the door of Movement 3—the transition that turns a person who is committed to Christ into someone whose life is fully surrendered to him. How will churches like Fox River Christian help their people navigate the transition from Close to Christ to Christ-Centered—perhaps the greatest spiritual chasm of all?

Just as importantly, how will you?

CHAPTER 9

Movement 3: From Close to Christ to Christ-Centered

W hat's love got to do with it?"
Pose Tina Turner's famous question to those in the midst of Movement 3 and you'll get their unanimous answer: "Everything." Love has everything to do with it—at least when "it" is the shift from a quasi-independent Close to Christ relationship to a fully surrendered Christ-Centered life.

"Your love for one another," Jesus said, "will prove to the world that you are my disciples" (John 13:35 NLT). The Bible makes it clear that the central character requirement of a disciple is love, an idea further expanded upon by Christ when he said, " 'You must love the Lord your God with all your heart, all your soul, and all your mind.' This is the first and greatest commandment. A second is equally important: 'Love your neighbor as yourself' " (Matthew 22:37 – 39 NLT).

Loving God and loving others is at the heart of the Christian faith, as Jesus makes clear, and so we, along with Christians throughout history, have defined spiritual growth as *the progress made in increasing in our love of God and love for others.* One of the surest signs we are becoming more Christlike is an increase in love—and in the actions inspired by that love. In Movement 3, Christians wrestle with the final phase of this journey—which began at its earliest point with the self-reliant, "I'm in charge" Exploring Christ segment, then advanced to the more personal but somewhat restrained, "Jesus-is-in-the-passenger-seat-but-I'm-still-driving" Close to Christ relationship. Movement 3 serves as the tipping point between the Close to Christ segment, whose faith is strong but still a bit at arm's length, and the thriving faith of a fully surrendered Christ-Centered life—a life marked by love.

The key to this final movement is found in one of the several hundred statements we included in the REVEAL survey, a statement that reads: "I am willing to risk everything that's important in my life for Jesus Christ." We have found, in church after church that we surveyed, that the higher the percentage of congregants who "very strongly agree" with this statement, the more likely it is that we will find visible evidence of spiritual momentum within their church. In fact, a high percentage of positive responses to this one statement virtually guarantees correspondingly high levels of agreement with beliefs, strong personal spiritual practices, high levels of outreach, and ongoing statistical evidence that this church is a spiritually mature, Christ-Centered church.

So if that one statement is a key marker of mature, Christ-Centered people, what is it that inspires someone to "very strongly agree"? What is it that motivates people to "risk everything" and yield control of their lives to Jesus?

As we sought answers to these questions, a pastor from a church in the United Kingdom provided an interesting perspective on this point by pushing back on what "willing to risk everything" might mean for those who read it. He said to us, "I don't think you understand. When people in the UK read this, they think of martyrdom. They think of someone chopping off their heads." Certainly, we acknowledge Europe's much longer—and sometimes persecution-prone—history. (Few who have visited Rome's Coliseum, for instance, will forget their guide's description of the lions' days-long starvation before confronting the Christians.) We pointed out to him that his congregation's low responses to this question were being compared to an international benchmark, one that reflected this cultural bias. Still, his comments fueled our curiosity. What makes the answer to *this* statement a distinguishing mark for vital churches?

We came to the conclusion that it all boils down to an underlying concept that runs all throughout the Scriptures—the idea of sacrifice. As the Bible describes it, love is most clearly marked by this single characteristic—it is a *sacrificial* love. Jesus tells his disciples: "Greater love has no one than this: to lay down one's life for one's friends" (John 15:13). And in his first letter to the churches, the apostle John writes: "This is how we know what love is: Jesus Christ laid down his life for us. And we ought to lay down our lives for our brothers and sisters" (1 John 3:15–17). It should come as no surprise to us that our love of God and our love for others grows in parallel with an increasing willingness to sacrifice ("risk everything")—for this is exactly what Jesus taught us. What we found, as we studied the REVEAL results, is that as people grow spiritually they make tradeoffs. They are more willing to sacrifice in order to grow in their relationship with Christ—a relationship that is defined by love.

So love—which is the essence of a Christ-Centered life—grows in concert with a willingness to sacrifice. Jesus sacrificed himself for us. In Movement 3, people decide to sacrifice themselves for Christ—at least, they "very strongly agree" that they're willing to do so. To the UK pastor's point, does this necessarily involve martyrdom or the choice to die for one's faith? That's a tough question to answer. But when we asked him an easier question—which is whether he'd like to see higher responses to the "willingness to risk everything" statement—he said he would indeed.

Let's help him—as well as all the rest of us—by examining what it takes to inspire this "risk everything" kind of sacrifice. We'll begin with the list of spiritual catalysts most likely to motivate Close to Christ people to fully surrender their lives to him.

Seventeen Catalysts Lead to Surrender

Seventeen catalysts are particularly influential in Movement 3, when the ultimate goal is a heart that willingly sacrifices everything for the sake of Christ. These catalysts, therefore, represent the decisions believers need to make so that their relationship with Christ can advance from one that is personal, characterized by daily connection and interaction, to one that is identity defining, with Christ serving as the central source of life's direction and the motivation for daily decisions (chart 9-1).

To better understand the distinct character of Movement 3, it's helpful to compare and contrast its list of influential catalysts with the lists assigned to prior movements. For example, while there's great similarity between the important personal spiritual practices of those in Movements 2 and 3, the frequency of the practices in Movement 3 increases yet again. In fact, five of the seven practices on the list are *daily* habits in the lives of these believers.

The increasing regularity of these personal spiritual practices is directly related to the two insights we see when we compare the most influential catalysts of Movement 3 with those of the other two movements:

Insight 1: It's All about Movement of the Heart. The faith of the more mature believers in Movement 3 is characterized by increasing emotional depth, which builds on the intellectual trust in core Christian beliefs and spiritual practices that were established in the earlier movements.

The Most Influential Catalysts for Movement 3

Spiritual Beliefs and Attitudes

Giving Away My Life
Christ Is First
Identity in Christ
Authority of the Bible
Stewardship

Church Activities

Serve Those in Need through My Church
Additional Teaching/Worship Service

Personal Spiritual Practices

Reflection on Scripture (frequent to daily)
Bible Reading (frequent to daily)
Tithing
Solitude (frequent to daily)
Prayer to Confess Sins (daily)
Journaling
Prayer to Seek Guidance (daily)

Spiritual Activities with Others

Evangelism
Spiritual Mentors
Serving Those in Need on My Own

CHART 9-1: From the twenty-five most influential spiritual growth catalysts, seventeen emerge as the most significant in Movement 3 when people surrender their lives to Jesus. Note that fewer catalysts are related to organized church activities than the other categories.

Insight 2: It Takes Place Largely Outside of the Church. Since Movement 3 begins with the Close to Christ segment, which is already heavily invested in efforts independent of the church to grow in relationship with Jesus, it's not surprising that the church's direct influence is minimal in this movement. Instead, daily dedication to personal spiritual practices paves the way for wide-ranging outreach activities.

Let's delve more deeply into these insights to see how pastors and church leaders can inspire and motivate greater risk taking and a sacrificial lifestyle among those who are Close to Christ.

Insight 1: It's All about Movement of the Heart

Attitudes that express love of God dominate Movement 3, far exceeding the influence of spiritual beliefs. In fact, as you will read later in this chapter, only one statement that qualifies as a core Christian belief—accepting the authority of the Bible—is among the five most influential catalysts in this movement. As we explained in earlier chapters, though, this should not suggest that beliefs have decreased in importance. It simply means that intellectual beliefs no longer have the power they once had to motivate significant spiritual growth for those in Movement 3. Like seeds planted deep in the heart, beliefs are now bearing fruit in attitudes and emotions that reflect the character of Jesus Christ.

Earlier, we drew attention to the parallel paths of love and sacrifice. We should note, though, that Movement 3 is not the first time these two elements appear in parallel. It is simply that in this most mature movement of spiritual growth, they *soar dramatically higher*—which makes them defining characteristics. When we look at the attitudes that express love of God, for instance, the percentage who "very strongly agree" escalates from 40 percent to almost 80 percent (chart 9-2).

There is a similarly sharp trajectory (chart 9-3) with attitudes that express willingness to sacrifice. In fact, willingness to "risk everything" doubles to over 50 percent. And attitudes about sharing faith, financially supporting God's work, and making time available to serve the community rise in similar fashion.

Love of God Rises Significantly between the Close to Christ and Christ-Centered Segments

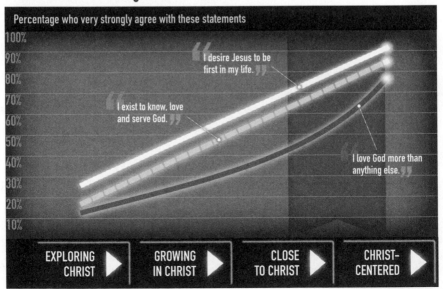

CHART 9-2: As people advance from having a personal relationship with Christ (Close to Christ) to being fully surrendered (Christ-Centered) in Movement 2, they are much more willing to agree with statements that indicate an increasing emotional commitment, such as putting Christ first in their lives.

Willingness to Sacrifice Increases Dramatically in Movement 3

Percentage who very strongly agree with these statements

60%
50%
40%
30%
20%
10%

I am willing to risk everything that is important in my life for Christ.

I feel fully equipped to share my faith with non-Christians.

My first priority in spending money is to support God's work.

I give away my time to serve and help others in my community.

| EXPLORING CHRIST ▶ | GROWING IN CHRIST ▶ | CLOSE TO CHRIST ▶ | CHRIST- CENTERED ▶ |

CHART 9-3: The percentage of people who are willing to agree with statements about surrendering the most important aspects of life to God rises significantly between the Close to Christ and Christ-Centered segments. This demonstrates a spiritual shift from a self-centered identity to an identity defined by a relationship with Christ.

As mentioned in chapter 5, the experience of spiritual growth can be viewed as a progressive release from the dark side of the human condition, not unlike the painful transition of addicts away from their drug of choice. In Movement 3, the steep slopes of "very strong agreement" with these attitudes about love and sacrifice suggest a wholehearted rejection of things like power, fame, or fortune—things that the world holds dear. These attitudes may also be propelled forward by a forthright, wholehearted *acceptance* of Christ's deep and abiding love—a dramatic understanding of the close, personal relationship he seeks with each of his followers.

There are few parallels in our human experience to this level of Christ-Centered love and intimacy. One of the closest, perhaps, is the relationship of a mother to her newborn baby. I (Cally) am reminded of the birth of my own daughter, who entered this world squalling her little lungs out. What a shock she was—mainly because everyone, including my doctor, was convinced we would be adding a second boy to our family!

But there she was—outraged at this unexpected disturbance from the safe world of the womb. With her bright red face and flailing miniature hands, she was clearly unconvinced that all of this was a good idea.

Not knowing what else to do, I began to sing one of the more nonsensical lullabies—"Hush, little baby, don't say a word; Mama's gonna buy you a mockingbird." (Who came up with this absurd lyric? Are mockingbirds even for sale?)

Now, more than twenty-three years later, I can still remember the moment that followed singing those lyrics as clearly as I remember what I just ate for lunch. My daughter went immediately silent. Her eyelids flew open, her now-quiet face transformed by two big, baby-blue eyes. She looked directly at me, and I knew what that look was saying. "I know you." Not "I love you." Or even "I trust you." Her eyes said, "I know you. I've heard your voice. I've sensed your presence." It was a look of stunning recognition, as if she were thinking; "*Now* I get it."

This "I know you" moment can serve as a metaphor for the transition from being Close to Christ to leading a Christ-Centered life. Similar to the dramatic shift we see in attitudes about love and sacrifice in Movement 3, this moment of recognition ignites a sharp upward-sloping trajectory of love and willingness to sacrifice. Spiritually, until that "I know you" moment, we're only remotely aware of a voice and a presence that is out there, muffled, and (we mistakenly think) relatively irrelevant to our existence. Then suddenly we "get it." In interviews with Christ-Centered people, we find they can often name specifically what they had to sacrifice in order to make Jesus the focus of their lives. Certainly spiritual surrender can occur without this kind of decisive moment, possibly more as the result of progressive growth in our understanding of God's care and provision for our lives. There is no single, one-size-fits-all path to spiritual maturity. But however they get there—whether through a gradual path of spiritual maturing or a flash of Holy Spirit–inspired clarity—mature believers in Christ come to understand that they are now done with the old world, and ready to move on to the new.

It might be tempting to assume that what I'm describing is simply the "born again" experience that happens earlier in the spiritual continuum. And for some people, this event may parallel that experience in some ways. But the spike in attitudes pertaining to love and sacrifice that we see in Movement 3 suggest that something very special occurs at this point of surrender to Christ—something that triggers a deeper level of love and devotion in the human heart.

People in Movement 3 progressively abandon darkness and fully embrace the light of Christ. Which means the research is telling us there is hope—an important message for frustrated church leaders who may fear that the world is doomed to rotate on a predominantly self-indulgent axis until Christ returns.

We see that hope in these charts and numbers, because Movement 3 relies on *attitudes*—and through God's grace, attitudes can change. In the previous chapter, we quoted a pastor who said, "When human intentionality cooperates with the Holy Spirit, spiritual transformation happens." What does that mean, exactly? What can we, as church leaders, do to help move the hearts of our people so they love Christ more? How can we help them love him so much they are willing to "risk everything"? At least part of the answer lies in the second insight derived from the most influential catalysts for Movement 3—that this movement is triggered by experiences that, for the most part, happen outside of the church.

Insight 2: It Takes Place Largely Outside the Church

First, let's take a look at what the data does *not* say. Certainly, there is a great deal of conjecture about the impact a life crisis has on spiritual growth. Many people believe that nothing is more spiritually catalytic than coming face-to-face with a personal or professional catastrophe—something directly at odds with our illusion of self-control. A variation on this theme is that we have to hit an emotional "wall" in order to fully surrender to Christ. Both of these explanations have their roots in the same assumption—that we must experience some kind of event that forces us to acknowledge our lack of control, which in turn inspires us to surrender whatever control we think we do have over to Jesus.

Our research, however, does *not* support these speculations. We pressed the issue in one-on-one interviews and searched our database for evidence that a crisis or an ordeal of any kind was a triggering experience for spiritual surrender. The data simply did not support the conclusion that one-time events—a traumatic experience or the breaking of an emotional wall—are prerequisites for a Christ-Centered life.

What the research *does* reveal is that people in this movement experience a deepening of their love for Christ, which seems to occur as the result of two outside-the-church activities: (1) a daily immersion in their personal spiritual practices, and (2) stepping out of their comfort zone in favor of increased outreach efforts.

The most compelling aspect of Movement 3's shift regarding spiritual practices, however, goes beyond the significant increase in their frequency. The data also underscores that there is an important change in "why" people engage in these practices—a dramatic shift in their attitude (chart 9-4).

For example, notice the jump in the percentage of those who now "very strongly agree" with the statement "I study the Bible to know God and the

Attitude and Action Related to Daily Spiritual Practices Increase Significantly in Movement 3

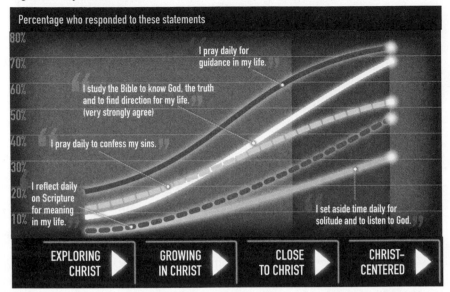

Percentage who responded to these statements

80%
70%
60%
50%
40%
30%
20%
10%

I pray daily for guidance in my life.

"I study the Bible to know God, the truth and to find direction for my life. (very strongly agree)"

"I pray daily to confess my sins."

I reflect daily on Scripture for meaning in my life.

I set aside time daily for solitude and to listen to God.

| EXPLORING CHRIST ▶ | GROWING IN CHRIST ▶ | CLOSE TO CHRIST ▶ | CHRIST-CENTERED ▶ |

CHART 9-4: Those in Movement 3 express increased agreement with a statement about why they study the Bible ("to know God"). There are also significant increases in daily reflection on Scripture, prayer, and solitude.

truth, and to find direction for my life." It increases to almost 70 percent! This is very consistent with our observation that those in this maturing spiritual movement are engaged in the discipline of studying the Bible — not simply to grow in knowledge or accumulate information — but to know God. At this point in their spiritual journey, reading the Bible is no longer merely an intellectual exercise. It's an effort to understand and connect with the heart of God.

Two additional factors also support the conclusion that there is a deepening of convictions and a more holistic approach to personal spiritual practices among those who are Christ-Centered. First, there is an increase in the number of people who spend time in solitude. One-third of those in Movement 3 specifically set aside time *every day* to "listen to God." A second practice they engage in is praying to confess sins — a daily activity for over half of those in this movement.

A similar pattern emerges when we look at outreach activities. Not only are Movement 3 people doing more outreach, they are also connecting the dots between "what" they're doing and "why" they're doing it (chart 9-5).

Two examples of alignment between heart attitudes and outreach activity are especially evident in this movement. The first is the correspondence

Attitude and Action Related to Outreach Increase Significantly in Movement 3

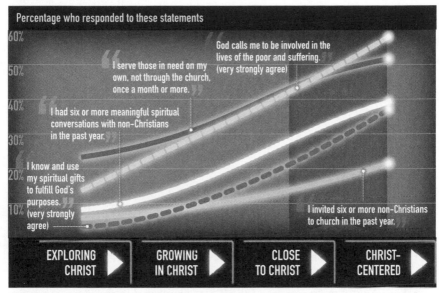

Percentage who responded to these statements

60%

God calls me to be involved in the lives of the poor and suffering. (very strongly agree)

50%

I serve those in need on my own, not through the church, once a month or more.

40%

I had six or more meaningful spiritual conversations with non-Christians in the past year.

30%

20%

I know and use my spiritual gifts to fulfill God's purposes. (very strongly agree)

10%

I invited six or more non-Christians to church in the past year.

EXPLORING CHRIST ▶ | GROWING IN CHRIST ▶ | CLOSE TO CHRIST ▶ | CHRIST-CENTERED ▶

CHART 9-5: Those in Movement 3 express increased agreement with statements about God's call to serve the poor and the need to use spiritual gifts. Their participation in regular outreach activities, such as having faith-based conversations with non-Christians, also increases significantly.

between people who are "serving those in need on my own" and the increasing percentage who "very strongly agree" that "God calls me to be involved in the lives of the poor and suffering." A related parallel is the increasing number of people involved in evangelism (having meaningful spiritual conversations with nonbelievers) and the corresponding rise in the number of people who "very strongly agree" that "I know and use my spiritual gifts to fulfill God's purposes." All of these trends indicate an increased confidence: knowing what God wants of them and then acting on it.

One final note of interest here is that of the seventeen catalysts, only two church activities show up. Not surprisingly, given the newfound passion for outreach they have, the number one church-related catalyst for those who are Christ-Centered is "serving those in need through the church." Should church leaders respond to this by providing an expanded menu of serving and outreach opportunities? Perhaps. But before we encourage that step, let's reduce our list of catalysts down to the top five—giving us a better idea of the highest-impact actions church leaders can take to inspire their people to willingly risk everything for Christ.

The Five Most Influential Spiritual Catalysts for Movement 3

The list of top five catalysts for Movement 3 is dramatically different than the short lists we had for Movements 1 and 2. In fact, in this movement toward becoming a mature Christ-follower, there is only one spiritual catalyst shared in common with the prior two movements — reflection on Scripture. The rest of the list puts an exclamation point on our observation that this, the final movement of spiritual growth, is almost entirely driven by inner heart transformation. The transformation we find among those in this segment is rooted in deeply held convictions that are lived out in practice in such a way that they have become integrated with the rest of life. Movement 3 people are moving from the Close to Christ's personal, but still somewhat reserved, relationship with Jesus to a fully surrendered Christ-Centered life by:

- Giving away their lives (I am willing to risk everything that's important in my life for Jesus Christ)
- Deciding that Christ is first (I desire Jesus to be first in my life)
- Embracing an identity in Christ (I exist to know, love, and serve God)
- Believing in the authority of the Bible (I believe that the Bible has decisive authority over what I say and do)
- Reflecting on Scripture daily (instead of frequently)

These are the five most significant, high-impact spiritual growth catalysts for Movement 3. They represent the decisions and actions that define people who are daily surrendering full control of their lives to Christ, as opposed to those who are still making many decisions on their own terms (chart 9-6).

As we look at the catalysts individually, note the varying impact each of them has on heart transformation. The top three heart-related catalysts stand head-and-shoulders above numbers four and five. In fact, the top catalyst — the willingness to "risk everything" — has *three times* the impact of those bottom two factors, belief in authority of the Bible and reflection on Scripture.

To put these impact-related distinctions into perspective, let me (Cally) once again draw on my husband's foreign travel. We'll think of the catalysts as stopping points in a journey toward an exotic, faraway location, but this time, we'll travel in a totally different direction. Imagine that we're traveling to an oil rig in the Gulf of Thailand. Departing from Chicago's O'Hare airport, our first stop is Tokyo, where we arrive after thirteen hours of travel. Then Bangkok is another seven-hour plane ride beyond Tokyo. Once there, we'll travel by helicopter to the platform of the oil rig.

The Top Five Spiritual Catalysts for Movement 3

Christ-Centered

Close to Christ

Growing in Christ

MOVEMENT 3

MOVEMENT 2

Giving Away My Life SPIRITUAL BELIEF/
I am willing to risk everything that ATTITUDE
is important in my life for Christ.

Christ Is First SPIRITUAL BELIEF/
I desire Jesus to be first in my life. ATTITUDE

Identity in Christ SPIRITUAL BELIEF/
I exist to know, love and serve God. ATTITUDE

Authority of the Bible SPIRITUAL BELIEF
I believe the Bible has decisive
authority over what I say and do.

Reflection on Scripture SPIRITUAL PRACTICE
I reflect on Scripture for meaning
in my life. (frequent to daily)

CHART 9-6: The top five spiritual catalysts are listed in order of importance for Movement 3. These five factors represent the combination of catalysts that are most predictive of movement from Close to Christ to Christ-Centered.

In this scenario, Tokyo represents the willingness to "risk everything" — to give away our lives. That thirteen-hour leg of the trip covers by far the greatest distance toward the destination, just like the willingness to "risk everything" has the greatest influence on Movement 3's journey toward Christ-Centeredness.

Bangkok represents the next important leg of the trip, just as the second and third catalysts represent significant, but second tier, spiritual influences for Movement 3. So while Tokyo remains the most efficient first stop (and the willingness to "risk everything" remains the most influential catalyst), Bangkok advances us toward the oil rig destination in a significant way, just as the second and third heart-related catalysts represent important spiritual "stops" in Movement 3.

As for the last two catalysts, they rank among the top five, but their potential impact pales in comparison to the first three. They're like the last leg of the trip toward the oil rig—certainly important (it would be tough to get there without that helicopter!), but covering much less spiritual ground compared with the big advances of the first three catalysts.

At this point, our travel analogy has brought us full circle—back to the UK pastor's problem with the willingness to "risk everything" statement. Clearly, it is essential for people moving toward Christ-Centeredness to agree with this concept, but the question of "how" remains. We asked earlier whether increased outreach options might be the answer to promote this type of sacrificial living. Would offering a big menu of serving opportunities influence people who are Close to Christ to surrender their lives to Jesus? Indeed, the research does suggest that expansive serving opportunities have the potential to catalyze growth in mature Christ-followers. But serving does not appear to be the *key* catalyst. Yes, it's important. But it's not what matters most.

How the Church Can Help

Like so many things in life, the solution, we think, is both easy and hard. Easy to know what to do and easy to put it into words. But very hard to implement.

Here's the easy part. Church leaders need to be crystal clear that the number one goal for their congregants is to help them grow into followers of Jesus Christ.

That's easy to say. But it's very hard to do, even if everyone in your congregation says, "Sign me up. I'm in!" The long haul of spiritual growth is challenging, and it's very difficult for people to persevere, putting aside worldly temptations day after day to walk through life as a follower of Christ. Also, it's hard for churches to hold them accountable. Like doctors, church leaders can tell people how to lead healthier lives—they can even be role models of a Christlike lifestyle—but they can't make people adopt and live up to a new set of life values.

Unfortunately, churches often make things harder still by obscuring the goal—to become more like Christ—with a complicated assortment of activities. For instance, encouraging people to:

- Attend teaching and worship services every week.
- Meet frequently with small community and Bible study groups (often requiring follow-up communications and homework).

- Serve the church a couple times a month.
- Serve those who are underresourced on a regular basis.
- Invite friends, coworkers, and family to church, special events, support groups, etc.

When the church incessantly promotes all the things people should *do*, it's very easy for them to lose sight of the real goal—which is who they should *become*. Of course, describing who they should become reverts back to the relatively easy part of this equation: they should move *away* from being self-centered and move *toward* becoming Christ-Centered.

We think the most effective thing a church can do to help people on the challenging journey to becoming Christ-Centered is to devote every ounce of energy and every resource at its disposal to making that happen. This means making it crystal clear that guiding and supporting their people along the road of spiritual growth is the number one objective of the church and that no other objective comes close. That's something, again, that's easy to say—but amidst the daily demands of weekend services, elder meetings, staffing challenges, and resource decisions, is very hard to do.

First Baptist of Orlando is a role model of this strategy, which senior pastor David Uth summarizes in a statement he routinely makes to his six thousand congregants: "We're not here to make you Baptists; we're here to make you disciples of Christ." This statement may sound glib, but it reflects the idea that the goal is not to inspire people to fall in love with the church and all of its activities; the goal is to help them fall in love with—and surrender their lives to—Jesus.

In all of its teaching and communication, First Baptist is direct and unambiguous about the discipleship goal of its ministry. But that's not their real distinctive. What distinguishes First Baptist, and other thriving churches like them, is their persistent, overarching commitment to that pursuit. In part 3, you'll find many stories and details from these best-practice churches that illustrate how they live out this commitment in everyday ministry. But for now, the salient point is this: *everything* starts by committing to the life-changing (not activity-creating) goal of discipleship and making it the top priority for all ministry efforts. The resolve of best-practice churches to achieving this objective is so steadfast that they risk letting people walk out the door—in fact, they *encourage* them to do so—if becoming a follower of Christ is not a commitment they're willing to make.

We see a similar type of resolve in other leaders who accomplish seemingly impossible tasks. John F. Kennedy put a man on the moon. Vince Lombardi grew a professional football dynasty in an off-the-beaten-path town in northern Wisconsin. Martin Luther King Jr. inspired a nation deeply entrenched in its prejudices to rethink its values and embrace equality regardless of race. Less dramatic but creating enormous cultural impact, CEO Steve Jobs regularly catapults Apple to the top of *Fortune*'s most-admired list with wildly successful technical innovations, like Macintosh computers and the iPad.

Each of these difficult achievements began with clear, unambiguous goals. JFK famously declared, "We will put a man on the moon in this decade." Lombardi said, "Winning isn't everything; it's the only thing." King gave voice to the aspirations of all African Americans in his "I have a dream" speech—describing the goal in concrete terms: that our children would not be judged by the color of their skin, but by the content of their character. Steve Jobs constantly reminds employees that "real artists ship," meaning that delivering working products on time is as important as innovation and design. What's important is that every one of these leaders used simple words to articulate difficult goals—goals that were far from easy to accomplish.

As a pastor or leader in the church, you may wonder, are these comparisons really relevant? After all, while putting a man on the moon may be tough, it's easy to assess whether or not the goal was achieved. And businesses can point to measurable sales and stock performance to judge success or failure. Even in Dr. King's case, we can point to such achievements as the passing of the Civil Rights Act of 1964 as a significant milestone. But growing a person's heart for Christ seems to be a different kind of endeavor. We can't see it happening, and measuring progress is problematic, to say the least.

But that's what this book is really all about. We are trying to give church leaders measurements—like attitude statements about a person's willingness to "risk everything"—that will help determine whether or not that individual is making progress in an area as intangible and abstract as spiritual growth. Underlying all of this, though, is an understanding that these measurements are merely tools that guide and describe what is, at heart, a mysterious and miraculous process—the transformation of people who are far from God into wholehearted, Christ-Centered disciples.

Circling back to the UK pastor who wants to know how to help his people grow in their love of Jesus, so much so that they're willing to "risk everything," we would say this: Five years of research findings point us to one singular conclusion—that the most essential decision a church leader makes is not what kind of worship service to offer or what kind of small-group system to build. It's the decision to lead his or her church with an unyielding and unequivocal commitment to a very easy-to-say, very hard-to-accomplish goal—which is, to do whatever is humanly possible to move people's hearts toward Christ.

If the UK pastor makes that kind of commitment—and prays for God's wisdom and guiding hand to help make the decisions necessary to achieve that goal—we believe his congregation's "willingness to risk everything" will rise in response.

Vanilla Ice Cream and Spiritual Growth

If your local ice cream parlor could sell only one flavor, it would sell vanilla. This isn't just because vanilla ice cream is the most popular flavor, although that is true. It's because vanilla ice cream is *hugely* popular; in fact, it's twice as popular as the second favorite flavor, which is chocolate. In turn, chocolate is twice as popular as any other ice cream flavor available. So your ice cream parlor would choose vanilla. Hands down. No contest.

Church pastors have an equally compelling option. If they could do only one thing to help people at all levels of spiritual maturity grow in their relationship with Christ, their choice would be equally clear. They would inspire, encourage, and equip their people to read the Bible—specifically, to reflect on Scripture for meaning in their lives.

Reflection on Scripture is the spiritual equivalent of vanilla ice cream because its influence on spiritual growth far exceeds the potential impact of other catalysts. A simple review of the top five spiritual catalysts for each of the three movements supports this statement, because reflection on Scripture is the only catalyst that appears on each list (chart 9-7, page 168).

This means that when we consider the most significant spiritual catalysts across the entire continuum, the Bible's influence transcends *all* the other catalysts, much like vanilla ice cream's popularity dwarfs all other flavors.

Hands down. No contest. When it comes to spiritual growth, nothing beats the Bible.

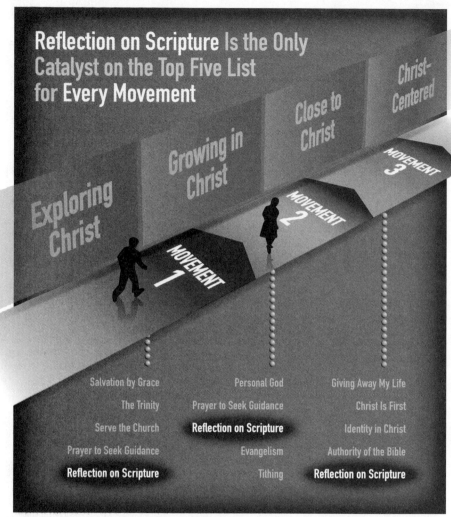

CHART 9-7: Reflection on Scripture is the only spiritual catalyst out of the most influential twenty-five that appears on the list of top five spiritual catalysts for *all three* spiritual movements.

CHAPTER 10

Barriers to Spiritual Growth: The Stalled and the Dissatisfied

No matter what the journey — traveling foreign lands, nurturing children toward adulthood, achieving expertise in a chosen field — progress depends, at least in part, on overcoming the various obstacles along the way. That's a given in any kind of journey. And spiritual growth is no exception.

As REVEAL participants shared how they combat barriers to their own spiritual growth, it provided us with some valuable insights. We began identifying the obstacles they shared with us, while also looking for clues to how people overcame these obstacles. But before we get into our findings, it may be helpful to hear directly from several men and women who took the time to write us notes that expanded on their personal frustrations.

"I am a Christian but my spiritual growth has been stalled for several years now," wrote one person. "I do take responsibility for some of that. My life has become quite hectic, and maintaining a consistent quiet time has been hard. In short, I am desperate for my relationship with Jesus to return to what it once was. I don't like the way I am fading away, but I don't seem to be able to get back."

"I serve as a leader and mentor," confided another. "I have for a long time. I am alone and isolated at church relationally; I am giving to those in need but not being fed in a meaningful or personal way by anyone."

A third person wrote only half-a-dozen words, but in doing so, spoke volumes. "I'm flailing," this churchgoer admitted, "but nobody knows it."

Two Barriers to Spiritual Growth

From the earliest days of our study, two specific barriers to spiritual growth have surfaced among the congregants of every participating church: being *stalled* and being *dissatisfied*.

Barrier 1: Being Stalled. In every congregation, there are people who select the word *stalled* to describe the pace of their spiritual growth, from a list that also includes the options "rapid," "moderate," "slow but steady," or "I'm content with my spiritual growth." The percentage of self-described stalled congregants in any given church ranges from the low single digits to numbers in the mid-twenties. In total, stalled people represent 13 percent of the REVEAL database, although almost everyone— *92 percent of those surveyed*— report they have experienced being stalled at some point in their spiritual journey.

Barrier 2: Being Dissatisfied. Every congregation also includes people who express some level of dissatisfaction with "the church's role in my spiritual growth." On average, the dissatisfied represent 18 percent of a church body, but this number varies widely among churches, from the low single digits to more than half of the congregation.

That these two groups exist is hardly breaking news for church leaders. But learning that the stalled and dissatisfied represent fairly healthy percentages of every congregation can be discouraging—even when strategies exist for turning around such realities. In some ways, it's like visiting the dentist for a routine checkup, only to discover that you have several cavities and need a crown. Even knowing that the problem can be fixed doesn't take away the sting of the damage!

It's easy to avoid such confirmation of dental problems, at least for a while, because the deep-down damage is invisible. It might be equally tempting for church leaders to look the other way and avoid dealing with these problems, because the deep-down spiritual damage is often hard to see. It's easier to focus on surface issues—like attendance and giving numbers—and just ignore the grumbling e-mails and other symptoms of spiritual-growth problems.

However, if you're thinking of skipping this chapter (just like the one-third of Americans who avoid the dentist each year), we would encourage you to keep reading. Remember the encouragement of Jesus: "Fear not!" We believe the insights of the REVEAL survey about the stalled and dissatisfied are actually more *encouraging* than discouraging. Toward that end, let's begin with two observations that should lift the spirits of every church leader eager to help the spiritually adrift get back on course.

Observation 1: The Stalled and Dissatisfied Overlap

Not surprisingly, the stalled and dissatisfied groups are not completely independent of one another (chart 10-1). When people are spiritually stalled, it's not unreasonable to suspect they might also express dissatisfaction with their

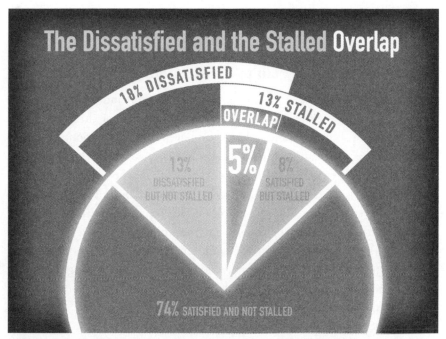

CHART 10-1: There is an overlap between the 18 percent of people who are dissatisfied and the 13 percent who are stalled. Five percent of the total sample are both stalled and dissatisfied. Adding together the percentages high-lighted within the circle shows that 26 percent of the total sample falls into the stalled and/or dissatisfied groups.

church, just as a student struggling to learn a difficult subject might criticize the competency of the teacher.

If, as you read the statistics above, you mentally tallied the 13 percent of those stalled and the 18 percent of those dissatisfied and concluded that over 30 percent of an average church congregation falls into these categories, we want you to know that it's not quite that bad. That number is too high. In fact, there is a 5 percent overlap between the two groups, meaning that 5 percent of an average congregation reports being both spiritually stalled *and* dissatisfied with the church's role in their spiritual growth. The fact is that most stalled people (the remaining 8 of the original 13 percent) blame themselves, not the church, for their predicament.

Adding all three numbers in the highlighted sections (13 percent + 5 percent + 8 percent) creates a total combined average of the stalled and dissatisfied group of 26 percent. This means that, on average, 26 percent—or about one of every four congregants—are either stalled, dissatisfied with the church, or both. The more important number, however, is the one in the large section that is not highlighted. That number—74 percent—reflects the sizeable majority of people who are growing spiritually and are satisfied with how the church is helping them do that—which is good news for church leaders.

Observation 2: They Plan to Stay in Church

And here's more good news. While it's tempting to conclude that the stalled and dissatisfied are either shopping for another church or thinking about checking out of church life altogether, most have no such intentions.

True, 10 percent of all churchgoers say they are "unsure," "probably," or "definitely" leaving the church in the near future, but the large majority (80 percent) of those individuals fall into the "unsure" camp. And among this 10 percent, we find the dissatisfied group is well represented. Still, by far the majority of those who are dissatisfied express no desire to leave. In fact, 63 percent of those who are dissatisfied and 79 percent of those who are stalled say they intend to stay at their church. And remember, even among those who fall into the 10 percent who are considering leaving the church, most of them (80 percent) remain "unsure."

That the vast majority of the stalled and the dissatisfied have no plans to leave the church should be a great encouragement for church leaders. It means that these struggling and/or frustrated people are worth the church's time, effort, and resources—even though the investment required may be considerable. These are people who haven't given up on the church, even if some of them are not especially happy with it. And they haven't given up on Jesus, even though some don't have much spiritual traction. This makes understanding their unique characteristics a worthy endeavor for all who are called to lead people—including the reluctant and recalcitrant—to follow Christ.

Getting to Know Those Who Are Stalled

While it's helpful to know that one out of every eight people (13 percent) in any given congregation is spiritually stalled, we find it even more interesting to study the spiritual profile of this group. The stalled reside in every segment on the spiritual continuum, yet the majority of them come from the less mature side of the continuum (chart 10-2).

In fact, the spiritual profile of the stalled comes into even clearer focus when the four segments are lined up, one after the other, for comparison with the total sample. As you can see, the dominance of the Growing in Christ segment is undeniable (chart 10-3).

Those Who Are Stalled Come Primarily from the Less Spiritually Mature Segments

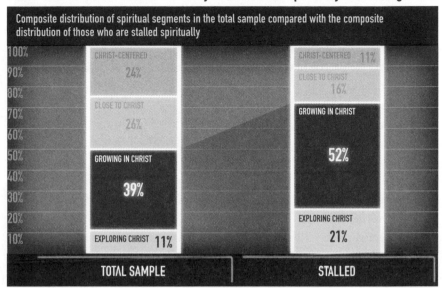

CHART 10–2: The less mature segments represent 50 percent of all people in the REVEAL database (11 percent are Exploring Christ; 39 percent are Growing in Christ). But they represent 73 percent of those who are spiritually stalled (21 percent are Exploring Christ; 52 percent are Growing in Christ). So most stalled people fall in the less mature segments.

The Growing in Christ Segment Dominates the Stalled Group

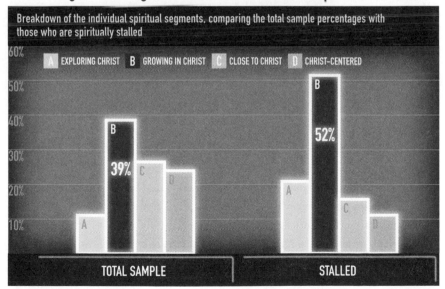

CHART 10–3: The set of bars on the left shows that the Growing in Christ segment is the largest of the four segments on the spiritual continuum. But it clearly dominates the stalled population, indicated by the set of bars on the right, visually eclipsing the rest of the segments.

While all the segments are represented in the stalled category, the Growing in Christ segment casts a remarkably tall shadow over the rest of them. This is important to note so that we can clarify the distinctions between what it means to be spiritually *stalled* versus spiritually *growing*. So, to provide the clearest possible profile of what it means to be stalled, we will focus exclusively on the characteristics of those who are stalled within the dominant Growing in Christ segment.

The stalled within this segment share three defining spiritual characteristics:

Characteristic 1: The Stalled Invest Little Effort in Their Faith. Even taking into account their lack of spiritual maturity, they invest much less personal time and effort in their faith than those who are not stalled.

Characteristic 2: The Stalled Are Less Connected to and More Disappointed in the Church. They are simply not well connected in the church. Across the board, they don't participate in church activities as often as others and they are much less satisfied with their church experiences.

Characteristic 3: The Stalled Say They're Too Busy. The primary reason for their low faith investment and church connection is simple: they feel they are too busy. Busy with what? Often it's simply the normal daily grind of life.

Let's take a closer look at these characteristics and how they play out in the churches we studied.

Characteristic 1: The Stalled Invest Little Effort in Their Faith

A comparison of personal spiritual practices between those in the Growing in Christ segment who are stalled and not stalled puts a spotlight on one of the most distinguishing barriers to spiritual growth. Those who are stalled make very little effort to communicate with God on a regular basis (chart 10-4).

In fact, the differences between the behaviors of the stalled and the not stalled are significant across *all* spiritual practices, from Bible engagement to prayer and solitude. And although this chart addresses only the Growing in Christ segment, comparisons between the stalled and not stalled in *every* segment echo this conclusion. The bottom line is this: little investment equals little growth — no matter what the level of spiritual maturity.

Once again, this finding — that little investment equals little growth — should not surprise us. In fact, the Scriptures consistently affirm that the process of spiritual growth isn't automatic or passive — it sometimes requires great effort. In 1 Corinthians 9, Paul uses two athletic metaphors — running a race and boxing against an opponent — to emphasize the importance of enduring effort and perseverance in the Christian life. Again, in Luke 8:15 we find Jesus

Stalled People in the Growing in Christ Segment Are Much Less Likely to Engage in Spiritual Practices

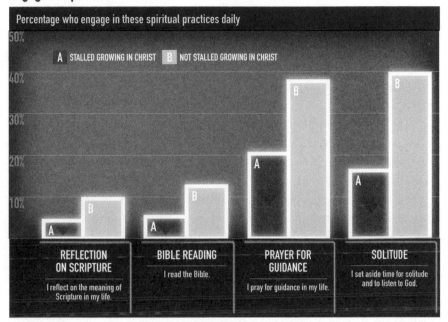

CHART 10–4: When compared with those who are *not* stalled, those who are stalled in the Growing in Christ segment are much less likely to engage in personal spiritual practices.

teaching his disciples that it is not enough to simply hear God's Word and respond to it half-heartedly. The seed that produces a lasting harvest falls on good soil, representing "those with a noble and good heart, who hear the word, retain it, and by *persevering* produce a crop" (emphasis added).

We all know the importance of persevering to reach a goal in any endeavor we undertake. So when my twelve-year-old daughter declared, "I want to quit!" after a particularly difficult piano lesson, I (Cally) wasn't all that surprised. Up to this point, she had loved playing the piano, but it had recently become a source of anxiety in her life, competing with other interests for her time and attention. She had stopped practicing regularly and had begun to grow angry and frustrated—with the piano, with her teacher, with my regular reminders to practice—but most of all, she was angry and disappointed with herself. She was stalled, and at the time it seemed easier for her to quit than to figure out how to get started again.

To be honest, I was less concerned with whether she continued playing than with her motives for quitting. I didn't want her to simply give up from sheer frustration. So, in a stroke of brilliant parenting, I agreed on the spot that she could quit—on one condition. I asked her to spend twenty minutes every day during the next week practicing the piano. If she would commit to practicing for one additional week and still wanted to quit after that, I would support her decision.

She agreed. And she didn't quit. In fact, she continued taking piano lessons until she went to college six years later. Sure, there were a few more bumps of frustration along the way, but whenever she buckled down and recommitted herself to the discipline of daily practice, she got herself back on track.

Why did this work? Because she loved the music. Her love for the music led her to *persevere* and reengage with the practicing required to enjoy the music. Playing the piano tapped into a passion that was renewed by a daily discipline of practice.

This same dynamic may explain the power personal spiritual practices have to catalyze growth in a spiritually stalled heart. When we allow God's grace to motivate our efforts, our daily disciplines renew our hearts and transform our thoughts, attitudes, and actions one day at a time. Engaging in personal spiritual practices *reinforces* our love for Christ and *rekindles* our belief in his love

Stalled People in the Growing in Christ Segment Believe in the Trinity and Salvation by Grace, but Struggle to Believe in a Personal God

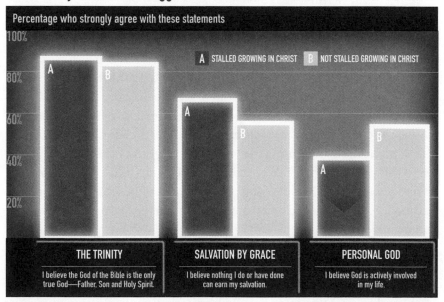

CHART 10-5: Whether or not they are stalled, those in the Growing in Christ segment tend to express belief in the Trinity and salvation by grace. However, those who are stalled are less likely to believe that God is active in their everyday lives.

for us. It is our belief in that love and God's faithfulness that keeps us strong in the face of life's burdens and pressures.

So if we know that additional effort will most likely aid the process of spiritual growth, why don't those who are spiritually stalled just buck up and try harder? Digging more closely into the data, we find that their low interest in spiritual practices may be a direct result of a weak belief in a *personal* God (chart 10-5). While those who are stalled claim to believe in the Trinity as firmly as those who are not stalled (and even *more* firmly in salvation by grace), they seem less convinced that God is actually active and present in their personal lives.

And this makes perfect sense. If we doubt that God is really active and present in our daily life, we are far less likely to connect with him in prayer or reading the Bible. However, the connection issues for the stalled run deeper than the spiritual practices alone.

Characteristic 2: The Stalled Are Less Connected to and More Disappointed in the Church

Those who are spiritually stalled also tend to participate less in church activities than those who are not stalled, and, like the level at which they engage in personal spiritual practices, this lower level of community connection appears across the board in multiple church activities (chart 10-6).

One of the most significant gaps, however, surfaces in small-group participation. For those who are Growing in Christ, small groups seem to be particularly important to the growth process. They are the primary resource people in this segment have for forming friendships and mentoring relationships that help them grow in faith. The fact that just over one-third of those who are stalled participate in small groups—compared with half of those who are not stalled—indicates that when people stall in their faith, these important early relational connections are not being made. And their absence has real consequences for spiritual growth.

Further, those who are stalled and *do* continue to participate in church activities, including the one-third who are involved in small groups, are demonstrably less *satisfied* with their experiences than those who are not stalled (chart 10-7). Again, these deficits in satisfaction occur in all church activities. And the differences are significant, ranging from 30 to 40 percent lower than the satisfaction levels of those who are growing spiritually.

The profile that emerges is one of less invested, underengaged people who are disappointed with the church—and probably disenchanted with God.

Stalled People in the Growing in Christ Segment Are Less Likely to Participate in Church Activities

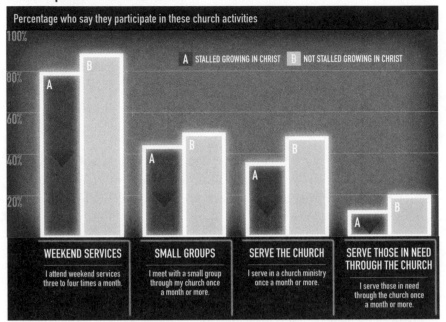

CHART 10-6: When compared with those who are *not* stalled, those who are stalled in the Growing in Christ segment are less likely to participate in church activities, reporting lower weekend service attendance, serving, and small-group participation.

Who are these stalled people? At first, we might be inclined to think that these are the people who have been knocked off track by one of life's curveballs—the loss of a job or the end of a significant relationship, for instance. Many church leaders seem to be convinced that these stalled people are the same individuals who show up at church recovery groups or call to arrange appointments for pastoral care. Our research, however, does not support these observations.

Certainly, people struggling with life crises are likely to wrestle with the idea that a good God is present in the midst of their troubles. But these individuals who seek out help or complain to church leadership may be akin to the proverbial squeaky wheel—meaning the volume of their voices can give a misleading impression about the strength of their numbers. Because they are being seriously challenged by life and are seeking support from pastors and churches, it is possible for us to miss the fact that they are not the only ones treading water.

Stalled People in the Growing in Christ Segment Are Much Less Satisfied with Church Activities

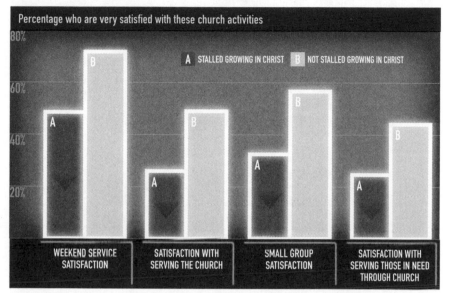

Percentage who are very satisfied with these church activities

A STALLED GROWING IN CHRIST   B NOT STALLED GROWING IN CHRIST

| WEEKEND SERVICE SATISFACTION | SATISFACTION WITH SERVING THE CHURCH | SMALL GROUP SATISFACTION | SATISFACTION WITH SERVING THOSE IN NEED THROUGH CHURCH |

CHART 10-7: When compared with those who are *not* stalled, those who are stalled in the Growing in Christ segment are distinctly less satisfied with their church activity experiences.

Yes, the stalled can include those who are in difficult seasons of life. But our research shows that a significant number of the stalled (we estimate at least half) are simply … busy.

Characteristic 3: The Stalled Say They're Too Busy

According to all survey respondents who report they have been spiritually stalled, the most significant contributing factor to this condition is a "lack of discipline in spiritual practices" (chart 10-8). But issues like a fast-paced life and conflicting responsibilities also rank near the top of the list of contributors, which may explain *why* people struggle with a lack of discipline.

The findings suggest that many of the spiritually stalled are simply overwhelmed by *normal* life. Not by the things that turn life upside down, like grief or depression, but by the daily demands of commutes, cranky bosses, dirty diapers, and financial shortfalls.

This observation is reinforced by looking at the list of things people tell us helped them become "un-stalled" (chart 10-9). At the top of the list, no surprise to any of us, is connecting with God through spiritual practices. But a

Why People Say They Stalled Spiritually

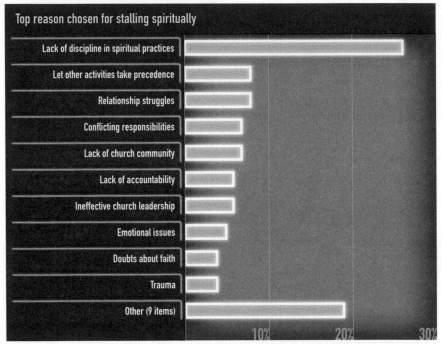

Top reason chosen for stalling spiritually

- Lack of discipline in spiritual practices
- Let other activities take precedence
- Relationship struggles
- Conflicting responsibilities
- Lack of church community
- Lack of accountability
- Ineffective church leadership
- Emotional issues
- Doubts about faith
- Trauma
- Other (9 items)

10%   20%   30%

CHART 10-8: Most people say they have stalled at some point in their spiritual development, and many report a "lack of discipline in spiritual practices" as the primary reason. However, several reasons indicate that everyday busyness contributes to a stalled spiritual life, such as "let other activities take precedence."

close second is "came to grips with the issue on my own," a response that seems quite consistent for those who are the victim of issues related to the daily grind.

Speaking of the "daily grind," no one who lives in the Chicagoland area would ever describe the driving pace between the suburbs and the city at 5 p.m. on a workday afternoon using the word *rush*. Instead, we creep along at a snail's pace, frustrated by the glow of red brake lights and drivers impatiently maneuvering to change lanes to gain the advantage of a few feet. We feel boxed in and helpless, knowing that there's nothing we can do to move any faster toward our destination. Except wait and hope that traffic will eventually ease—and wonder if next time, we shouldn't just take that commuter train that whizzed by.

This is how those who are stalled feel—boxed in and trapped by their schedules and commitments. They are unable to see any real options that would break through the logjam of their lives to create spiritual momentum. So they just wait, hoping that at some point the demands of life will ease or an alternative streamlined path will magically materialize.

What People Say They Did to Get "Un-Stalled"

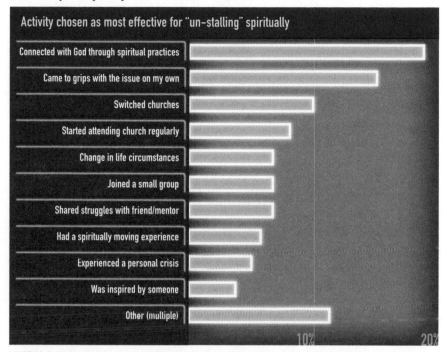

Activity chosen as most effective for "un-stalling" spiritually

- Connected with God through spiritual practices
- Came to grips with the issue on my own
- Switched churches
- Started attending church regularly
- Change in life circumstances
- Joined a small group
- Shared struggles with friend/mentor
- Had a spiritually moving experience
- Experienced a personal crisis
- Was inspired by someone
- Other (multiple)

10%   20%

CHART 10-9: When asked what they did to "un-stall" their spiritual life, many reported connecting with God through spiritual practices or coming to grips on their own with the issue that was compromising their spiritual momentum

That's the challenge to the church — to create the spiritual equivalent of the commuter train. To provide a path that helps those who are stalled circumvent the crush of life's "rush hour," and puts them in a position to grow spiritually, despite circumstances that seem determined to block their way.

What if we could offer credible options, for instance, to the survey taker who wrote to us, "I'm at a time in my life when I'm stretched to the limit with full-time work, a four-hour daily commute, and taking care of elderly parents"? How can we help the single mom of three more effectively overcome the obstacles she faces? A single mom in our survey asked this question: "Is there a way to connect congregants who can only come on the weekends? I can't come midweek. I feel alone at church." How can we respond to her?

To be stalled is to be disillusioned. But most of those who are stalled seem less disillusioned with the church or in God than they are with their own lives. Most recognize the connection between their life circumstances and their lack of spiritual traction. They just have no idea what to do. So how can we respond to them? What's the innovative church strategy to reach these people and inspire them to invest in the activities, relationships, and practices they need to help them grow?

The good news is that such strategies exist. But before we focus on responding to those who are stalled, let's take a closer look at those who are dissatisfied with the church's role in their spiritual growth. As we will see, just as the stalled and dissatisfied overlap in congregations, the best ideas for how to address their issues and needs also overlap. So let's unpack what makes the "dissatisfied" so dissatisfied. Then we'll conclude with some barrier-busting strategies that can activate spiritual momentum for both groups.

Getting to Know Those Who Are Dissatisfied

Like the stalled, the dissatisfied also show up in every spiritual segment. Unlike the stalled, however, there is no dominant segment that defines this group (chart 10-10). In other words, people seem to be similarly satisfied or dissatisfied with the church, regardless of where they are on their spiritual journey.

Still, there is an interesting story behind these numbers. When the results from the first Willow Creek survey were analyzed, we were quite surprised to find a significant level of dissatisfaction among the church's most mature believers. And as the survey results expanded beyond Willow Creek, we found this pattern of dissatisfaction across all spiritual segments continued — confirming that this wasn't something unique to our church. In every church we surveyed, the most mature believers were just as likely to be dissatisfied as new believers and those still exploring faith in Christ.

Why were we so surprised to find dissatisfaction among mature believers? Traditional market research experience would tell us that satisfaction with the church should *increase* (and dissatisfaction decline) as people become more engaged spiritually. This is because, in the marketplace, satisfaction tends to increase among the most loyal customers of any brand or service. Someone who is a big fan of cappuccinos, for instance, is likely to be a loyal and satisfied customer of his or her chosen vendor, like Starbucks or the local coffeehouse down the street. Logic would suggest that, similarly, as a person's relationship with Christ grows and matures, satisfaction with his or her chosen church should also rise.

That's not, however, what we found. In fact, as we have mentioned already, the level of dissatisfaction exists on a relatively equal basis regardless of spiritual maturity. In fact, dissatisfaction even *increases* slightly in the most mature Christ-Centered segment.

No Segment Stands Out As Having More or Less Dissatisfied People

Composite distribution of spiritual segments in the total sample compared with the composite distribution of those who are dissatisfied with the church's role in helping them grow spiritually

	TOTAL SAMPLE	DISSATISFIED
CHRIST-CENTERED	24%	26%
CLOSE TO CHRIST	26%	24%
GROWING IN CHRIST	39%	36%
EXPLORING CHRIST	11%	14%

CHART 10-10: The distribution of dissatisfied people in the four segments on the spiritual continuum mirrors the distribution of all people in the REVEAL database.

Keep in mind that this dissatisfaction is *not* a measure of people's feelings about their church leadership or the activities at their church. It is, very specifically, a measure of people's feelings about the church's role in helping them grow spiritually. And with that in mind, we probably should not have been surprised at our survey results. Given that most churches try to serve the spiritual needs of all people with a one-size-fits-all strategy, it makes sense that most churches only *partially* address the needs of any particular group — creating this fairly balanced pattern of satisfaction and dissatisfaction across the spiritual continuum. To put it simply: No one is altogether happy — or unhappy — with the church's role in fostering spiritual growth because the church is serving all segments equally well. Or not.

The most distinguishing characteristic of the dissatisfied lies in what they are most dissatisfied *about*. If those who are dissatisfied could hand the church a job description, five requirements would top their list of priorities (chart 10-11). These requirements emerge from a list of nineteen statements rated by all survey respondents in the areas of importance and satisfaction. (For the list of all nineteen statements, see "What Do People Want the Church to Do Better?" on page 189).

These five priorities help us grasp some of the most critical things people want from a church. They indicate the top five areas in which dissatisfied

The Dissatisfied Have Five Top Priorities for the Church

—Help me understand the Bible in depth

—Help me develop a personal relationship with Christ

—Challenge me to grow

—Church leaders model how to grow

—Help me feel like I belong

CHART 10-11: The dissatisfied would like the church to respond to these top five priorities. Their desire for more help in understanding the Bible in-depth leads the list.

churchgoers believe their churches need to improve. But this list is more than just a reflection of what is most wanted or needed by the dissatisfied. Two additional insights make it especially important that church leaders pay attention to the items on this list.

Insight 1: The Satisfied and Dissatisfied Share the Top Two Priorities

Broadening our base—from those defined as dissatisfied to the entire database of 250,000 survey respondents—only reinforces the importance of the top two priorities on the list (chart 10-12). Not only do both groups choose the *same* two statements; they even list them in the same order. For the dissatisfied—and *all other churchgoers as well*—"Help me understand the Bible in depth" is the number one priority. "Help me develop a personal relationship with Christ" is number two.

This means that those who are dissatisfied are not just chronic complainers with needs distinct from the rest of the congregation. Instead, their highest felt needs reflect the *same* needs we find within the rest of the church body. To be sure, the dissatisfied are much *unhappier* than the average congregant with their church's performance in addressing these priorities. Typically, their unhappiness gauge is more than twice that of other congregants. But the top priorities of the dissatisfied are far from isolated, independent gripes about the church. In reality, they are bellwethers for the concerns of the entire church.

Our reviews of hundreds of church reports rarely reveal an inconsistency in these findings. Time after time, we see correspondence between the highest priorities for the dissatisfied congregants and the priorities of the aggregate

The Dissatisfied Share the **Same Top Priorities***
for the Church as Everyone Else

TOP FIVE CHURCH PRIORITIES: Total Sample

Help me understand the Bible in depth.
Help me develop a personal relationship with Christ.
Help me develop my prayer life.
Help me in my time of emotional need.
Provide a clear pathway to guide growth.

TOP CHURCH PRIORITIES: Dissatisfied Group

Help me understand the Bible in depth.
Help me develop a personal relationship with Christ.
Challenge me to grow.
Church leaders model how I grow.
Help me feel like I belong.

CHART 10-12: Everyone in the database reports the same top two priorities for the church as the dissatisfied group, which means church leaders should feel confident that increasing their teaching and support related to these issues would address the concerns of most congregants.

*Note that these lists of top priorities differ from the top five things each segment wants from your church presented in part 1 (pages 34, 35, 68, 94). That's because the lists in part 1 reflect only levels of importance. The lists here reflect two things: levels of importance *and* levels of satisfaction. This means that the most important benefits with the lowest satisfaction are those that lead the list.

church body. In some ways, this should be encouraging to church leaders. Because addressing the top priorities for one will, in fact, address issues of concern for all.

Insight 2: All Segments Share the Same Top Two Priorities

Not only do we find the same top priorities for the dissatisfied and the satisfied, those top priorities don't vary much across spiritual segments (chart 10-13). In other words, regardless of whether people are still Exploring Christ or are more mature, Christ-Centered believers, one of their highest hopes is that the church will help them develop a personal relationship with Christ. Helping people understand the Bible in greater depth is one of the top two priorities for those who are dissatisfied *across all the believer segments*.

How, then, should churches respond based on these insights? Well, our findings suggest that if a church were to focus exclusively on these two objectives—helping people develop a personal relationship with Jesus and helping them understand the Bible in depth—they would not only address the issues that are important to the dissatisfied people in the congregation, they will address the needs of the church congregation as a whole, irrespective of a person's spiritual maturity.

The Dissatisfied in All Segments Echo these Same Priorities

Less Mature Spiritual Segments			More Mature Spiritual Segments		
Dissatisfied Exploring Christ	Dissatisfied Growing in Christ	Dissatisfied Close to Christ	Dissatisfied Christ-Centered		
Help me feel like I belong	**Help me develop a personal relationship with Christ**	**Help me understand the Bible in depth**	**Help me understand the Bible in depth**		
Help me develop a personal relationship with Christ	**Help me understand the Bible in depth**	Church leaders model how to grow	Church leaders model how to grow		
Help me in my time of emotional need	Challenge me to grow	Challenge me to grow	Challenge me to grow		
Provide a clear pathway to guide growth	Church leaders model how to grow	**Help me develop a personal relationship with Christ**	**Help me develop a personal relationship with Christ**		
Help me develop a prayer life	Help me feel like I belong	Provide a clear pathway to guide growth	Provide a clear pathway to guide growth		

CHART 10–13: Regardless of spiritual maturity, dissatisfied people want more support from the church in developing a relationship with Christ. Dissatisfied people in all segments (Exploring Christ, Growing in Christ, Close to Christ, and Christ-Centered) share a desire for more help in understanding the Bible.

The bigger question, of course, is "How"? How do church leaders actually do this? How do they re-engage the stalled and satisfy the dissatisfied? We believe the answer can be summed up in two words: the Bible.

How the Church Can Help

It shouldn't surprise us in the least, but our research confirms what church leaders have known for centuries: the Scriptures are the key to breaking through the barriers encountered by both the stalled and the dissatisfied. Those who are stalled *need* the Bible; those who are dissatisfied *want* the Bible. It should encourage us, as church leaders, to know that the remedies for the two barriers to spiritual growth have their roots in the same resource—the simple power of God's Word. In part 3, you'll read inspiring accounts of how churches successfully bring the Bible to life for their people, helping their stalled and dissatisfied people move beyond the barriers that have long impeded their spiritual growth. Typically, we find that they foster this movement toward renewed spiritual growth by applying two simple strategies, both of which involve Bible engagement beyond the walls of the church.

The first strategy is to create a small-group curriculum to complement and extend the teaching from weekend services into experiences of deeper reflection during the week. (Some churches even include children's and youth ministries in this process, to equip families for dialogue on fresh spiritual topics between services.) This practice has the potential to accomplish two things—first, to raise the value of small-group participation for the unconnected stalled people by connecting the study to weekend content; and second, to encourage the more comprehensive biblical study sought by the dissatisfied. Based on a number of REVEAL churches that have embraced this approach and then resurveyed their congregations, we find consistent evidence of that progress on many fronts, including declining percentages of stalled and dissatisfied people. (You may recall the story of Fox Christian Church, for instance, from chapter 8.)

A second strategy that churches are utilizing is making use of the many innovative Bible-study options that are now possible through Web-based platforms and widespread availability of the Internet. These resources are more than just slick software packages. Consider, for example, the simple Daily Devotion videos recorded by the leaders of a Methodist church in Myrtle Beach, South Carolina. Posted each day on the church's website, these videos are popular with the nine-hundred-member congregation—and those who watch a new video each day will eventually walk through the entire Bible in one year. Does this really work? While it is difficult to prove a direct cause-and-effect relationship, we believe the answer is "yes." The survey results of this church indicate outstanding personal spiritual practices, including 58 percent who report a daily personal solitude experience with God.

While the Web enables us to establish simple and inexpensive strategies using a bit of creativity and innovation, there are also some more comprehensive, professionally designed technical platforms available for churches. These offer individual spiritual growth plans for their congregants, including customized recommendations for next steps. One example of this is Engage, an interactive web- and mobile-device-based churchwide system. A core component of the Engage program is the Engage Life Survey, which allows an individual to personally apply some of the findings of the REVEAL study. Congregants who participate in Engage receive personalized spiritual growth plans in response to a short survey that gauges the best next steps for their spiritual development. These next steps can range from a customized Bible engagement plan to specific growth opportunities provided by the individual's church, like education classes or serving opportunities. Besides providing help with personal spiritual development, Engage also facilitates online interaction within a church community, including opportunities for social networking and full support for group life activities.

Options like these — whether they are simple Web-based devotionals or more comprehensive platforms that facilitate personal spiritual growth plans — may be the key to real breakthroughs for the very busy stalled and the frustrated dissatisfied groups in your congregation. Both of these strategies, of course, require that church leaders put increased emphasis on helping their people break away from their Sunday-morning-only routines. If those who are dissatisfied continue to depend exclusively on a single hour of weekend teaching to help them grow spiritually, they will remain dissatisfied. If those who are stalled stay unconnected with the community of faith and unaware of alternative spiritual growth options more compatible with their lifestyle, they will remain stalled. But today's churches are much better positioned than they were in the past to help both groups find ways to meet their needs.

Does that mean that the stalled and dissatisfied are likely to disappear? No. But we hope that as churches seek to engage these groups, we will see a measurable decline in their numbers, and any decline is good news for church leaders — and for the kingdom of God.

What Do People Want the Church to Do Better?

Churches offer many opportunities — weekend services, small groups, serving experiences, mission trips, classes, and more. All of these activities are offered with a single end goal in mind — that somehow the activity will help people grow spiritually.

The REVEAL survey identifies nineteen statements that reflect the various ways the church contributes to that goal. Every person who takes the REVEAL survey rates these statements based on their importance to spiritual growth and satisfaction with the church's role in each specific area. From those ratings, the nineteen statements were ranked in the order of the survey-takers' perception of the greatest shortfalls — and opportunities — for the church. They are:

- Help me understand the Bible in depth.
- Help me develop a personal relationship with Christ.
- Help me develop a prayer life.
- Help me in my time of emotional need.
- Provide a clear pathway to guide growth.
- Challenge me to grow and take the next steps.
- Help me feel like I belong.
- Provide strong programs for children.
- Model how to grow.
- Encourage accountability.
- Provide a chance to grow with others.
- Encourage me to take responsibility for my own growth.
- Empower me to go out "on my own."
- Inspire a sense of church ownership.
- Provide compelling worship.
- Set clear expectations.
- Incorporate Communion [Eucharist] into worship services.
- Promote a strong serving culture.
- Provide a chance to serve those in need.

PART 3

Spiritual Leadership

CHAPTER 11

The Spiritual Vitality Index

W*e found them."*

The longer we stood there welcoming people—shaking hands, putting faces with the names we knew, making introductions—the more those three words echoed in our minds. After five long years, here they were, gathering at Willow Creek: the pastors of the churches representing the most vibrant, spiritually alive congregations among the five hundred churches that had, to that point, participated in the REVEAL survey.

We had invited this group together because the analysis of their REVEAL survey results indicated something special was going on in their churches. According to their numbers, they were among the top 5 percent of all churches surveyed in terms of their congregants' spiritual growth. We knew the factual results were conclusive, and that something quite remarkable set these congregations apart from all the others we'd surveyed—including our own. But when it came to the leaders of those churches, we had to wonder: Would they be as remarkable as their survey results?

The only way to find out was to meet them in person. So we arranged an all-day meeting that started with a dinner the night before, on the Wednesday after Labor Day 2008. I (Greg) was so nervous I could barely stand still long enough to greet our guests. One after another, those who had accepted our invitation walked through the door—thirteen senior pastors, as well as members of their teams, representing just over half of the top twenty-five REVEAL churches.

By the first break the next morning, we were absolutely positive that these were the individuals we'd been looking for. Despite all our second-guessing, behind the impressive survey statistics were equally impressive leaders—individuals who had much to share about how to help people grow in a relationship with Christ.

What convinced us? For one thing, in spite of their churches' great diversity of sizes, locations, and cultures, we sensed these leaders' hearts were all in the same Christ-centered place. As they interacted, they did not discuss church growth strategies; there were no conversations, for instance, that began, "We did this and our church grew by X percent." Instead, they discussed the importance of embedding the Bible into the hearts of their congregants. They talked about helping people move from simply knowing Jesus to surrendering their lives to him. Their own personal devotion to that work was so extraordinary that it set this group apart from the hundreds of pastor gatherings I have participated in over the last two decades. Indeed, just being among them made that Thursday one of the greatest days of my life.

These church leaders also pursued common strategies—which was somewhat surprising. We thought we would find that some achieved their results through creative small-group strategies, others with far-reaching local and global serving programs, and still others through dynamic teaching. What we found instead was a group of leaders extraordinarily in sync with one another, pursuing very similar strategies to advance the spiritual growth of their people. They also shared a common passion: a single-minded focus on making disciples of Christ. We saw in them a living illustration of the verse: "Love the Lord your God with all your heart and with all your soul and with all your mind" (Matthew 22:37).

That's why we considered this such a big deal. We had begun the REVEAL work five years earlier. As it developed, we started to dream of finding—through fact-based evidence—churches that were spiritually thriving. We believed that if we could find them, we could learn from them. We could share what we learned with others. Five years of effort. Then, within a single day, we were in the midst of something quite incredible. We really *had* found them.

The chapters in part 3 are dedicated to unpacking what we believe is the greatest gift REVEAL has to offer—the story and strategies of how best-practice churches like these most effectively inspire spiritual growth.

The Story Behind "Best Practices"

Every journalism student quickly learns the tried-and-true checklist for capturing the facts, called the "Five W's (and one H)": who, what, where, when, why, and how. Interestingly, that formula originated more than a century ago, when Rudyard Kipling wrote:

I keep six honest serving-men:
(They taught me all I knew)
Their names are What and Where and When
And How and Why and Who.[1]

Now this verse-turned-media-staple can help to clarify REVEAL's measurement of spiritual vitality within individual congregations. Using the "Five W's (and one H)" formula, we can describe the facts that enabled us to identify REVEAL's best-practice churches—an exercise that is important for two reasons.

First, the unique contribution of REVEAL is its quantitative foundation. (That's a fancy way of saying we didn't make this stuff up.) Every step taken toward this point of identifying best practices was fact-based, not opinion-based. So we hope you will read and study the stories of these churches with at least a measure of the kind of respect you would accord to reports of medical or scientific breakthroughs that have an objective basis for their results and conclusions.

In addition, ticking through the facts should help to reinforce the bull's-eye focus of this work—which is not really so much about the church. It's much more about *the people who attend the church.* REVEAL looks through its statistical microscope to assess the spiritual vitality of a congregation. It is through *that* lens—not the lens of church size or resources or notoriety—that we identified churches doing the best job of growing people into followers of Christ. It is our hope that an overview of that process will reinforce your confidence in the value and wisdom of the best-practice strategies pursued by these outstanding REVEAL churches.

Confidence, of course, should not be assumed. People want to "kick the tires" before they accept information and advice, especially on challenging issues. I (Cally) was recently reminded of that when, during a routine medical procedure, a friend discovered she had cancer of the appendix. She turned first to family and friends for comfort, then to the Internet for facts and advice from people in a similar circumstance. That readied her to seek out the medical experts who could recommend and carry out whatever next steps she chose to take. This process of due diligence—the gathering of facts, advice, and recommendations from experts—gives my friend the confidence she needs to pursue a course of action. While her faith in God minimizes her fear of what

---

[1] Rudyard Kipling, "The Elephant's Child," *Just So Stories* (Garden City, NY: Doubleday, 1902), 65–84.

lies ahead, it is her confidence—based on due diligence—that gives her the courage to act.

Similarly, we hope you will trust the guidance offered by these churches because you understand the effort to find them was rigorous and comprehensive. Toward that end, we offer a synopsis of the facts, using the "Five W's (and one H)" formula to make sure we communicate the full story. We'll begin with "What?"

What Defines Best Practices?

It is important, first of all, to understand which factors we include in the measurement of spiritual vitality—and why they are included—because that quality is the yardstick for determining which churches are "best." Every church that takes the REVEAL Spiritual Life Survey receives a measure called the Spiritual Vitality Index (SVI) in the report that summarizes their results (chart 11-1).

The SVI is the number in the center of the triangle. It is based on a scale of one to one hundred and indicates how a church's congregation compares to the rest of the churches in the REVEAL database. This comparison is made in three categories of attitudes and activities vital to spiritual growth: the church's role, personal spiritual practices, and faith in action.

* *The Church's Role.* This category assesses the congregation's satisfaction with a few key church attributes that are most catalytic to spiritual growth—for instance, how the church helps people develop a personal relationship with Christ, understand the Bible in greater depth, and challenges them to grow.

* *Personal Spiritual Practices.* This category assesses those spiritual practices most critical to spiritual growth across all three movements, including reflection on Scripture and prayer for guidance.

* *Faith in Action.* This category includes factors significant to the more mature movements of spiritual growth, such as evangelism, serving those in need, and the degree to which congregants are willing to risk everything for Christ.

You may wonder why and how the factors in these three categories were chosen. The answer tracks back to the origin of every fact and finding in *Move*, which is the definition of spiritual growth based on Jesus' words in Matthew 22:37–39. We define spiritual growth according to this great commandment,

Spiritual Vitality Index for Church ABC

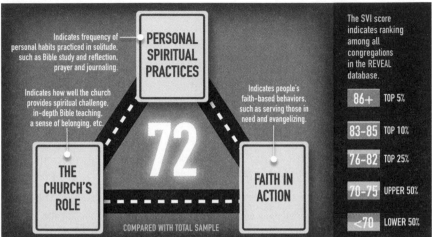

Indicates frequency of personal habits practiced in solitude, such as Bible study and reflection, prayer and journaling.

PERSONAL SPIRITUAL PRACTICES

Indicates how well the church provides spiritual challenge, in-depth Bible teaching, a sense of belonging, etc.

72

Indicates people's faith-based behaviors, such as serving those in need and evangelizing.

THE CHURCH'S ROLE

FAITH IN ACTION

COMPARED WITH TOTAL SAMPLE

The SVI score indicates ranking among all congregations in the REVEAL database.

86+	TOP 5%
83–85	TOP 10%
76–82	TOP 25%
70–75	UPPER 50%
<70	LOWER 50%

CHART 11-1: The number in the center represents the REVEAL Spiritual Vitality Index (SVI) for a typical church. It benchmarks key measures related to spiritual growth for an individual congregation against the total database. These measures fall into the three categories shown on the triangle: Personal Spiritual Practices, Faith in Action, and the Church's Role. The SVI scale mimics an academic grading scale, so 72 reflects an average spiritual vitality score.

which means spiritual growth occurs when love for God and love for others increase. Based on the research, the factors in the Spiritual Vitality Index are those that are most catalytic to advancing growth in attitudes about love of God and love for others.

Using these catalytic factors, we compare the responses of each participating church to the responses of the thousand churches in the REVEAL database. So, the Spiritual Vitality Index—which is the yardstick we use to determine which churches are "best"—is based on congregant responses to questions about the most influential catalysts of spiritual growth benchmarked against all the churches in the database. A church is considered "best practice" if it receives an SVI score of 86 or higher out of a possible 100, which means it ranks in the top 5 percent of churches in the REVEAL database. How to interpret SVI scores is explained in the following section.

How Does the Spiritual Vitality Index (SVI) Work?

One way to think about the SVI is to reflect back on your high school report cards. If you got an overall grade in mathematics of 80, that grade reflected assessments of multiple factors like class participation, homework, and special projects, as well as test scores. Similarly, the SVI of 72 on chart 11-1 reflects the impact of multiple factors related to spiritual growth. SVI scores are intentionally similar to academic grading scales, in that scores in the high eighties and nineties (top 5 percent) indicate strong spiritual momentum in a church, much like academic grades in the high eighties and nineties indicate top-of-the-class performance. Likewise, SVI scores between 75 and 85 are above average, and scores between 65 and 75 — the range into which most churches fall — are average.

We sometimes feel reluctant to talk about numbers within the context of REVEAL. Even though I (Cally) know that statistics are key components of any well-grounded, credible research effort, I've wrestled with how to focus on the heart of spiritual growth and still deal with the necessity to share the numbers (see "The Cringe Factor," page 209). Reconciling these two factors — the heart and the numbers — played an important role recently in a situation with my son who, at 6 foot 10 inches tall, towers over most people. But the issue had nothing to do with his height. It was his weight.

When he left for college, his 220 pounds looked almost insufficient on his long, lanky frame. College added a few pounds, and by the time he married six years later, he weighed 240. Eight months after the wedding, he topped 280.

This significant weight gain suggested his problem was more *internal* than external, less about the number on the scale and more about a new life situation creating circumstances that led to poor choices, like eating too much fast food and not exercising regularly. His solution was not to go on a crash diet — to merely change the number on the scale — but to join a weight-management program that included a significant support system of weekly counseling and encouragement.

Today, he's back down to 220. But the number itself is far less important than the changes that have taken place in his attitudes and behaviors. His weight has changed because his heart has changed.

The Spiritual Vitality Index serves as a scale that helps you "weigh" the spiritual hearts of your people. Yes, the resulting numbers can identify problems and opportunities — and yes, they can track progress. But they can't make that progress happen. The goal of REVEAL, therefore, is not to help church leaders ramp up their numbers. The goal is to help church leaders change hearts. (Although as hearts change, there is good reason to believe numbers will inevitably change as well.)

The beauty of the SVI — and its greatest distinction — is that it does not measure church *health* as much as it measures the *hearts* of the people attending the church. Two observations underscore this very important point:

* *Traditional church operations and activities have no bearing on the Spiritual Vitality Index.* This means that organizational factors — like church finances, staffing, and infrastructure — play no role in the SVI assessment. Attendance or congregant satisfaction with organized church activities — like weekend services and small groups — also have no impact on the SVI. In fact, the SVI puts more weight on things that happen outside the church building than within its walls — like personal spiritual practices and faith in action, which includes evangelism and serving the underresourced. Individuals may participate in these activities, or decide to take a pass, based on factors like family status or work requirements that have little to do with their church life.

* *The Spiritual Vitality Index takes into account people's spiritual attitudes and habits that may have little to do with the church they currently attend.* Because the SVI puts so much weight on people's attitudes and activities that occur outside of church settings, it takes into account spiritual attitudes and habits that may be derived from a personal history that has little to do with their current church. For instance, among congregation members who grew up in families that regarded church attendance as merely a weekly habit instead of a core value, personal spiritual practices are unlikely to be part of the daily routine. For those who grew up in a community with strongly reinforced Christian values, on the other hand, a solid grasp of core Christian beliefs may have been established early in life.

The key is that the Spiritual Vitality Index gives church leaders a current spiritual health snapshot of their congregation that is much broader than a measure of their experience with the church. How, then, does the church fit into the picture? The mathematics grade referenced earlier can once again serve as an analogy. When you studied math, the expertise of the teacher and the school's environment certainly contributed to your mastery of the subject. But unless you did the homework and put those skills to use outside the classroom, your command of the fundamentals and ability to usefully apply them later in life is likely limited.

So it goes with spiritual growth. While the local church is incredibly important as the principal motivator, teacher, and role model for spiritual growth, a person's spiritual maturity is as much — or more — a reflection of what they do in their everyday lives than what they do within the church building.

Who Are the Churches at the Top of the Spiritual Vitality Scale? (And Where and When Did We Find Them?)

We opened this chapter by describing our excitement—back in the fall of 2008—as we met pastors and leaders from among REVEAL's top-5 percent churches. These churches represented a good cross section of the twenty-five churches most effective at fostering spiritual growth within their congregations, and they have since provided the foundation of the information we present in the next five chapters. Certainly, they are not the only churches we could tap for such information, as many additional churches have earned this best-practice designation since 2008. Conversations with all of these pastors and leaders continue to enrich the inventory of insights derived from REVEAL—and to reinforce the validity of the survey's overall findings.

The most remarkable characteristic of these churches is their incredible diversity (see Appendix 4: "Who Are the Best Practice Churches?" page 265). They range from a church with weekend adult attendance of 220 located in the poorest zip code in Detroit, to a church from the Dallas suburbs where the 9,000 who attend on weekends support one of the highest tithing rates in the nation. Two churches are African American and seven are multicultural. Many are nondenominational, but four Assembly of God and two Baptist churches are included. Locations range from rural Montana to the gritty streets of Far Rockaway, New York; and while some come from the heavily churched Bible belt, one church is from a community where regular church attendance hovers at only 4 percent. A 400-person church on the outskirts of Chicago has the most dangerous street in the US in its backyard. This is an all-volunteer church with no paid staff. The senior pastor is a dentist.

You'll soon get to know these churches and pastors through the stories and strategies they generously share. But before digging into how they create such extraordinary spiritual momentum, let's reflect a moment on this portfolio of amazing geographic, denominational, and cultural diversity. Such a heterogeneous profile was neither intentional nor expected. It simply emerged from the research, bearing witness to a great God who works with equal effectiveness in the darkest, poorest corners as he does in the wealthiest, most privileged enclaves. The pastors who serve within all of these environments have much to share about how to best enable God's Spirit to thrive—no matter what the circumstances of your church.

First, though, we need to cover one final element of our "Five W's (And One H)"—the *why*.

Why Measure Spiritual Vitality?

Do you weigh yourself once a week? Check your blood pressure? Or watch the stock market? (It's probably better to check your blood pressure *before* you check the stock market.)

Whether you're calculating the length of a trip or assessing your child's aptitude for college, the measurements you use all have one thing in common — they are arbitrary. Someone made them up. Throughout history, humankind has created measures to track progress, gauge effectiveness, and provide benchmarks of health, wealth, size, distance, and countless other quantifiable interests.

While it is true that every factor in the Spiritual Vitality Index is derived biblically from the great commandment and is also based on verifiable facts, the index itself is a human creation. It was crafted by a thoughtful, intentional, trial-and-error process aimed at measuring the spiritual well-being of the people within a congregation. Why invent the SVI? Three reasons:

* *To respond to pastor feedback.* Many of the earliest REVEAL church pioneers expressed frustration with wading through a forty-plus-page report. Specifically, they wanted something that would sum up their findings and show how their people compared to other congregations. Now the SVI is near the front of each REVEAL report.

* *To identify best practices.* Much of REVEAL's early work was done to identify pastors leading churches that clearly excelled at spiritual growth, so that we could learn from them and perhaps even find a "silver bullet" or two that might be helpful in transforming churches into more effective agents for Christ.

* *To understand church patterns.* Is every church unique? Yes. But one objective of this work was to identify patterns of church effectiveness related to spiritual growth. Could the SVI help churches understand spiritual effectiveness the way the Body Mass Index (BMI) helps doctors classify people as underweight, normal, or obese? While there are countless combinations of height and weight, the BMI classifies people into categories that indicate whether intervention is necessary. Could there be similar distinct classifications of church effectiveness? If there were only a handful of problematic patterns, it would be much easier to suggest solutions. It also would be easier to emulate patterns that consistently lead to genuine progress.

We quickly addressed the first two issues. Now, every church that takes a REVEAL survey receives a one-page, net-it-out summary featuring their Spiritual Vitality Index. In addition, the SVI identified best-practice churches, enabling us to share the lessons learned from them.

In response to the third issue — understanding church patterns — what follows are the most recent findings from the Spiritual Vitality Index. These are four distinct patterns of church effectiveness — patterns that, interestingly enough, bear some similarity to the BMI classifications for personal health and fitness.

Four Patterns of Church Effectiveness

Talking with pastors about their REVEAL survey results is always interesting. Recently, within the same week, we spoke with the leaders of a three-thousand-person church in Nebraska, two medium-size churches in California and Virginia, and the first REVEAL church in South Africa. Helping church leaders to connect the dots as they walk through their REVEAL results is an incredible gift and real privilege. Clearly all these pastors care deeply about their people. It's heartwarming to hear them talk about their passion for helping people grow in a relationship with Jesus — and heartbreaking when things aren't going particularly well.

Based on these countless conversations and our review of hundreds of REVEAL reports, distinct patterns of church effectiveness clearly *do* exist. Although most of REVEAL's contribution relies on its meticulous adherence to quantitative data, it is *qualitative* interpretation that best showcases these patterns. So, starting with the most discouraging example, then building toward its knock-your-socks-off, high-energy counterpart, here are the four distinct church patterns, each one based on spiritual effectiveness.

Pattern 1: The Apathetic Church (SVI score typically under 60)

"It's hard to know you're stalled if you don't know there's a journey." So said the pastor of a large church in Missouri during our conversation with his leadership team about their congregation's SVI score of 54 out of 100 (chart 11-2).

His remark triggered bittersweet laughter among his colleagues because it summed up the irony of his congregation's profile. Only 8 percent had chosen the word *stalled* to describe their pace of spiritual growth, yet the evidence was clear throughout the pages of their report that most of the congregation was

Spiritual Vitality Index for an Apathetic Church

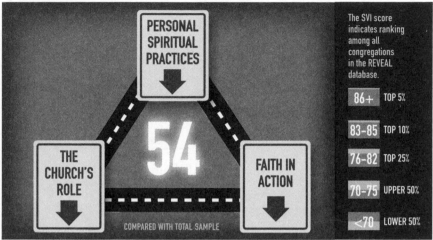

CHART 11-2: This Spiritual Vitality Index of 54 represents a congregation in the lower half of the REVEAL database. The arrows pointing down next to the three categories of spiritual catalysts depict a congregation that measures more than 20 percent below the REVEAL database average.

spiritually immobile. Reinforcing this picture were facts about their Christian beliefs, which — in spite of regular church attendance over a period of years — were far below average. The down arrows on their chart show that personal spiritual practices were also well below average. And the category of faith in action (serving, evangelism, and attitudes about their willingness to risk everything for Christ) was similarly sobering. Their journey toward developing a relationship with Christ was nonexistent. Motionless.

In the spirit of the BMI analogy, an unfortunately high percentage of REVEAL churches (an estimated 20 percent) fall in this category that might be described as spiritually "underweight." Typically, these are older congregations with a long-tenured history of regular church attendance; yet two-thirds of the congregants fall within the Exploring Christ and Growing in Christ segments. This pattern of spiritual growth (perhaps better described as spiritual standstill) is incredibly challenging. The roots of apathy run deep.

Pattern 2: The Introverted Church (SVI score typically in high 60s)

"Are they growing a relationship with the church or a relationship with Christ?" Leaders of introverted churches often pose such a question. Their congregations report strong attendance records and above-average personal

Spiritual Vitality Index for an Introverted Church

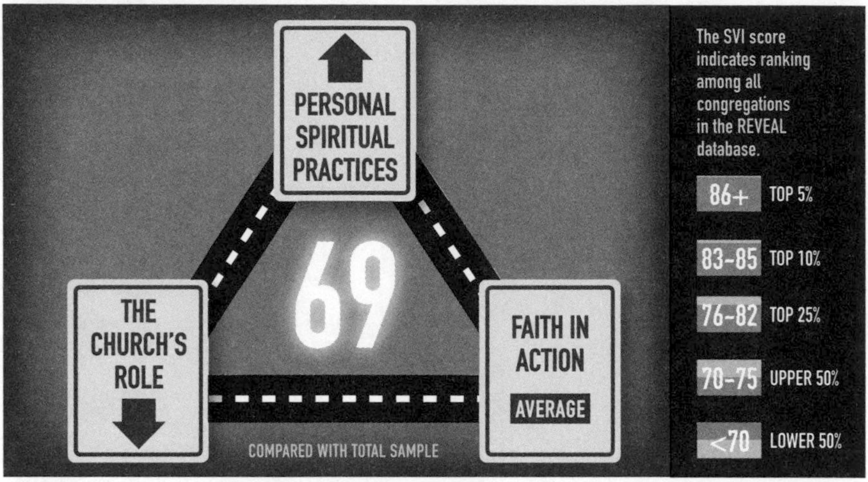

CHART 11-3: This Spiritual Vitality Index of 69 represents a congregation that is average, but the arrows pointing down indicate an introverted spiritual profile. While their personal spiritual practices are strong, their faith in action is not and they are unhappy with their church. These results tend to reflect a congregation that is inwardly focused on growing their faith but is not living it out.

practices, but fail to demonstrate an increasing love of God in their attitudes or in their faith-in-action behaviors (chart 11-3).

We call them introverted because their faith is insular, typically focused on developing strong biblical knowledge, but lacking the emotional connection of a walk with Jesus. That connection is what turns us outward into the world as his ambassadors. Instead, these congregants turn inward, frequently expressing frustration with their church (note the down arrow on the Church's Role) for lacking the capacity to advance their journey with greater inspiration and education. An estimated 15 percent of REVEAL churches fall into this category.

Their cry is for the church to "help me understand the Bible in depth." But that's not what they need. Using the BMI analogy, these people are spiritually "overweight." What they need is spiritual exercise, not more feeding.

Pattern 3: The Average (and Average-Plus) Church (SVI score typically in the 70s)

"I've never been average in my life." Hard-charging pastors do not often receive seventy-ish SVI scores with great joy. More often than not, their immediate reaction is denial — similar to the pastor who made this comment and who leads a bustling "average" church. Denial is understandable. These leaders

Spiritual Vitality Index for an Average Church

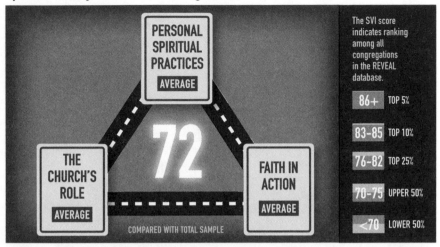

CHART 11-4: Most congregations fall within an average SVI range of 65–75 with no arrows on the triangle pointing either down or up. This means all the spiritual vitality measures included in the index are within 20 percent of the average for the benchmark database of 1,000 churches.

frequently shepherd large, dynamic ministries. But the painful truth is that, collectively, their congregants are spiritually average (chart 11-4).

No arrows going up or down on the SVI triangle is the classic picture of an average congregation. That means none of their findings set them apart from the rest of the database, either positively or negatively. Beneath every average SVI lies a story. And often, that story centers on opportunities to re-energize personal spiritual practices, since these churches typically have high percentages of new believers (the Growing in Christ segment).

However, the real opportunity for average churches lies in the lower left corner of the triangle: the Church's Role. Remember, the factors underlying this category are not the overall satisfaction measures for the church or senior pastor. The Church's Role reflects satisfaction with the most critical things a church does to help people grow spiritually, such as challenging them to grow and take next steps or helping them understand the Bible.

Churches that do those things well produce an SVI profile called "Average-Plus" (chart 11-5). These churches have congregations that are spiritually average, *but* they also have something very important that most average churches lack: a strong platform of permission.

High marks on the Church's Role mean a congregation has great love and respect for the church and its leadership, which suggests they give the church

Spiritual Vitality Index for an Average "Plus" Church

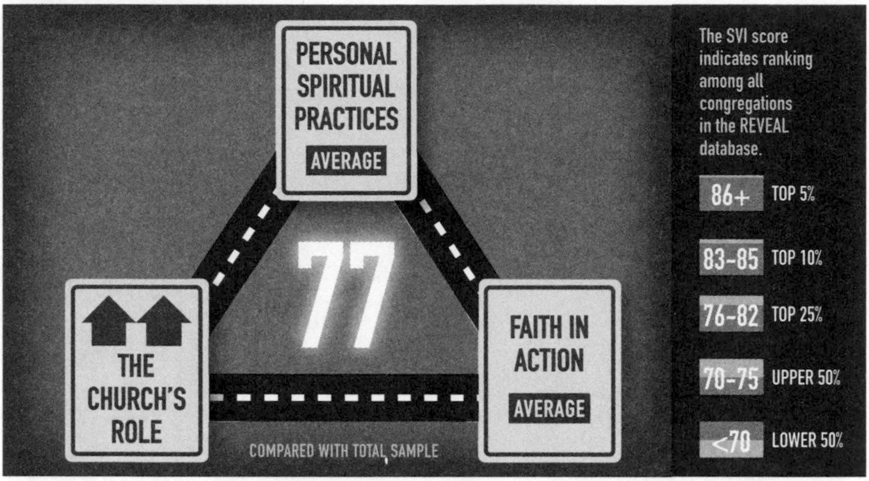

PERSONAL
SPIRITUAL
PRACTICES
AVERAGE

77

THE
CHURCH'S
ROLE

COMPARED WITH TOTAL SAMPLE

FAITH IN
ACTION
AVERAGE

The SVI score
indicates ranking
among all
congregations
in the REVEAL
database.

86+ TOP 5%

83-85 TOP 10%

76-82 TOP 25%

70-75 UPPER 50%

<70 LOWER 50%

CHART 11-5: This average "plus" profile represents a congregation that is clearly happy with the church's role in helping them grow spiritually, even if the rest of the SVI measures are average. This profile indicates that church leaders are greatly respected so congregants would be likely to follow them on whatever spiritual growth pathway they decide to advocate.

significant latitude and permission to lead them in new directions. Churches like the one depicted in chart 11-5—a large Wesleyan church in Michigan—can lead with confidence, knowing their people will gladly follow. So for the majority of churches that show up as average, the greatest opportunity may be to recharge its leadership corps around spiritual growth and turn up the arrows on the Church's Role. People are much more likely to embrace spiritual guidance and direction from a church they hold in high esteem.

In the BMI context, this might be akin to upping one's exercise from a jog around the block a few times a week to training for a marathon—moving from spiritually average to elite.

Pattern 4: The High-Energy Church (SVI score typically 85 or above)

"Christianity is not a spectator sport." This quote from the pastor leading the Spirit of God Fellowship on the outskirts of Chicago defines the character of the top REVEAL churches. If you attend one of these churches expecting to just sit in a pew on Sundays, you will eventually be encouraged to go elsewhere. These churches are on the move, growing people up in Christ and releasing them to have impact for the kingdom. Their tolerance for spiritual lethargy is low (chart 11-6).

Spiritual Vitality Index for a High Energy Church

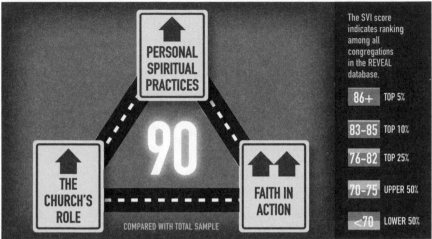

CHART 11-6: The arrows pointing up in all three categories of spiritual catalysts indicate a high-energy congregation that is committed to growing into Christ-Centered disciples. Their investment in personal spiritual practices, their faith in action, and their love of the church are all above average. The two arrows pointing up on faith in action represents attitudes and activities that exceed the benchmark average by more than 50 percent.

There is good news for *all* churches underlying this very impressive pattern of spiritual effectiveness—and that is the fact that these high-energy churches are not unique. They come in all shapes and sizes across the country, in many denominational formats and cultural combinations. Chapters 12 to 16 showcase lessons learned from them, specifically regarding four best practices and one overarching principle we call Christ-Centered leadership. Whether these high-energy churches are small or large, rural or urban, black or white or mixed races and cultures, they pursue these four best practices: they get people moving, embed the Bible in everything they do, create ownership, and pastor the local community.

* *They get people moving.* These churches clearly communicate a pathway of next steps that launches newcomers on a spiritual journey—a pathway that is strongly endorsed and supported by the senior leadership of the church. The pathway's framework varies and is often customized to reflect individual church circumstances, but there is *always* a pathway. And the expectation that all congregants will experience and follow this pathway is unmistakable and unavoidable.

* *They embed the Bible in everything they do.* Dedication to Bible engagement flows from the pulpit to the water cooler, with all leaders modeling

biblical literacy and learning as a core value in the church and in their lives. This commitment goes well beyond providing Bible studies and classes. In these high-energy environments, God's Word is the central axis around which every discussion, activity, and decision revolves.

* *They create ownership.* Most churches encourage volunteerism to support ministry needs, but these churches take the concept of serving the church to a whole new level. They inspire congregants to own the vision of the church — to adopt it as a part of their very identity. "I don't go to church; I am the church" could easily be their motto.

* *They pastor the local community.* These are churches of high expectations. Church leaders and congregants alike are knee-deep in addressing local community needs, frequently partnering with other churches and nonprofit organizations to identify and resolve issues that would otherwise languish for lack of attention and resources. They are pillars of great influence, bringing the heart of Christ to their communities as a natural by-product of living out their faith in authentic devotion to him.

Wow. Feels a bit overwhelming, doesn't it? And here's the kicker — churches that do these four things radically well range from being incredibly well-resourced to having minimal means. They can be small, understaffed urban churches or rural churches thriving in the middle of nowhere. How do they pull it off? What's their secret?

Their strategies and success stories — as well as a few notable failures — lie ahead.

The Cringe Factor

There's something about rating churches — and then ranking them in comparison to one another — that makes me (Greg) cringe. It's just the wrong way to talk about churches. Long ago, one of my mentors taught me that comparison can easily undermine community. Whenever I compare myself to someone else, or compare one person or organization with another, I am in danger of destroying their precious common ground. And if there's one thing that's completely clear in Scripture, it's that Christ desires unity among the members of his body. There's no room for us to say (or even think), "I'm better than you." That's just wrong.

So how do we reconcile this cringe factor with the truth — which is that we intentionally looked for churches that seem to be doing a better job than others at helping people grow spiritually? Do we let ourselves off the hook because our motives are pure? Because we are willing to admit we don't have all the answers? Because we just want to learn from them?

We think the simple answer is "yes." We chose to tolerate — and ask you to tolerate with us — some uneasiness with this process because our quest itself is honorable. It's not to publish a Who's Who of best-practice churches. It's not to give out Oscars for best performance. And it's certainly not to keep what we learn to ourselves.

We want to learn and we want to share what we learn. In a description usually associated with economic (rather than spiritual) growth, we want everything we learn to be a "rising tide that lifts all boats." Because all churches can do better. And all churches, we believe, would desire the opportunity to do exactly that.

CHAPTER 12

Get People Moving

So we tell others about Christ, warning everyone with all the wisdom
God has given us. We want to present them to God, perfect in their
relationship to Christ.

Colossians 1:28 NLT[1]

The military uses boot camp to turn civilians into soldiers. Baseball uses
spring training to test new players and try them out in different positions.
Many colleges require freshmen to attend orientation week so they can become
familiar with their new environment and a new set of expectations.

These short-term launching pads into life experiences are analogous to the
first best practice found among the most spiritually effective churches in the
REVEAL database. They get people moving by providing a high-challenge, non-
negotiable path of first steps to engage people in a process of spiritual growth—a
process that will ultimately lead them to become followers of Jesus Christ.

To be clear, this practice is *not* about providing a comprehensive, detailed
spiritual road map that guides someone who is Exploring Christ toward
becoming Christ-Centered. Instead, this is the spiritual equivalent of jump-
starting a car: an action that charges up the multiple parts of an automobile's
internal combustion engine so it can get itself moving. That's what this practice is all about—jump-starting *movement*—because these churches recognize
that one of the greatest challenges to spiritual progress occurs right at the out-
set, and that by employing this practice, they tackle what may be the biggest
obstacle to spiritual growth, which is overcoming inertia in order to take those
first steps—to just get moving.

---

[1] Each chapter in part 3 opens with a verse chosen by pastors as the most reflective of the biblical basis
for that best practice.

This spiritual jump start shows up in a variety of programmatic forms among the top churches. The four-class, "baseball diamond," Purpose-Driven model referenced in chapter 7 clearly influences many of the approaches used. Various combinations of classlike experiences provide the basics of the Purpose-Driven formula—including an introduction to church vision, core Christian beliefs, spiritual practices, and opportunities to connect with others through serving and/or small-group structures. But some very effective churches offer different jump starts—like orientation programs that focus strictly on building up biblical literacy and spiritual practices. Or they use various other experiences, like the well-regarded ten-week Alpha® program that introduces people to the basics of Christianity.

However, it would be a mistake to dismiss this Get People Moving best practice as something that can be addressed by simply introducing a series of classes or an orientation program. There's a much bigger shift at work here—we call it the "Get People Moving" paradigm shift—from "more is better" to "less is more." This implies that a major change may be required in the traditional philosophy of how to lead a church.

The "Get People Moving" Paradigm Shift

A paradigm shift is a substantive change in basic assumptions. At times people use this phrase inappropriately, exaggerating the magnitude of a change that really isn't particularly noteworthy. The Get People Moving best practice, however, warrants the description, because it poses a challenge with far-reaching consequences to the traditional church mindset.

Churches are as guilty as other sectors in society in thinking that more, by definition, is better. Understandably, they strive to provide multiple ministry options to newcomers—from support and recovery programs to a wide range of small-group and ministry serving opportunities, including outreach efforts that impact their local communities or global issues of injustice and poverty. Nowadays, thanks to an Internet platform that makes ministry resources widely and easily available, churches large and small have the ability to offer rich menus of next steps—steps that enable people to map their preferred pathway of spiritual growth.

Based on findings from the most effective churches, however, this "more is better" way of thinking is not the best route for people who are new to a church, and it is particularly unsuitable for people who are taking their first steps to explore the Christian faith. Instead of offering a ministry buffet with multiple tempting choices of activities and studies, these churches make one singular pathway a virtual prerequisite for membership and full engagement with the church. Their reason for doing this tracks back to the paradigm shift that is the hallmark of REVEAL: Spiritual growth is not driven or determined by activities; it is defined by a growing relationship with Christ. So the goal is not to launch people into an assortment of ministry activities; it is to launch them on a quest to embrace and surrender their lives to Jesus.

For these churches, the less-is-more approach is the way to activate that quest for people who are new to their church. In practical terms, they implement this approach using three key strategies, each one representing a shift to a new way of thinking about how to lead a church.

Three Key Strategies to Get People Moving

It is not the *form* of the spiritual jump-start program that determines whether or not people get on track with a process that will lead them into a growing relationship with Christ; rather, it is how the program is executed. Based on our review of the top REVEAL churches, three key strategies make all the difference.

Key Strategy 1: *Make the destination clear.* People leave these jumpstart experiences crystal clear about two things. First, they know that the church's top priority is to do everything within its power to help them grow into devoted disciples of Jesus Christ. Second, they know how the church defines what it means to be a disciple.

Key Strategy 2: *Make the spiritual jump start non-negotiable.* A newcomer does not warm a pew long before realizing that participation in the jump-start program is expected and assumed. From verbal announcements at weekend services to written collateral about church priorities, the jump-start pathway is prominently featured as a centerpiece opportunity and implied necessity for congregants.

Key Strategy 3: *Make the senior pastor the champion.* The senior pastor strongly promotes and encourages newcomers to make attending the jumpstart program a top priority and, in most cases, teaches one or more of the sessions. Especially when it comes to casting the vision of the church, this is not something typically delegated to the staff or volunteers.

Fortunately, the pastors themselves have a good deal to say about why Get People Moving is one of the top priorities for their churches and how, amidst all the daunting daily demands of running a church, they are able to so effectively execute against these three key strategies.

Strategy 1: Make the Destination Clear

"We are called not to sit and watch, but to join God in his work so that others can become saved and healed. That requires a real sell-out to Jesus, so I preach it. I preach a high bar of discipleship ... I want people not to toy with Christianity, but to really jump in."

So says Jeff Richards, who leads East Valley Foursquare Church, a thriving three-hundred-person congregation in rural East Helena, Montana. But when Jeff first arrived ten years ago, the church was more failing than thriving. Weekend attendance hovered around fifty. The discipleship bar was pitifully low—people just came to services; very few rolled up their sleeves to do anything, and the church had little community impact. But freshly inspired by Henry Blackaby's *Experiencing God*®, Jeff was determined to grow a congregation of deeply devoted Christ-Centered disciples. So he introduced the Blackaby curriculum and tenaciously took all core members through it. Attendance fell to forty.

Jeff was undeterred, and so—it seems—was God. Through circumstances that Jeff describes as miraculous, he found the resources to distribute a book written by a radically saved former prison inmate to 3,500 households and to invite the entire community to hear the author's testimony. Three hundred and fifty people showed up. Thirty-five gave their lives to Christ that night. It was a turning point for the church. "God fed that," Jeff says.

Today, he continues his dogged pursuit of disciple making, insisting that all newcomers—including veteran Christians—experience the Alpha® course, and then go through *Experiencing God*. Serving is an immediate next step, and journaling is another big emphasis. That's a tough sell ("It's hard, especially where we live, because so many struggle with reading"), but being tough doesn't faze Jeff. Because he knows the destination. He knows where he wants his people to go—and he's pretty sure he knows how to help them get there.

"It's just about hearing what God is saying," he says. "Having a Christ-Centered heart means you have to follow the Lord no matter what, even if it's going to hurt your numbers. Eventually, inevitably, it's going to be exactly what God wants."

In a nutshell, that's the destination that Jeff—and the rest of these very effective pastors—communicate to their people. That they want them to grow Christ-Centered hearts so they will follow the Lord "no matter what." So they can do "exactly what God wants."

The paradigm shift in this strategy is that pastors need to make it clear to newcomers that the church's agenda for them—their destination—is to know

Christ and surrender their lives to him. In other words, the church's agenda is not to assimilate them into a variety of church activities. This may sound harsh, but prodding congregants to plug into multiple church activities may too often suggest to them that the end goal is the activities themselves.

Jim Reed, senior pastor at New Life Community Church in Danville, Virginia (a recent addition to the list of best-practice churches), puts it this way: "We say we are Christ's followers—and that means we are literally following Jesus, and Jesus was going somewhere. He moved through his life in a very specific manner, so that ultimately, God's complete purposes could be fulfilled in his life." This is the destination these most effective churches want for their people—the destination inspired by Jesus—that, ultimately, God's complete purposes would be fulfilled in their lives.

Strategy 2: Make the Spiritual Jump Start Non-Negotiable

Steve Milazzo admits he struggles at times to convey the spiritual jump-start process to his 850 congregants as the priority it needs to be. "I tend to like the big events," says the senior pastor of Bethlehem Assembly of God Church in Valley Stream, New York. "The outreach stuff—getting the crowds to make an initial decision to follow Christ. That's who I am."

Fortunately for Steve, "People-moving is taking hold in my staff—so they'll remind me. My staff will say, 'Pastor Steve, how does that event fit into the big picture?' or 'Did that leader go through the Purpose-Driven process—does he know his gifts?' My staff is very good about reinforcing this process of doing ministry." (This is, by the way, verification of the need for a church's staff to be on board, from the beginning, with whatever Get People Moving initiatives the pastor inaugurates.)

This church's jump-start process uses two pathways, both starting at the newcomers' reception and introductory class. Then congregants go into either a new believers' foundational process, which Steve leads for its five-month duration, or into a series of Purpose-Driven 101–401 classes.

Why does Steve devote so much time to these early efforts to get people moving? Because, like so many pastors leading top REVEAL churches, he knows it works. So does First Baptist in Orlando, where senior pastor David Uth promotes a series of three "spiritual development classes" that start with a two-hour class required for new members—a class that's offered ten times a year. "I'll be there," he says, and without fail this leader of a six-thousand-person congregation shows up to field questions and kick off the classes, which cover church vision, core beliefs, spiritual practices, and opportunities to connect—which, in their case, refers to life groups that serve as the source for much of the church's spiritual momentum.

First Baptist directly attributes their strong REVEAL results to these classes (which more than six thousand people have attended), saying they work because people know what they're getting into. The numbers bear this out. Among churches in America, the average retention rate is 35 percent. If a new-member class is offered, it goes to 72 percent. When the class is required, like it is at First Baptist, the retention rate rises to 80–85 percent.

At the opposite end of the country, in Fremont, California, Harbor Light Church's senior pastor, Terry Inman, invented his own six-week series of classes called "Doorway." His passion for newcomers was born out of recognition that the people walking the streets of his community looked quite different than his white middle-class congregants—they had darker skin, long beards, and wore turbans and robes. He knew his quest to increase the meager 4 percent of people regularly attending church in that community had to be creative, so he encouraged his congregants to interact with their foreign-born neighbors. He even had church leaders personally deliver coffee mugs to the homes of every visitor to his Harbor Light Church within twenty-four hours of his or her first visit. Today, 50 percent of first-time visitors typically return to the thousand-person church, creating a congregation that is truly multicultural—a fact celebrated by the eighty international flags hanging in their entryway. Terry himself teaches the Doorway classes so he can cast his vision of multinational faith, leadership, and service.

Pastors Marcus Ways of Christian Gospel Center Church of God in Christ in Detroit and Michael Moore of Birmingham's Faith Chapel Christian take a different approach, offering eight- to ten-week new-membership tracks that focus on building a foundation of biblical literacy and engagement. Pastors Steve Gallimore of Tennessee Valley Community Church in the small town of Paris, Tennessee, and David Bish of Tri-County Church in rural Pennsylvania use the Purpose-Driven pathway, modified in Tri-County with personal follow-up coaching and at Tennessee Valley with a "Fresh Start" connection for new believers.

Whether they use or customize standardized formats like the Purpose-Driven or Alpha programs, or they invent their own approaches, virtually all of these very effective churches offer some version of a spiritual jump start. It may be a bit of a stretch to say they're nonnegotiable, since churches aren't really in a position to require or enforce mandatory attendance on newcomers. But based on the resources and the prominence given to these efforts, the message is clear that these first steps are considered essential building blocks for spiritual growth—as important to those who are new to church as the basics of reading and arithmetic are to first graders.

The paradigm shift for church leaders is to move away from promoting a plentiful buffet of ministry opportunities to newcomers and instead provide them with a "plated dinner" of high-challenge, non-negotiable first steps. While this conflicts with a natural tendency to leave newcomers alone—to let them become familiar with the church on their own terms for fear we might scare them away—all of the findings from REVEAL show that what newcomers really want is challenge and clear spiritual guidance—not anonymity and spiritual mush.

Strategy 3: Make the Senior Pastor the Champion

Jorge Vega calls himself the "spiritual father" of his multicultural Full Gospel Tabernacle church in Far Rockaway, New York. A father, he says, leaves footprints—marks on a person's life. In his view, that influence and authority can't be delegated, a perspective undoubtedly reinforced by the high percentage of families in his 350-person church who are missing fathers. "I feel as strongly about being involved in my people's first steps of faith as I did about being at the births of each one of my sons. As a pastor, you are the heart of your church. There's nothing more important than transferring the spirit of your ministry into the hearts of others."

His strength of conviction shows up in a twenty-four-session membership curriculum, which he launches by describing a church vision born directly out of his own testimony. "I'm a former pastor's son who became an alcoholic and considered suicide. I did some major backsliding from how I was raised. I tell my story one-on-one with all new members so they can believe in God's love and power to transform. I want them to see how God can change a life, so they can believe it's possible for them."

Jorge Vega's story may be unique, but his personal commitment to convey to newcomers that God has the power to transform lives—and that the purpose of his church is to help them experience that transformation—is not. Senior pastors of the most effective churches champion these jump-start programs regularly from the platform, and more often than not, they contribute personal time and energy to ensure their success. In this circumstance, their role is not unlike the coach who looks into the eyes of nervous rookies to cast the vision and inspire the momentum for a winning season.

In fact, the Get People Moving best practice reflects a significant shift in mindset for senior pastors—from thinking about their role as a shepherd who is primarily devoted to spiritual teaching and leading a congregational flock, to a role devoted more to spiritual coaching, modeling, and vision casting.

The coaching analogy applies equally well to all three strategies. First of all, great coaches certainly "make the destination clear" by describing the objective of the season and identifying the obstacles to achieving the objective. Actually, this is one of the most significant roles a senior pastor can fulfill—to spell out the vision of leading a life surrendered to Christ and to model how to navigate the demands of daily life as a follower of Jesus.

Great coaches are also active on the sidelines of the preseason jump-start experience, encouraging rookies and envisioning new opportunities for veteran players. In a similar way, senior pastors are in the unique position to win the immediate respect of church newcomers, be they seekers or longtime Christians. Like all great sports coaches, they can inspire those who are new (or returning) to the "game" of leading a Christ-Centered life to give it a try.

In sports, of course, the jump-start experience is non-negotiable; if you don't show up, you don't make the team. Senior pastors don't have it quite that easy—certainly, they can't demand that people attend an orientation event. But their commitment to dedicating time to new congregants will go a long way toward making the spiritual jump start a "can't miss" occasion.

Finally, a sports coach is also the greatest champion of the team, not only at the beginning of the season but throughout its ups and downs. The coach is the one who tells it like it is, but always inspires those he or she leads to never give in to discouragement or defeat. That sounds like a textbook definition of an outstanding senior pastor—one who is much more than a teacher of biblical doctrine and director of multiple ministries. A critically important role of a senior pastor, then, is to be a great spiritual coach—someone who leads his or her people to play the game of their lives for Jesus Christ.

Equating the role of a senior pastor to that of a sports coach may initially feel simplistic—or perhaps even seem to diminish the critically important eternal implications of a pastor's work. The analogy intends neither of those things; it simply borrows some of the steps that lead to championship teams and applies them to the path toward spiritual growth.

Such steps may take some getting used to—or even create a bit of anxiety, at least initially. The recognition that newcomers need to hear a clear explanation of the vision of the church and its discipleship agenda sooner rather than later, for instance, is typically a paradigm shift for senior pastors. So is their congregants' need to hear that message from the senior pastor, rather than from church associates or volunteers with little decision-making authority or leadership clout. These shifts may generate concerns that such bold, up-front declarations early in the church exploration process may be off-putting to seek-ers—that they may drive away more people than they attract. But best-practice pastors—like Rick Gannon who leads the flourishing three-thousand-person Palm Valley church in Mission, Texas—disagree.

The "Get People Moving" Dilemma: Will We Scare Them Away?

"Our goal all along has never been about church growth; it's always been about health," Rick says. "I don't have to sit by my kids' bedsides at night and pray that they grow. If, as a parent, I just make sure they're healthy, they will grow. When I took this church, it was not very healthy. I fought a lot of ugly, hard battles. The reason it worked is we never focused on growth, just health."

Rick didn't care whether or not his church grew in numbers. In fact, just like Jeff Richards, whose story you read earlier in this chapter, the number of people attending his church shrank while he waged some of those "ugly, hard battles." But numbers weren't the objective—they weren't Rick's destination. The objective was to challenge his congregation and help his people grow in a relationship with Christ. Rick, like so many best-practice pastors, still teaches the first class of Palm Valley's jump-start program—because, he says, he wants to look into the eyes of those who are uncertain, and to make this invitation clear: if they want to become a disciple of Christ, they are welcome. If not, they should probably look elsewhere.

That's a paradigm shift for many church leaders, and there's more para-digm shifting to come.

CHAPTER 13

Embed the Bible in Everything

All Scripture is inspired by God and is useful to teach us what is true
and to make us realize what is wrong in our lives. It corrects us when
we are wrong and teaches us to do what is right.

2 Timothy 3:16 NLT

Church leaders should bleed Scripture when they're cut."
So says Todd Wagner, senior pastor of Watermark Church in Dallas,
Texas. His descriptive language reflects an attitude that is pervasive among
best-practice churches—one that views the Word of God as much more than
a teaching tool or source of guidance for life decisions and self-improvement.
For these churches, the Bible is less a resource than it is a defining characteristic
of their church culture—something they look to as a gauge and mirror for
everything they say and do.

In practical terms, Todd knows what a congregation that "embeds the Bible
in everything" looks like and how it behaves. He explains that no matter what
situation they face, people who attend these churches constantly ask themselves, "What does God's Word have to say about this?" This has to be second
nature, he says, tackling problems and processing issues starting *not* from one's
own wisdom, but from what God has to say. "Because you're not in charge of
your life," says Todd. "We report to the King. So our first question should be
'What does the King have to say about that?'"

Churches like Watermark—those that embed Scripture in everything
they do—go well beyond offering Bible classes and devotional guides. They
approach and adhere to the Bible as the central and highest value guiding
church direction and priorities. This best practice qualifies as a paradigm
shift—from viewing the Bible primarily as a resource tool to positioning it

as the DNA of the church, the thing that defines the identity of its very heart and soul.

The "Embed the Bible in Everything" Paradigm Shift

It is with caution that we describe this best practice as a paradigm shift. For many church leaders, this may seem like hyperbole — a gross overstatement, like saying the need to exercise or to eat a balanced diet is a paradigm shift within the context of good health. Exercise and a good diet are well-known and accepted standards of behavior for healthy living, not new thoughts that challenge basic assumptions. Likewise, church leaders may think that embedding the Bible in everything is a well-known and accepted standard for most churches — a natural by-product of church leadership and more like conventional wisdom than a breakthrough ministry concept.

But the REVEAL database begs to differ. If churches typically embedded the Bible in everything, then people's behavior regarding Bible engagement wouldn't vary much from church to church. On the contrary, however, the percentage of congregants who say they reflect on Scripture for meaning in their lives every day ranges from a low of 3 percent to a high of 42 percent. The average for all database churches is 21 percent, whereas the average for best-practice churches is significantly higher, at 34 percent.

This wide variation suggests that there's a great deal of difference in terms of attention and deference given to the Bible among the thousand REVEAL churches, and that best-practice churches are embracing the Bible in unique and effective ways. These Bible-embracing efforts fall into three key strategies, and each one represents a shift to a new way of thinking about how to lead a church.

Three Key Strategies to Embed the Bible in Everything

All churches and church leaders love the Bible. As best-practice pastor Marcus Ways put it, "The Bible is God in paperback form — everything we need is there!" Within Scripture we find the voice of God providing comfort, encouragement, and inspiration. We find God's wisdom and advice about how to handle whatever needs and obstacles confront us. What's not to love?

But transitioning that love to congregants who have mixed levels of trust, experience, and confidence in reading and interpreting the Bible for themselves is not easy. This is the distinction of the best-practice churches—not their *love* of Scripture, because that's common to all churches. It's how they *execute the transition of that love* to their congregants. Based on our review of the top REVEAL churches, three key strategies appear to make that happen.

* *Make the Bible the main course of the message.* While there is great debate over the most effective way to teach God's Word, a number of best-practice churches lean toward the expository-teaching style. However, the most important takeaway about teaching from best-practice pastors is that they all start the preparation of their messages with Scripture. Even if their teaching is topical in nature, their goal is to transfer a life application from Scripture. Their starting point is the Word, followed by application to the world.

* *Take away the excuses.* Best-practice churches make Bible engagement practical, meaningful, and accessible—something that can fit even into the busiest schedules.

* *Model Scripture as the church's foundation.* Everywhere you turn in best-practice churches, you see the Bible as core to the church and its leadership. This includes everything from weekend services to serving experiences to leadership selection and training—virtually every ministry activity is founded and depends upon biblical truth for guidance and inspiration.

Why and how do best-practice pastors so effectively embed the Bible in everything through these three strategies? Let's tap into their experience and learn from their best advice.

Strategy 1: Make the Bible the Main Course of the Message

The poster-child pastor for serving up the Bible as the "main course" may be Marcus Ways, who leads Christian Gospel Center Church of God in Christ in Detroit, Michigan—a church with weekend attendance of 350 and the highest Spiritual Vitality Index score in the REVEAL database. He teaches five times a week:

* *Sunday Bible school.* All members participate in classes that deliver practical Bible instruction. Marcus ends class time with a half-hour review to make sure everyone is on the same page.

✱ *Sunday worship service*. Marcus ministers and teaches at the regular weekend service.

✱ *Sunday leadership development*. Short sessions help lay leaders learn how to process and present a biblical message or theme; the goal is to change them from passive listeners to active participants in the Word.

✱ *Bible Institute Hour*. Marcus created the curriculum used in this midweek class for all sixty-six books in the Bible. Every session starts with a fifteen-minute Q&A, because he gauges effectiveness by the quality, quantity, and diversity of the questions he receives.

✱ *Pastoral teaching (Friday evening)*. Marcus offers congregants doctrinal teaching about core Christian beliefs and concepts, like salvation, the Trinity, and eternity. The goal is to give them a biblical basis for the doctrines of the church—what they believe and why.

"This is the vein of our church—Bible teaching and Bible-based ministry," says Marcus, who founded his church twenty years ago with a vision dedicated to making the Bible "the source and reason for everything we do."

His teaching style is unapologetically expository, which means he starts with the Bible, rather than a life experience, as the source of the lesson. In other words, he interprets Scripture directly for life application rather than cluster Bible verses around a life experience, like parenting, to teach a topical message. This models going to the Bible in an open-minded way, in a search for what God's Word has to say, irrespective of life circumstances.

Why is he so devoted and adamant about immersing his people in Scripture? Because he believes that unless the Bible is internalized, "... you get empty vessels. When the testing time comes, they fall apart because there's no substance for them to stand on. So we're committed to the longer, slower route. It's the more difficult path, but it is definitely more fruit bearing."

On the other hand, Russ Austin, senior pastor of Southpoint Community Church in Jacksonville, Florida, a recent addition to the REVEAL best-practice churches, takes the topical teaching approach. He says it works better for him to start with a real-life situation and then work the topic back to Scripture. But he shares the same goal as Marcus. "If I can't get them to the Word of God," Russ says, "then I've failed. If I haven't gotten them to a place where they know how to fish rather than having caught a fish, then I've failed to get them to the place where they can succeed. This is the challenge we make to people regularly—if your business is failing or your marriage is failing or you're failing as a parent, the principles for getting things back on track are in the Word of God. The reason you're failing is you don't know and apply the Word of God."

Knowing the Word of God is the goal all best-practice pastors have for their congregants, even though they may use different techniques for communicating and transferring their love of Scripture. Many use expository teaching, but a number use topical teaching or a mix of both methods. In the end, however, they all want the same thing—not just to inspire people to study God's Word, but to love and internalize it—so that, as Marcus says, there is "substance for them to stand on" when life gets tough.

It may seem odd to suggest that the need to teach from the Bible is a paradigm shift for senior pastors. But two issues emerging from REVEAL data reinforce our concern that love for and knowledge of Scripture is not being transitioned to church congregants as effectively as we would all like. The first issue tracks back to observations made in earlier chapters about the incredible power that reflection on Scripture has to catalyze spiritual growth. Truly, if a church could do only one thing to help people grow in their relationship with Christ, it would be to get them immersed and in love with God's Word. The second issue is the wide variation and generally low numbers of people (only about one out of five) who reflect on Scripture daily. Even among those in the Christ-Centered segment, fewer than half open their Bibles every day.

Paradigm shift or not, the evidence is clear. Challenging people to engage with Scripture more intentionally and more frequently would advance the spiritual growth of most, if not all, people attending church today.

Easy for you to say, you might be thinking, especially if you knew that I (Cally) have never taught the Bible. But I have real empathy for those who do, based on my ten years as an adjunct professor at a local college. I taught an introductory corporate finance class, a prerequisite for all business-related degrees, and I began every semester by looking into a sea of reluctant and anxious faces. The class was reputed to be pretty tough, and it's fair to say that my students both dreaded the class and just hoped to survive it.

But I wanted to make them *love* finance. You see, I love numbers—for me, digging into profit-and-loss statements and balance sheets is like doing a big jigsaw puzzle; I thoroughly enjoy the challenge of unraveling the story behind the numbers. So, in a limited way, I can appreciate the struggle of pastors eager to turn on spiritual light bulbs for people when they teach on the weekends; they want to help people fall in love with God and his Word, not confuse them—or worse, bore them—with Scripture that can seem abstract and intimidating.

What's the secret to transitioning a love for something that seems abstract and intimidating to people averse to receiving it? Based on my finance class experience, I had a hunch about the answer—and then getting to know these best-practice pastors confirmed my gut instinct. It's not about teaching technique—expository or topical or whatever. I don't think it's even about creating insightful life applications from Scripture.

In fact, it's not a specific approach or a particular program that makes a subject come to life. It's you. In my finance class, it was me. My passion for using numbers to unlock what makes an organization tick was far more important than any technique or textbook I used. Your passion for using Scripture to unlock the glorious mysteries of our faith will carry the day, regardless of whether you're an expository or topical teacher. REVEAL's best-practice pastors have teaching styles that vary as much as their personalities. But they have in common a deep passion for the Word of God. And that, they say, is the secret for transitioning a love of Scripture to our congregations—making sure we show up each and every day with that passion burning in our hearts, so that we can help them embrace the power God's Word has to transform their hearts.

Strategy 2: Take Away the Excuses

Even in light of a pastor's passion, convincing people to cram anything more into their busy schedules can be an uphill battle. So best-practice churches get creative by providing a variety of avenues to help their congregants grow in biblical literacy, competence, and confidence.

Many go the traditional route of offering Bible classes off-line from normal weekend services. These range from midweek classes, like Marcus Ways's Bible Institute Hour described earlier, to a university-style curriculum with multiple options, such as Gateway Church's Gateway Equip, which runs four nights a week, thirty weeks a year.

Others take away the excuses in simpler ways. For example, at Bethlehem Assembly of God, senior pastor Steve Milazzo asks his people to sign a 10/10 covenant, which means they commit to:

- Read the Bible for ten minutes a day.
- Pray ten minutes a day.
- Connect with ten people in a small group.
- Pray for ten people to accept Christ.

Steve says the purpose of having them sign the covenant is not to create the activities—it's to create intentionality and an opportunity for them to experience their faith outside of the church. "You do the ten minutes because it will change your life," Steve explains. "People don't realize that faith isn't about making a commitment to attend services. It's about allowing the Holy Spirit to change who you are on the inside — the transformation that occurs only by God, not by us."

Watermark Church uses a high-tech twist to encourage Bible engagement. Their Join the Journey program is a Web-based daily Bible reading plan, developed not by church staff, but by the congregants themselves. They volunteer to provide a daily reflection on a Scripture passage that's assigned to them, including a brief description of who they are and what's important in their lives. People sign up to receive these daily reflections by email — so it's community building, practical and easy. Most importantly, since the program was launched at Watermark, the number of people reading the Bible daily has doubled!

Other approaches to inspiring regular reflection on Scripture include Gloucester County Community Church's free quarterly distribution of the "Word for You Today." The New Jersey church's senior pastor, Bruce Sofia, incorporates its themes in his messages often enough to reinforce the need for his 2,500 congregants to engage in Scripture on their own. At Tennessee Valley Community Church, Steve Gallimore provides individual tools like the *Power Up* devotional journals to his five-hundred-plus NASCAR-fan congregants in Paris, Tennessee.

While the range of strategies is wide, best-practice churches share a focused and firm commitment to get their people to engage with the Bible in an ongoing fashion. Whether they have enough resources to field a Web-based devotional program or multiple tracks of Bible classes — or they choose to follow a simpler path, like the 10/10 covenant — their expectation is that people will connect with God in a personal way, through his Word, in between weekend services.

The paradigm shift here is from a mindset that weekend services must carry the burden of transformation to a mindset that what happens between services is the lifeblood of transformation. In other words, the more time people spend engaged with God outside the church, the more likely they are to grow as disciples of Christ. This shift motivates church leaders to be inventive, flexible, and deliberate about creating strategies to take away the excuses that limit people to a spiritual life defined solely by Sunday morning.

Best-practice churches do this because they believe their primary role is to be the launching pad for spiritual growth, rather than as the rocket that carries people to a Christ-Centered life. Their job is to open the door to allow "the Holy Spirit to change who you are on the inside," as Steve Milazzo explains it, because although transformation happens within a person, it can happen outside, as well as inside, a church building.

Strategy 3: Model Scripture as the Church's Foundation

In case this idea of modeling Scripture as the foundation of the church seems abstract, Watermark's Todd Wagner offers a practical application: "You have to constantly heat up the value of going to the Word for guidance, decisions, and inspiration," he says. "It starts with me and how I lead." Some examples of that leadership include the following action items:

- *Take time at staff meetings* for people to share what they're learning from the Bible and share verses they're memorizing. Whatever topic is under discussion, ask leaders for verses to inform the dialogue.
- In leadership development groups, *use case studies* about thorny issues like marital fidelity, racism, or workaholism, asking first "What would you do?" And then follow up with the question, "Where do you find that in Scripture?" This may initially throw people off balance, because they're so used to attacking issues within their own frameworks and it's not (yet) second nature to say, "Let me start with what Scripture has to say about that."
- *Take church members to God's Word* whenever they come to you about any question, issue, or problem. Our first question in all circumstances should be, "What does God's Word say about that?"

This might seem a daunting proposition if your church culture is less open and direct than Watermark's. Nonetheless, holding staff and lay leaders accountable, at least at some level, for using a biblical context to solve problems and counsel congregants is a consistent behavior pattern found in best-practice churches.

Southpoint's Russ Austin puts it in simple terms: "How the Bible is treated by the leaders is more important than teaching what the Bible says." That sounds like a paradigm shift to us.

The "Embed the Bible in Everything" Dilemma: Can It *Really* Become the New Normal?

The word *normal* means conforming to a standard. Synonyms include words like *customary, typical, ordinary, usual,* and common. Wouldn't it be something if hearing Scripture quoted at the water cooler, the coffee bar, and in the church lobby was as customary, typical, ordinary, usual, and common as it is to hear it from the pulpit?

The truth is: *It's not normal.* Unless you are part of a best-practice church, where it's not necessarily a sure thing, but it's definitely more likely to occur.

When we hear the term "new normal," it's usually in the context of an aftershock; for example, the "new normal" of air travel security in the wake of the September 11 attacks or the "new normal" of modified financial habits that followed the recession that began in 2008. Something shakes up the environment so dramatically that it settles into a new formation that is distinctly different from the old one.

Everything in REVEAL points to the need for us to shake things up — to create a "new normal" for the church — one that doesn't include people sleepwalking through decades of church attendance as Bibles collect dust in church pews. Can churches that embed the Bible in everything become the norm, rather than the exception? Absolutely — that's what we've learned from the best-practice churches. But we've also learned that a shock to the system may be required, because the numbers show current church expectations and standard operating procedures will need to be upended to make it happen.

Another synonym for "normal" is healthy. Having normal blood pressure is a good thing. Having Scripture flow through the "vein of a church" (per Marcus Ways) would also be a good thing.

"Church leaders need to bleed Scripture when they're cut," says Todd Wagner. That's what it means to embed the Bible in everything.

We know it can be done. It starts with us.

CHAPTER 14

Create Ownership

> Now these are the gifts Christ gave to the church: the apostles, the prophets, the evangelists, and the pastors and teachers. Their responsibility is to equip God's people to do his work and build up the church, the body of Christ. This will continue until we all come to such unity in our faith and knowledge of God's Son that we will be mature in the Lord, measuring up to the full and complete standard of Christ.
>
> *Ephesians 4:11–13 NLT*

Jesus Christ was countercultural. He rocked the ancient world, teaching about humility, compassion, and service in a legalistic society ruled by kings and caste systems. He came to earth to save us, to be sure, but he also came to bring God's kingdom here on earth by challenging and changing two characteristics that define a culture: its beliefs and its behaviors.

Two thousand years have passed, and the change Jesus wanted to see—a shift from a culture of self-absorption to one of self-sacrifice—isn't going particularly well. While Christian beliefs may be widespread, there is little real evidence among Christians of the countercultural behaviors implicit in those beliefs. The fact is that the humble, compassionate behavior we might expect from Christ-followers seems to rarely distinguish their everyday encounters in neighborhoods, corporate hallways, or traffic jams.

This disappointing truth—that Christian beliefs don't necessarily translate into Christlike behaviors—is the target of the Create Ownership best practice. This best practice is all about creating ownership of a set of values that represent the vision and mission of the church—which, according to Scripture, is to go and make disciples.

If best-practice churches create such ownership—meaning that their congregations buy into the vision of discipleship—does that result in behavior change? Are the members of these congregations self-sacrificing people? Do they divorce less, file more honest tax returns, and demonstrate greater kindness in their daily interactions with others? We do not know, because such measurements aren't part of the REVEAL survey. However, based on multiple measures of attitudes and behaviors, we *do* know that best-practice congregations embrace a value captured by the phrase emblazoned on the purple t-shirts worn by those who attend Tri-County Church in DuBois, Pennsylvania: "I don't go to church. I *am* the church."

I am the church. The church *creates ownership.* What do these abstract concepts really mean? When these values are actively engaged, how do they shape a culture? Rather than describing the dynamics of cultural and organizational transformation conceptually, allow us to illustrate it with a simple story.

Several years ago, I (Cally) was traveling with my then nine-year-old daughter on Southwest Airlines. Typical of a Southwest flight plan, getting from Chicago to San Diego required multiple ups and downs between home and our final destination. My sweet Charlotte had a sinus cold that I was treating—unsuccessfully—with over-the-counter medications. Her ears were completely blocked when we began our descent into St. Louis. Tears streamed down her face from the pain of the eardrum pressure. "It hurts!" she cried, not in muffled tones.

The flight attendant came quickly alongside with warm compresses, but my daughter's distress was unabated. I could almost see the wheels turning as the attendant searched for alternate solutions. "What's her name?" she asked.

Answer in hand, she stepped into the center of the aisle with her microphone. "I need your attention," she announced to the entire cabin. "We have a very special guest on this flight named Charlotte, and I want you to help me let her know how much we care about her and how grateful we are to have her aboard."

Then, in a lovely Southern drawl and with a voice worthy of Grand Ole Opry attention, she belted out a country ballad dedicated to telling this miserable little girl how happy Southwest was to be taking care of her. Everyone on board burst into applause, and my now-distracted daughter smiled and soaked in the loving attention from this plane full of strangers.

The flight attendant wasn't employed to sing to crying children. She didn't sing because it was a job requirement. She sang in response to an expectation created by a corporate culture that puts a high priority on making flying a fun experience for everyone—including unhappy nine-year-olds. She wasn't required to sing, she was *empowered* to sing; because at that moment, she didn't just work for Southwest Airlines. She *was* Southwest Airlines.

This idea of empowerment is a cornerstone of the Create Ownership best practice. And it's a paradigm shift for churches that have simply set the bar of expectations too low for their people. Too many churches are satisfied to have congregations filled with people who say they "belong" to their church—who attend faithfully and are willing to serve or make a donation now and then. But that belonging bar is not high enough; simply belonging doesn't get the job done for Jesus. The people who get the job done are those willing to embrace a value—and maybe even wear t-shirts stating *I am the church.*

The "Create Ownership" Paradigm Shift

Bruce Sofia, senior pastor of Gloucester County Community Church in Sewell, New Jersey, knew there was a problem. "Two years ago our church leadership team acknowledged we had a flaw in our philosophy," he explains. "We were doing great on the outside—with lots of growth in attendance and activities—but we weren't developing disciples who modeled Christ. All our ministries were need-specific and too often independent of the whole. We felt this produced immature believers, people coming to church to get their needs met—very self-centered. The focus was on what was in it for them, rather than what they were doing for Christ and others. The disciplines necessary to take the next step of growing in Christ and contributing to the church as a whole were missing in their lives."

Today, Bruce's church is among the top 5 percent of REVEAL churches, churches whose congregations are far from self-centered. In the aggregate, over 70 percent of best-practice congregants serve their church—and 50 percent serve those in need on their own, at least once a month. Over 60 percent tithe. More than one-third had at least six meaningful spiritual conversations with non-Christians in the past year. All of these percentages are markedly higher than averages for the rest of the REVEAL database—in most cases, at least 50 percent higher.

By and large, these people are living out the vision of their church, adopting the values of Christ into their lifestyles inside and outside of the church walls. We would suggest this means the pastors of these churches recognize, like Bruce does, that merely belonging is not enough. Showing up for weekend services and participating in select ministries that may appeal to a person's special interests are insufficient standards for growing as a disciple of Christ.

Importantly, almost 70 percent of those belonging to best-practice congregations strongly agree that, "I cannot grow as a Christian unless I am an active member of a local church." They can't imagine living out their faith absent that context, because (in the spirit of Tri-County's slogan) they don't just go to church, they *are* the church. Its values and vision infuse their identities.

Best-practice churches are living, breathing organisms. They are filled with people who gather together and then disperse into their communities to live out the commitment to Christ that binds them together. In practical terms, these churches create ownership by using three key strategies, each one representing a shift to a new way of thinking about how to lead a church.

Three Key Strategies to Create Ownership

When it comes to inspiring and equipping people to live out the values of Christlike behavior, the natural inclination for church leaders is to reach for traditional levers such as volunteer programs, small groups, and training for the lay leaders who lead these programs. Not surprisingly, best-practice churches take advantage of all these levers. However, in the countercultural spirit of Jesus, their goal is not to build up these programs. Their goal is to *change behavior*. Specifically, Bruce turned his congregation of 2,500-plus weekend attenders who "belonged" to the church into Christ-followers who "owned" the church's discipleship vision by employing three behavior-changing strategies found in best-practice churches:

* *Empower people to be the church.* This is the priesthood-of-all-believers strategy, aiming to break down the mindset that divides pastors and congregants. Blurring those dividing lines involves assigning high levels of ministry accountability to lay leaders and using creative ways to inspire people to experiment with Christlike behavior in their everyday lives.

* *Equip people to succeed.* It's not enough to simply empower people. Establishing high standards for performance and accountability is critical, as is educating and giving congregants the tools they need to meet those standards.

* *Hold people accountable.* Best-practice churches understand that their attenders need spiritual mirrors, which means safe, relational networks that help them navigate the ups and downs of an expanding walk with Christ. Many invest significant time and resources in small-group infrastructures to provide that support.

Let's turn now to some of the practical ways best-practice churches execute these three strategies to inspire their congregants to own and live out the vision of the church.

Strategy 1: Empower People to Be the Church

Empowerment takes place when people feel they have the authority to live up to a set of expectations. Best-practice ingredients for a successful empowerment strategy include inspiration, modeling, and clarity of purpose about what the expectations include.

David Bish, lead pastor of Tri-County Church who coined the "I don't go to church; I *am* the church" motto of this best practice, empowers people to live into this vision in three practical ways:

* *Preach it!* Teaching is imperative. "I am the church" is central to Tri-County's annual vision-casting series.

* *Reinforce it!* Beyond the teaching, Tri-County dedicates a wall in their sanctuary to visual images that illustrate what "I am the church" looks like. They distribute the aforementioned t-shirts on which the phrase is prominently featured. And they distribute response cards regularly, to capture and communicate stories congregants share in answer to the question, "How were you being the church this week?"

* *Do it!* Being the church also has a corporate "doing" component. Every fall hundreds of attenders don their t-shirts and join together for a weekend of community serving.

Bruce Sofia's Gloucester County Community Church takes this behavior modification a step further. Several times a year the church creates short-term challenges — each one designed to inspire congregants to experiment with a spiritual behavior and then to share stories about their experience. For example, a "Power on the Spot" challenge encouraged congregants to pray immediately with and for distressed people who crossed their paths. The goal was to do this at least once a week for a six-week season, with the hope that a short-term focus might make instantaneous prayer a more routine behavior. Weekend storytelling reinforced the "we're in this together and we're not crazy" spirit of the effort.

They also used a short-term challenge to heighten the congregation's awareness of spontaneous promptings of the Holy Spirit. At a weekend service, congregants received envelopes containing undisclosed amounts of money. The goal of each participant was to respond, within forty days, to a Spirit prompting to donate the unknown dollars. Subsequently, congregants were asked to submit cards answering the question, "Why did God prompt me to do this?" Nearly 70 percent of them returned the cards, many with stories of Spirit-inspired matches between a stranger's financial need and the exact amount of money contained in the envelope.

Bruce also asks congregants to exchange names and pray for specific people who are far from God to come to faith. These covenant campaigns are branded with phrases like "Through the Gate in 2008" and "Cross the Line in '09." Often after services, congregants introduce Bruce to guests using special signs or whispers to let him know he's meeting a "Through the Gate" or "Cross the Line" person.

Another way many best-practice churches fortify their empowerment culture is by tapping lay leaders for significant ministry roles. For example, Marcus Ways runs the Christian Gospel Center Church of God in Detroit, Michigan, with a handful of staff and a thirty-person, all-volunteer leadership team. These are not individuals who simply provide advice; they actually lead every major ministry initiative. Todd Wagner's large Watermark Church in Dallas also has a high level of lay leadership; in fact, Watermark's children's ministry was their only ministry that began by hiring a paid staff leader.

Not surprisingly, volunteer hours run high at the best-practice churches; people giving twenty to twenty-five hours a week on top of full-time jobs are not uncommon. In fact, Michael Moore of Faith Christian Chapel in Birmingham, Alabama, says he often has to counsel his four thousand congregants not to let their volunteering fervor interfere with daily work obligations. His back-up teaching pastor, by the way, is Birmingham's chief of police—an individual who undoubtedly manages an already-busy schedule.

These concepts are not necessarily unique. They represent, however, an intentionality on the part of best-practice churches to empower their people to behave inside and outside the church as stakeholders and contributors to Christ's countercultural vision. This constitutes, we believe, a mental shift for church leaders.

It is also a very big deal. Everything in REVEAL tells us that people want to be challenged. Instead of handing them the proverbial fish, they want us to provide them with a fishing line so they can find out what it's like to catch one on their own. If we do that—if we help people experience life as a Christ-follower, whether through short-term behavior challenges or substantive ministry assignments—we'll catch a lot more fish for Jesus than if we keep doing so much ourselves.

Strategy 2: Equip People to Succeed

Tim Gray started The Bridge Community Church in rural Missouri in 2006 with eight people and $156. Today, his church of four hundred is anchored on a cell family model that is flourishing, largely because he equips cell leaders for success. While Tim's leadership requirements may seem quite ambitious by normal church standards, his disciplined approach provides food for thought about what people who lead within their church are willing to do to serve Christ.

Tim's cell leaders, for example, receive thirty-five hours of training in Bible teaching, pastoral care, and biblical counseling. This is *after* they've experienced the fourteen hours of training required to become a church member. Members also sign a covenant allowing someone to mentor them and committing to mentor someone else. Tim defends these high standards, saying, "We are commanded to go and make disciples, not members or pew dwellers. But empowering people is not enough. You don't just hand over the car keys without making sure your child has driver's training. You cheat your church if you give away leadership and don't train the leaders. People *want* training. Our mission is to equip as many as possible to be capable of equipping others."

Terry Inman, senior pastor of Harbor Light in multiethnic Fremont, California, agrees. "Church leadership is about equipping," he says. Terry regularly gathers new members of the church into a leadership development retreat experience, using it to assess strengths and passions and to provide one-on-one coaching on ministry serving and leadership options.

Fifty-three percent of congregants within best-practice churches strongly agree with the statement, "I know and use my spiritual gifts to fulfill God's purposes." The concept of spiritual gifts is not new, of course — in fact, it dates back to Paul's letter to the Ephesians, the source of the signature verse of this Create Ownership best practice. And it's certainly not unique to best-practice churches; in fact, just over 40 percent of all congregants say they use their spiritual gifts for God. But the very intentional focus of best-practice churches to equip their people — to prepare them to do something by arming them with training and tools — offers a message of encouragement to church leaders.

That message is to aim high. And to expect people to not only be willing to serve, but also to have an appetite for learning and training that will make them, as Tim says, "capable of equipping others."

Strategy 3: Hold People Accountable

"If people are in relationship with other Christians, growth is automatic," says Steve Gallimore, senior pastor of Tennessee Valley Community Church.

"Growth is automatic, because 'God talks' can happen." Like Tim Gray's cell groups, Steve's life groups are empowered to be ministers—a dynamic that exists in many best-practice churches. In fact, life groups are so important at First Baptist of Orlando that congregants are told if they have only one hour to spend on spiritual growth, they should attend their life group instead of weekend services!

If you've been wondering where small groups fit in the best-practice equation for spiritual vitality, this is it. That's because small groups provide the environment of relational trust necessary for true accountability.

Bruce Sofia realized this when his leadership team decided to introduce more discipline into their disciple-making efforts. One of their first moves was to shut down everything in the church and introduce their community strategy called "Circle of Friends." This means normal weekly activities (with the exception of weekend services) were preempted for six weeks to launch "Circle of Friends." This enabled people to participate in a small-group study based on a DVD curriculum supported by weekend messages. Bruce says the groups reinforced spiritual disciplines. People who rarely prayed were praying. People who never opened a Bible were reading Scripture.

But the best moments were what Steve Gallimore calls "God talks"—the authentic disclosures that allow people to share hurts and struggles. According to Bruce, those only happen in groups. "Being in a Circle of Friends—like Christ had his circle of friends—will make people face and resolve issues," he explains. Nowadays, he shuts down all adult ministries every eighteen months to reinvigorate their Circle of Friends with curriculum integrated with weekend services. In fact, the church promotes the effort widely, using billboards and banners throughout their community to draw newcomers into the church.

Seventy-five percent of best-practice congregants meet with a small group at least once a month, compared with 50 percent, on average, for the rest of the REVEAL database. Why?

The key is that best-practice churches expect small groups to go beyond providing community—which is the primary goal for small groups in most churches, where they are intended to provide a place to connect and form friendships. While those goals are important at all churches, the best-practice churches also expect small groups to be the place for "God talks"—where people "face and resolve issues."

This may be a paradigm shift for church leaders—to think that their small-group infrastructure could be much more than a strategy for helping newcomers make friends. Their small groups could actually be their most powerful organized activity for creating ownership of the church vision, by advancing its discipleship-making agenda.

But this caveat bears repeating: Best-practice churches are not striving to increase their number of participants in small groups. Numbers are not their goal. Their goal is accountability—providing a safe environment for coaching and counseling that helps people face and process issues.

Steve Gallimore explains it like this: "If you are not accountable, you will not change." The heart of his church is to help people change—to help them "come clean with God so you can become a useful vessel." The goal of best-practice churches is to provide their people with accountable relationships—which means a trust-based community of people who will help them look honestly in a spiritual mirror, so that they can get rid of the blinders that keep them from growing and becoming the most useful possible vessels for God.

The "Create Ownership" Dilemma: So You Say You Want a Revolution?

"Well, you know," said the Beatles, "we all want to change the world."

The Create Ownership best practice lays down the gauntlet. Do we want to change the world? Or not?

Because it would be a radical change if churches around the world focused on holding Christ-followers accountable for changing their behaviors. We have proven we can inspire people to belong to a church, but can we inspire them to *own* the discipleship agenda of Jesus? That agenda is the mantle of the church, dating back to Christ's resurrection when he told the disciples to "go and make disciples of all nations, baptizing them in the name of the Father and of the Son and of the Holy Spirit, and teaching them to obey everything I have commanded you" (Matthew 28:19–20).

His message was countercultural and his final challenge to his followers was to make that message a reality. None of us are doing this perfectly. But the promise of REVEAL's best-practice churches is that it's possible to learn from one another, and, as a result, to do this in a much better way.

So let's get started. Because the reason we're leaders of Christ's church is that we actually *do* want to change the world.

CHAPTER 15

Pastor the Local Community

"You are the light of the world—like a city on a hilltop that cannot be hidden.... In the same way, let your good deeds shine out for all to see, so that everyone will praise your heavenly Father."

Matthew 5:14, 16 NLT

I don't pastor a church; I pastor a community."

This somewhat unconventional statement guides the ministry of Terry Inman, senior pastor of Harbor Light Church in Fremont, California. Note his use of the word *pastor* as a verb; he uses it instead of the word *serve* as a way to describe his relationship to the community. To serve—the term most often associated with how a church interacts with its community—means to be useful or to render assistance in some way. To pastor, on the other hand, is a broader concept. Derived from its original Latin roots with the meaning "to shepherd," to pastor means to take on the role of guiding, watching over, and protecting an entire flock.

We tend to associate the word *pastor* with the role and tasks of leading a church. The pastor's flock is his or her congregation. In Terry's view, however, his flock is not the church; it's the community. This view came to define Terry's ministry calling twenty years ago, after a week of fasting and praying this prayer: "Lord, where is the church going and what do we need to be doing?"

Do what you will be judged for.

That's the directive that came to Terry as a strong divine impression. This led him to the Matthew 25 passage that describes what will happen when Christ returns. In that passage Jesus says that, like a shepherd who separates the goats from the sheep, he will divide us into two groups based on how well we fulfilled this expectation: "For I was hungry, and you fed me. I was thirsty, and you gave me a drink. I was a stranger, and you invited me into your home. I was naked, and you gave me clothing. I was sick, and you cared for me. I was in prison, and you visited me.... I tell you the truth, when you did it to one of the least of these my brothers and sisters, you were doing it to me!" (Matthew 25:35 – 36, 40 NLT).

Terry structured the ministry resources at Harbor Light to respond to this clear and detailed command. As a result, Harbor Light has become a powerful voice and influence in its community. The church became a vital part of a coalition of forty other churches that now serves as the primary volunteer force for nonprofit organizations in three California cities.

That's how best-practice churches see their roles: pastors of their communities — people of God who not only *serve* their communities, but also step up to try to resolve problems like homelessness and addiction that plague their neighborhoods. They are plugged into community networks and are deeply involved in local issues. That's because they believe they are called to be shepherds — to guide, watch over, and protect, not just the people who walk through their doors, but all the people who walk the streets where they live.

To pastor the local community requires having skin in the game — not just to care about the community's pressing concerns, but to come to the table prepared to work with others in an effort to do something about those issues. This activist mindset sees things like the blight of poverty and injustice as affronts to Jesus and lives out the spirit of Matthew 25 to do whatever can be done to eradicate them.

The "Pastor the Local Community" Paradigm Shift

Hold on, you may be thinking. Aren't most church leaders committed to local service and impact? Isn't supporting the community a common goal in most ministry plans?

The goal may be common, but this best practice most certainly reflects a paradigm shift for many churches. You find it in the words of Jesus: "When you did it to one of the least of these ... you were doing it to me!" The clear implication is that Christ wants more than a simple mental expansion of a church's ministry field to include others in the larger community. He is asking us to look into the eyes of every man, woman, and child who needs food, water, shelter, or companionship. Then he asks us to serve them as though we were serving *him*. To dry tears because they are his; to feed and clothe the homeless because their needs are his; to care for the sick and dying because their pain is his. This is a paradigm shift, or at least a big step up, from a simple pledge to serve the local community. The magnitude of the Matthew 25 commitment is much greater—it asks us to serve anyone who is hurt or struggling as though we are directly serving Christ.

The degree of focus and intensity required to respond to this commitment is apparent in best-practice churches. You see it in their decisions about how to spend church resources, how to manage their personal calendars, and how to choose those who sit in the inner circle of church leadership. At these churches, it's clear that they get it—that Matthew 25 really does describe what's going to sort the sheep from the goats when Christ returns.

Best-practice churches pastor their local communities by bringing the same inspirational energy—and the same sense of high-priority ministry importance—to outreach strategies and initiatives that they bring to designing and executing weekend services. In practical terms, this approach is implemented using three key strategies, each one representing a shift to a new way to think about how to lead a church.

Three Key Strategies to Pastor the Local Community

The numbers back up the reality of the outreach culture in best-practice churches. In the REVEAL database of 1,000 churches, the percentage of people serving those in need through their church at least once a month ranges from a low of 6 percent to a high of 61 percent. The average for all churches is 26 percent. At the top-5 percent best-practice churches, however, the average percentage is significantly higher, at 41 percent.

Equally important is that these numbers reflect an outreach culture that is *ongoing*. In other words, it is not something that happens twice a year around the Christmas and Easter holidays. Outreach activities are once-a-month-or-more occurrences for two out of five congregants in these churches, according to the numbers above. Not surprisingly, almost three out of four also serve in a church ministry once a month or more, and the same number strongly agree with the statement: "God calls me to be involved in the lives of the poor."

Given the clarity of Christ's command in Matthew 25, we know why these churches place such a premium on community outreach. But how do they fit that into the daily demands of ministry? And how do they then inspire their people to make it such a high priority in the midst of their busy lives? Three strategies emerge as the ones that make this work.

> ✱ *Set a high bar for serving the church and the community.* Best-practice churches make it clear early and often that they count on congregants to

serve the needs of both the church and the community. The senior pastor sets the tone and pace for this commitment because—according to senior pastor Steve Gallimore of Tennessee Valley Community Church—"your people will care no more than you do; go no farther than you will. It's that simple."

✱ *Build a bridge into your local community.* Most best-practice churches establish strong relationships, and often partnerships, with other churches, nonprofits, and community leaders. They do this for two reasons: to stay in touch and involved with the most pressing community needs, and to generate the greatest possible impact by working shoulder-to-shoulder with others to address those needs.

✱ *Make serving a platform for the gospel.* "It's a no-brainer," says Barbara Sullivan, who copastors Spirit of God Fellowship in South Holland, Illinois, with her husband, John. Her comment acknowledges that best-practice pastors see a natural affinity between evangelizing and serving those who are struggling and broken—because people who feel hopeless have hearts that are fertile ground for Christ's message of grace and redemption.

Now let's unpack the practical ways these churches pastor the local community by executing these three key strategies so effectively.

Strategy 1: Set a High Bar for Serving the Church and the Community

The people attending Tennessee Valley Community Church (TVCC) are in the thick of their community—sitting on the Chamber of Commerce, canvassing economically depressed neighborhoods to identify and serve needs, and going into corners where you wouldn't normally find the church. Senior pastor Steve Gallimore is the number one champion for these efforts, saying he doesn't worry about community service distracting or compromising his people's commitment to serve the church because he keeps his foot on the gas pedal for *all* serving needs. This is his advice for church leaders:

✱ *Be a high-expectation church.* If people come to TVCC expecting to sit passively in the pews, they've come to the wrong place. Regular ministry serving is nonnegotiable and part of the membership covenant.

✱ *Preach the announcements.* Every weekend Steve brings the highest priority church needs to everyone's attention, connecting the dots between opportunities to serve and spiritual growth and responsibility to the church. Then he tells them to go to a central location called "Connection Point" after services, showing up there himself to shake hands so it's clear these needs are important to him.

* *Constantly monitor serving activity.* TVCC keeps tabs on how often and in what way people are serving, mostly to make sure they don't overextend themselves and burn out. Steve says he has encouraged a number of people to take a break from serving for a season because they were exhausting their energy and enthusiasm. Monitoring volunteer participation also helps ensure that people don't stay uninvolved.

* *Make it easy.* A volunteer strategy called "Try it for 20" teams up a serving rookie with a seasoned volunteer for a twenty-minute experience on the weekend. This encourages trial-and-error participation by offering people a temporary and convenient way to sample different serving ministries— and it ultimately results in more stable long-term volunteer commitments.

An additional way to make sure church needs aren't left behind as people take on demanding community obligations is to integrate serving within other church activities. Harvey Carey's Citadel of Faith Church in Detroit gets creative by occasionally incorporating surprise community outreach projects within weekend services. His multicultural congregation is put on notice to come to weekend services packing their gym shoes in their car, because they never know when Harvey will preempt the service and send them out for a community-based outreach activity.

Sometimes that involves an initiative called "Prayer on the Porch." Harvey dispatches congregants to homes already touched by the church's outreach— for instance, by receiving a free Bible (one of the eight thousand distributed in a single ministry year) or a school backpack. Congregants are commissioned to connect with the families and pray for their needs on the front stoop. Another out-of-the-box activity is "urban camping." Men and boys from Citadel grill hot dogs and s'mores on street corners known for drug deals, successfully disrupting drug traffic at a number of locations. These efforts reflect the heart of Citadel of Faith. Not accidentally, the word *citadel* refers to watching over the community—a crucial role for this church located in the poorest zip code in the poorest large US city and an apt descriptor for a church that aspires to be a city on the hill (Matthew 5:14–16).

A number of best-practice churches make serving an expectation for small groups. Bruce Sofia's Gloucester County Community Church (Sewell, New

Jersey), for example, requires its Circle of Friends to take on two serving projects every ministry season — one within and one beyond the church walls. Other churches — like Christian Gospel Center Church of God in Christ (Detroit, Michigan), Faith Chapel Christian (Birmingham, Alabama), and East Valley Foursquare (East Helena, Montana) — make serving the church and the community the primary purpose of small-group life.

The mental shift required to make sure all needs are met when a church truly pastors the local community is best captured in Steve Gallimore's advice: *Be a church of high expectations.* Set a high bar. That's the spirit of the best-practice churches. "If you're breathing, you're serving," says Jeff Richards of East Valley Foursquare. "We're going to get you out of a bib and into an apron," says David Uth of First Baptist of Orlando. (And they pass out the aprons to make sure people don't miss the point!)

As you're ramping up such pastoring initiatives in your community, don't assume that higher demands to serve beyond the church will diminish your congregants' desire and will to serve within the church. Trust the Spirit to grab their hearts — and inspire them to rise to the occasion to meet whatever challenges you put in their path.

Strategy 2: Build a Bridge into Your Local Community

It started with a monthly gathering of forty evangelical churches southeast of San Francisco, gathering to pray for the unique needs of their community. They prayed for the many lost people living in their neighborhoods where a mere 4 percent attend church. And they prayed for ethnic and cultural bridges to be built in a community known as the most diverse for its size in America. (Their public school system reports that its students speak 136 languages.)

Terry Inman and his fellow pastors felt the time had come to move from simply praying about community needs to taking the steps necessary to address them. They also decided that proclamation alone — and one church alone — wasn't going to create the wave of change that was required. So they joined forces. Here's what happened:

- They met with the mayor and local officials, who said the best way to serve the city was to partner with the nonprofits — organizations that were always in need of volunteers.
- They formed Compassion Network and pooled resources to fund an office in the city's Family Resource center, which already housed twenty-five other private and government agencies.

- Monthly donations from each participating church were used to fund a full-time administrator and four or five interns. Their job is to network the church congregations toward meeting the needs of people within the community.
- Today, all churches receive weekly emails posting volunteer opportunities—opportunities that are typically filled within hours. In 2008, Compassion Network received the local government's Nonprofit of the Year Award.

Compassion Network is only one channel for Terry's very serious response to Matthew 25. He could give you multiple examples of actions taken to address each one of Christ's six commands. Especially compelling is his perspective on visiting those in prison. "We have traditional prison ministries," he says, "but it dawned on me that most people without Christ are in some kind of prison—could be a prison of doubt or fear. The only way we'll reach them is to go to them in their prison." That's his broader view of Matthew 25—that "all those six things talk about getting out, getting out, getting out; I've been communicating that message from the pulpit and by example for twenty years."

While best-practice churches may not always be as organized or multifaceted as Compassion Network, many do partner with other community organizations, including other churches. Nick Honerkamp's New Covenant Church in Clyde, North Carolina (a recent best-practice addition), joined with thirty other churches to tackle their community's homeless problem, starting a shelter and supporting it completely with church funds and volunteers. This same group of churches, realizing that public school budgets were tight, pitched in to clean up school properties before the academic year began. Since this church partnership effort to support the schools in 2008, sixty-eight churches have joined together to adopt all the public schools in the county—a formal agreement that's the first of its kind in North Carolina. The churches have also partnered on ministry initiatives, like mission trips and pooling resources for a shared Vacation Bible School format and curriculum.

Nick, like several other best-practice pastors, requires all church staff to get involved with a community organization so the church can keep its fingers on the pulse of the greatest unmet needs in the area. That's the real difference we see in churches that go beyond the idea of serving (being useful) and see themselves as their community's pastor. They spend the time and resources to watch out for their flock—often by joining forces with others to deal with the greatest threats to public health and safety in their neighborhoods.

They see the needs. They own the issues. They join forces. Those three stepping-stones represent mental shifts for church leaders who currently define their flocks as the people sitting in the pews — and who currently confine their capacity to act on community issues to the resources of their individual churches.

Jesus modeled a different way when he fed the five thousand. First, he saw the need. Then he gathered the resources and asked God to bless them. He didn't focus on limitations or impossibilities. Best-practice churches suggest that we shouldn't either.

Strategy 3: Make Serving a Platform for the Gospel

The marginalized or the lost? Social justice or evangelism? That's a classic tug-of-war for church leaders as they wrestle with how to allocate their resources, time, and attention. Both initiatives are important. But which is primary? Which is secondary? Spirit of God Fellowship in South Holland, Illinois, is a best-practice church that doesn't see the two activities as independent choices. That's because they believe serving is the best way to reach people for Christ.

The founders of the church, John and Barbara Sullivan, are unassuming, down-to-earth people. In the 1970s, God called John, a local dentist, and his wife Barbara to found a church in South Holland, a relatively affluent suburb near Chicago. In 1980, the church began ministering to inner-city drug addicts in a treatment center south of Chicago. In 1988, the church founded Restoration Ministries in Harvey, a neighboring community widely known for drug addictions, gang violence, murder, and corruption (it was recently recognized for having the most dangerous street in America). They formed an independent board of directors to enable other churches to participate in these inner-city ministries. In the intervening decades, Restoration Ministries has helped transform thousands of lives by serving as a beacon of hope for a place and population written off by many as too far gone to recover.

A city on the hill, indeed.

Restoration Ministries now includes two live-in facilities for recovering addicts and twenty-eight programs for kids to seniors, including:

- *Boxing club.* Ex-addicts coach eighty kids in boxing. Their motto is that it's better to sweat in a gym than bleed on the streets.
- *Project Intercept.* This volunteer-led after-school program includes tutoring, art instruction, basketball, and a computer club. The gospel message is stressed in all activities.
- *Mentoring.* Former addicts provide mentoring at a local grammar school. This was the only school in Harvey to come off the state's aca-

demic watch list, an achievement directly attributed to the after-school and mentoring programs.

Spirit of God is certainly not the only best-practice church having a powerful influence for Jesus through outreach to marginalized people. East Valley Foursquare in rural Montana brings seven busloads of two hundred to three hundred disadvantaged children to church every weekend. The 350 congregants of Christian Gospel Center Church of God in Detroit host an active food pantry with a signature annual event that feeds three thousand people. Full Gospel Tabernacle in Far Rockaway, New York, has a prominent community presence that includes job fairs, parenting seminars, and partnerships designed to address the most pressing needs of five housing projects. Senior pastor Jorge Vega says, "Even the gangs know this is a place that helps the community. There are no bars on our windows."

Does this outreach to "the least of these" really spread the message of Jesus? Do those who benefit from the food, counseling, and hope for a better future eventually decide to follow Christ?

Spirit of God is a test case that suggests it does. They say at least eight thousand people have given their lives to Jesus through their ministry. Cofounder Barbara Sullivan is firmly convinced that serving those who are the most discouraged—who have hit bottom, beaten up by life—is the best platform for the gospel message. That's why she always sends nervous rookie evangelists to the drug rehabilitation house for their first attempts at a spiritual conversation with non-Christians. There they will find people with uncritical spirits, hungry hearts, and listening ears for the promise of salvation and redemption.

It's unlikely that any church leader doubts the truth of Barbara's observations. The difference for best-practice churches may be their intentionality in acting on that truth. And once that truth is internalized, it is amazing how creative these pastoring churches become in their efforts to get to know their community flocks. Some best-practice churches even build floats for local parades, in order to make people more inclined to give the church—and consequently, faith in Jesus—a try. In fact, Spirit of God actually won the best Memorial Day float award eight years running! As one pastor explains such efforts, "A step toward the unchurched is just showing up as a church that cares. Then they'll at least be open to checking us out."

Whether it's building floats, distributing food, or running a boxing club for disadvantaged kids, best-practice churches would tell you it all works—eventually—to start people down a path toward growing a relationship with Christ.

The "Pastor the Local Community" Dilemma: It's an Uphill Climb

"Acts of service, probably more than anything else, motivate people down the pathway of spiritual maturity," says senior pastor Terry Inman. "What has hurt us is that we have overly trained people in classrooms and have not given them hands-on experience. Scripture tells us we should not just be hearers of the Word, but doers as well."

The facts back him up. By all measures, the majority of Christ-followers fall far short in their others-oriented attitudes and behaviors. In earlier chapters, we've noted the gap between love of God and love of others; for example, in chapter 5 we observed that three out of four spiritually mature Christ-Centered people very strongly agree that they "love God more than anything," but less than one-third of them very strongly agree that they "have tremendous love for those I know and those I don't know."

With regard to others-oriented behaviors, on average 57 percent of all church congregants serve their church, 26 percent serve those in need through their church, and 39 percent serve those in need on their own (not through the church) once a month or more. This means that, in any given month, over 40 percent of congregants *don't* serve their church, almost 75 percent *don't* serve those in need through their church, and over 60 percent *don't* serve those in need on their own.

These facts must break a pastor's heart (and God's as well) — not only because it demonstrates the uphill climb to fulfilling Matthew 25, but also because serving the "least of these" is a tremendous catalyst of spiritual growth for all believers. This is especially true for those seriously pursuing a personal relationship with Christ and on the threshold of fully surrendering their lives to him. The disappointingly low numbers for people at all levels of spiritual maturity, when it comes to attitudes and behaviors related to "love of others," is arguably the single biggest failure of the church.

On the other side of the "biggest failure" coin, however, awaits "greatest opportunity." And best-practice churches are cheering the rest of us on with their encouragement and examples. The key difference is that these churches *don't let people off the hook*. Because their vision goes well beyond serving — instead, they are intent on *pastoring* their local communities, and they do that with passion. And through this expanded view of what it means to pastor, hearts within the congregation grow as well.

Is such a transformation possible? Of course. Is it always easy? Of course not. Church leaders need the wisdom of Solomon to sort through all the serving possibilities for church congregants and then to decide which of these are the top priorities. Setting a high bar is a fine ideal, but we need to be realistic, right? If we put too many options out there, will people either take on too much and burn out — or feel so confused and overwhelmed they'll stay on the sidelines?

As we ponder these questions, one of Solomon's proverbs give us food for thought: "Take a lesson from the ants, you lazybones. Learn from their ways and become wise!" (Proverbs 6:6 NLT). If the ants are the congregants in best-practice churches — where 73 percent serve the church, 41 percent serve those in need through the church, and 51 percent serve those in need on their own every month — the lesson to "learn from their ways" is that there's a lot of capacity in most congregations to step up and do more. So don't shrink back from bringing the needs of the church, the community, and the world to the attention of your people. Like the ants, when we work together using the resources God gives us, all those needs can be met.

CHAPTER 16

Lead from a Christ-Centered Heart

Love the Lord your God with all your heart and with all your soul and with all your mind and with all your strength.

Mark 12:30

On Sunday, October 29, 1989, I (Greg) walked into Willow Creek Community Church for the first time. I wasn't really sure I wanted to be there.

Earlier that year, I had read an article in *Time* magazine that said the church used "rock music, drama, and multimedia slide shows" and noted that congregants sat in "posh theater seats rather than pews." As a guy who had attended traditional hymn-singing, robe-wearing Lutheran churches all my life, I was skeptical. But my mom had sent me a copy of a book she had just read in her women's Bible study down in Houston. She really liked *Too Busy Not to Pray*, and she thought the author, Bill Hybels, led a church somewhere in Chicago.

I read the book and found it very useful—and solid theologically. So when a friend invited me to attend Willow, I reluctantly accepted. After making my way through the longest line of traffic I had ever seen moving toward a church service, I found a seat in the back of the auditorium and opened the program. The message for the day was, "The Rise of Satanism: Overcoming Satanic Opposition." I kid you not. Kind of a heavy topic for a seeker-sensitive church.

The opening music and drama sketch were well done. After that I watched the then thirty-seven-year-old senior pastor take the stage. His message centered on how we could know if someone had come under the control of Satan and, if so, what we should do about it. It was intense.

After nearly half an hour on this topic Bill took a turn, directing his comments to the "growing Christians" in the audience. He said that Satan knows he would never succeed in involving many of us in outright Satan worship, so instead, he has a Plan B. "He will simply try to take the edge off your full devotion to Christ," Bill said. "He will try to convince you that 80 percent or 90 percent or even 95 percent devotion is good enough. But it is a *lie*. Jesus demands *full* devotion. Ninety-five percent devotion is 5 percent short." Bill was adamant that the only way to live is with a sold-out heart, a sold-out head, and sold-out hands. He ended on a crescendo, challenging and imploring us to set our sights on a life of full devotion, a life with no compromise.

I was transfixed. My mind was racing and my heart was pounding. Time stood still. I had waited my whole life for someone to call me to that kind of commitment, that kind of absolute devotion. I could tell this pastor was completely serious. He passionately believed with his entire being that this was the only way to live. Totally sold out for God. Fully surrendered.

In the years since, in addition to getting to know Bill personally, I have had the privilege of meeting and working with many individuals who live out the kind of focus and passion I heard about that day. But when our team met with the top-5 percent REVEAL pastors in September 2008, we knew there was something different about this group. After spending some time together, the reasons behind that difference became increasingly clear.

In our conversations with these pastors, we shared with them our hypothesis of what they all had in common, then listened intently as they refined our thinking with their own insights and experience. The fruit of those discussions are the four best-practice strategies you read about in chapters 12 to 15. But it also became clear that these strategies were not the *only* things these churches had in common. Something else was going on in their midst, and after additional dialogue and reflection, we identified a fifth commonality—one that had nothing to do with strategy. It was all about the attitude these senior leaders shared: they were *consumed* with making disciples. Absolutely consumed. That was unquestionably their most important aspiration and the deepest desire of their hearts.

As we listened more carefully, three characteristics that contributed to this focus on making disciples became obvious: these leaders were disarmingly humble; they modeled a surrendered life; and they focused their energies on growing hearts rather than attendance.

Christ-Centered Leaders Are Disarmingly Humble

These top-5 percent pastors credit whatever transformation that occurs among their congregants not to their own efforts, but to God's presence, activities, and intervention. When we first contacted Rick Gannon of Palm Valley Church in Mission, Texas—one of the most spiritually catalytic churches in the REVEAL study—he admitted that our call had taken him by surprise. He was sincerely shocked that his church was among the top 5 percent of REVEAL churches; in fact, when asked what contributed to Palm Valley's amazing results, his entire leadership team was at a loss to explain why things were working so well. Their focus, instead, was on what they still needed to achieve. There was no sense of self-congratulatory accomplishment, just a desire to address their unfinished business.

Such humility was a consistent theme with the other senior pastors in the top-5 percent group. They did not feel particularly special. They said their churches still had lots of things that needed to be fixed. And they always pointed to God as the one who was making good things happen in their midst, many times in spite of the leaders themselves. In fact, they even resisted our efforts to try to find common trends or themes among them, insisting that any progress was only about God—his grace, love, and power.

These leaders were humble, so much so that they felt very uncomfortable when we tried to point out how their efforts contributed to the vitality of their congregations. They were living out Philippians 2:3: "Do nothing out of selfish ambition or vain conceit, but in humility consider others better than yourselves." We found this refreshing and encouraging. It would be wonderful if great leaders always reacted this way, but the reality is that most people, when told they are doing some things very well, are all too eager to elaborate on how they do them.

In listening to these leaders, though, we were reminded of Jim Collins's research on great companies detailed in his book *Good to Great*. He says one of the characteristics of enduring great companies is the presence of a "Level Five Leader," someone who demonstrates "the paradoxical combination of deep personal humility with intense professional will." Such leaders, he explains, "routinely credit others, external factors, and good luck for their companies' success."[1] These pastors clearly demonstrate similar humility.

Christ-Centered Leaders Model a Surrendered Life

Church leaders understand that people in their congregations are watching them, looking to see whether they are truly living out what they are preaching.

---

1. Jim Collins, "Level Five Leadership: The Triumph of Humility and Fierce Resolve," *Harvard Business Review* (January 2001).

Todd Wagner of Watermark Church in Dallas, Texas, puts it this way, "If we are going to create more disciples, then we need more people who say what Paul says, 'Follow my example, as I follow the example of Christ' " (1 Corinthians 11:1).

During our first gathering with these best-practice pastors, one point all of them agreed on was their need — and the need of other senior leaders — to model the life they were inviting their congregations to live.

"This is what we tell every member who joins our church," says Todd, "if you ever see us [leadership] do something inconsistent with Scripture, approach us. If you approach us and we rationalize it or blow it off, run for the hills. You do not want to be under that kind of leadership."

The behaviors of REVEAL's top-5 percent pastors appear to match their desire to model a Christ-centered life. We were struck, for instance, by how often in our conversations with them, these pastors referred to what they had been learning from God during their own personal time of reading and reflecting on Scripture. They don't just teach the Bible, they let the Bible teach them. Shape them. Form them. They are obviously eager to be with God and to learn more from his Word.

Pastor Terry Inman of Harbor Light Church in Fremont, California, says, "The most feedback I get from my congregation is not on my sermons; it is when I tell my own story about my walk with God and my family's walk with God." He understands that it is not his words, but his actions that speak the loudest. And he is intentional about letting his congregation in on how things are going in his relationship with God.

Transparency is key. What congregants see modeled in these leaders is not perfection so much as a work in progress. Leaders of the top-5 percent churches share their failures and their struggles. They let their congregations see their flaws so everyone can learn from their mistakes.

"If you were to poll our congregation and ask them about myself and the other ministers here," says Rick Gannon, "they would say things like, 'They are transparent. They're one of us. They're not perfect, but I want to be like them; I can follow them and follow Christ.' It's humbling to hear that, but it's also something that — if we don't hear it — we know we are in trouble."

Your congregation is watching, and you will inspire them when you share your own journey. When they see that you haven't figured it all out yet, that encourages them. And self-disclosure can mitigate the disconnect that sometimes develops between the person in the pulpit and the people in the pews. Living a Christ-Centered life becomes doable to the congregation. They think, "If you can do it, I can do it."

Christ-Centered Leaders Focus on Growing Hearts, Not on Growing Attendance

Typically, when a ministry leader or pastor meets his or her counterpart from another church, a question that is nearly always asked, within the first minute or so, is, "How big is your church?" We want to know how many people attend the church, and whether consciously or unconsciously, we use the answer to do a quick evaluation of the competency of the pastor or leader we're talking to. A small number creates one impression; a large one, another. To tell the truth, we esteem the leader of the larger church more than that of the smaller. It's not right, but that is what we do.

One of our concerns when we gathered the top-5 percent pastors was whether or not they would respect each other as peers, given the very different sizes of their congregations, which ranged from two hundred to over nine thousand. We hoped size would not be an issue, but we didn't know.

Turns out, there was nothing to worry about. Not only was size not an issue as it related to mutual respect, size was not something anyone even talked about. Ever. It was oddly absent from the conversation. It just was not relevant to them.

As the group continued to dialogue, it became clear why. These leaders were so focused on their primary mission — that of growing truly sold-out disciples of Jesus — that size was just not on their minds. They had a single objective: making disciples. And with such an appetite to see lives transformed, everything else takes a backseat.

"I've seen pastors look out over a mostly full sanctuary and say, 'Ah, it's not very good today,'" notes Rick Gannon. "Nobody on our staff would ever say that. Ever."

Now these folks do, of course, look at attendance information. It is just that it is not the main thing they focus on. They truly are not distracted with wondering how to increase attendance by 10 percent. They are obsessed, instead, with challenging their congregation members to move closer to Christ. To live a sold-out life. To surrender it all. Nothing else is as important as that.

The One Thing You Must Do

Less than two months after our first meeting with these top-5 percent pastors — on October 16, 2008 — we concluded a conference in which many of these individuals spoke to more than 1,500 church leaders. They focused on many of the concepts you have read about in this book, providing a wonderful, informative two days. Now that it was over, Cally and I (Greg) had a meeting in my office to debrief the conference.

Cally was on Cloud Nine. Happy, expressive, relieved. She was excited about what we accomplished and felt it was worth at least a small celebration. She was right. In many ways, this was a major milestone for REVEAL and the culmination of our work over the previous five years. Even more importantly, hundreds of pastors were headed back to their churches with fresh inspiration and the tools to put that inspiration to work.

I, on the other hand, was extremely discouraged. Not because it was all over. And not because I would genuinely miss the new friends I had made among the top-5 percent pastors. No, I was feeling low because as a pastor and leader in my church, I knew I had a lot of work to do. Let me explain.

After listening again to the stories of these great churches and their leaders, I saw with startling clarity how our own church needed to continue to change. We had already implemented some new strategies, many of them learned through interaction with the best-practice churches. But we could do more. We *had* to do more. Although this might be a challenge, however, this was not the reason for the sinking feeling I was experiencing.

No, the reason I was feeling so low that day — and for several days to come — was that it had become very clear to me that the first step toward helping Willow Creek to become more spiritually vibrant was for *me* to become more spiritually vibrant. I understood as never before the full impact of the phrase, "It starts with me."

I had to face the brutal facts. Although I loved God, and despite the fact that my spiritual growth was progressing more than at any other time in my life, I had just encountered a group of people who were significantly more focused and committed to their relationship with Jesus than I was. And that chasm — between where I was and where I wanted (and needed) to be — looked almost impossible to cross. The questions I had about the possibility of getting from here to there created an overwhelming sense of concern that was very hard to shake.

Up until then, I had thought our work with REVEAL would provide all the necessary insights and strategies to help me in my role as Willow's executive pastor. And that had, to this point, been the case. But on the day we concluded the conference, it became painfully obvious that those ideas and strategies would get me only so far. What had to happen — what was nonnegotiable — was that I had to pursue my relationship with Christ with even greater intensity, passion, and single-minded commitment.

Of all people, I now knew what it would take to pursue that relationship. I understood, because of the research I'd been involved in, what created catalytic growth. There was no getting around the fact that I must seriously commit myself to spending more time with God, to reading my Bible, to serving the poor, and to resurrendering my entire life on a daily basis.

The verse "Blessed are those who hunger and thirst for righteousness, for they will be filled" (Matthew 5:6) has guided me since that day. I needed to feel it in my body, like a craving for food and water. I needed to ache to be close to Christ, to give him everything, small and large. I needed to desire being with him more than I desired anything else.

I had to ask myself the question, "Am I consumed with becoming a disciple of Christ?" And on that morning, I had to be honest and say that I still had a long way to go.

So what about you? Do you hunger and thirst for righteousness above all else? Or do you relate—at least to some extent—to the feelings I was dealing with?

The journey to a spiritually vital church must begin within your own heart. After that, you can explore and implement the four best-practice strategies you've read about and pursue insights inspired by the other research findings. But if you get that order reversed—relying on strategies before working on your heart—beware. You cannot reproduce in others what you are not producing in yourself. The main thing you need to do—the one thing you *must* do—is fully within your reach.

You must surrender all.

Everything.

The first step to building a great, spiritually vital church is for you—and the leaders around you—to follow Christ with your whole heart every day of your lives. To die to your own agendas and follow Christ, one day at a time. To declare that your relationship with Christ is the most important relationship in your life. To pursue intimacy with Christ with your entire mind, body, heart, soul, and strength. To allow nothing, absolutely nothing, to stop you from this one main thing.

You can do this.

And for the sake of your congregation and those you lead, you *must* do this. You can try other paths, find a new strategy, perhaps, or hire some really talented staff members. But in the end, if your church is not led by people completely devoted to Jesus—people who prioritize their relationship with him above everything else—it will not work. It will not produce life. It will not change the world. And we all know how badly this world needs changing.

Throughout this book you have gained an appreciation for what is required to move closer to Christ, to move toward a deep intimacy with Jesus that produces a life characterized by deeper levels of love for God and others. At times, this journey may feel like it is all about something we must do, a step we must take all by ourselves and in our own power.

The really good news is that God is already moving toward us. This is a two-way street. And not only that, but he is way ahead of us. He has been pursuing us even before our first breath. When he first thought of you, before you were even conceived, his heart overflowed with love for you. And from the moment of your birth, he has been moving toward you with outstretched arms. Out of love, he has intervened in your life in ways you cannot begin to understand. His one agenda has been your redemption, and his longing is to be completely united with you in the most intimate relationship you will ever experience.

Remember what Paul wrote: "For I am convinced that neither death nor life, neither angels nor demons, neither the present nor the future, nor any powers, neither height nor depth, nor anything else in all creation, will be able to separate us from the love of God that is in Christ Jesus our Lord" (Romans 8:38–39). God's passion is *you*. Always has been, always will be. Every step you take toward him is matched by scores of his steps in your direction. You walk toward him; he runs toward you. He loves you and desires to give you everything you need—for your life and for your leadership.

God has taken the first steps. Now it's your turn. What are you waiting for? *Move.*

Appendices

1. What Is REVEAL?

A Research-Based View of the Spiritual Journey

REVEAL is a research-based view of how the spiritual journey unfolds, validated to date through survey input from approximately 250,000 congregants in 1,000 churches.[1] The distinction of REVEAL is its ability to "measure the unseen," using a research approach that assesses how people's spiritual attitudes, needs, and motivations align with spiritual behaviors.

REVEAL identifies a spiritual continuum comprised of four segments of people at different stages of spiritual development: Exploring Christ, Growing in Christ, Close to Christ, and Christ-Centered. REVEAL's deeper value, however, is found in its insights about what creates movement along the journey; for example, which church activities, beliefs, spiritual practices, or activities (evangelism, serving, etc.) are most influential to spiritual growth at different points along the journey.

A Spiritual Life Survey

The Spiritual Life Survey is a research tool local churches can use to assess the spiritual health of their congregations. The goal of the Spiritual Life Survey is to provide church leaders with a research tool equivalent to the finest research tool used in the marketplace at a small fraction of the marketplace cost. For more information, see Appendix 2, "What Is the REVEAL Spiritual Life Survey?" (page 261), or visit www.revealnow.com.

---

[1] For more information and a brief history of REVEAL, visit www.revealnow.com.

Three Books

Published in 2007, *Reveal: Where Are You?* describes the initial aggregate findings based on input from 5,000 surveys completed by seven different congregations.

A second book, *Follow Me: What's Next for You?*, published in 2008, expands on earlier findings about the four segments on the spiritual continuum by describing the spiritual catalysts most influential to movement along the continuum. The findings in *Follow Me* are based on input from 80,000 surveys completed by people in more than 200 congregations.

Focus: The Top Ten Things People Want and Need from You and Your Church, published in 2009, compares the drivers of satisfaction with the church and senior pastor (what people want) with the most influential catalysts of spiritual growth (what people need). Its findings are based on input from 80,000 people in 376 churches who participated in the REVEAL Spiritual Life Survey between September 2008 and February 2009.

2. What Is the REVEAL Spiritual Life Survey?

The REVEAL Spiritual Life Survey is a proven way to benchmark and track spiritual growth in a congregation. It moves beyond measures like attendance and financial giving to determine if your church is really making a difference in helping people become more like Christ. This anonymous, congregational online survey is easy to understand, simple to administer, and repeatable over time to monitor change. Its large database, which represents a quarter million congregants from a thousand churches, allows you to compare your results with other churches.

Should My Church Use This Tool?

When it comes to spiritual growth, we need to be able to measure the unseen. Churches who use the Spiritual Life Survey receive an in-depth understanding of their congregants' spiritual attitudes, motivations, behaviors, and satisfaction. The survey enables church leaders to track over time the movement of their congregation toward Christ, to see if ministry efforts and resource allocations are really contributing to the spiritual health of people in the church.

What Does the Spiritual Life Survey Provide?

Three surveys over five years: a baseline survey and two follow-up surveys. Follow-up surveys can be executed at any time within the five-year window.

A Spiritual Life diagnostic report, benchmarking your church's spiritual profile against the results of any prior surveys as well as other churches in the REVEAL database.

REVEAL WORKS, a four-step planning process tool to help your church leadership team develop an action plan that responds to your REVEAL findings.

Marketing collateral to help promote the Spiritual Life Survey to your congregation, including sample text for print and e-mail communication and other tools to increase awareness and participation.

3. Who Are the 1,000 Churches?

The findings in *Move* are based on 1,007 churches surveyed from September 2008 to March 2010. What follows is a brief overview of these churches.

Geography and Size

Charts A3-1 and A3-2 show the distribution of the 1,007 churches by geographic location and by size (based on weekend adult attendance).

Three out of the four geographic regions account for almost 90 percent of the churches, with the Midwest accounting for just over 35 percent. The Midwest is more strongly represented due to the influence of the states of Illinois, Michigan, and Ohio. The Northeast accounts for only 11 percent of the churches.

Geographic Location of the 1,007 Churches

Geographic Regions of the United States	Geographic Section	Percentage of the Church Sample
Base Size		1,007
Northeast	New England	3%
	Middle Atlantic	8%
Midwest	East North Central	26%
	West North Central	11%
South	South Atlantic	15%
	East South Central	4%
	West South Central	13%
West	Mountain	7%
	Pacific	13%

CHART A3-1: The 1,007 churches represented by the findings in *Move* are located across the country. The fewest, 3 percent, come from New England. The most, 26 percent, come from the East North Central Midwest.

Weekend Attendance of the 1,007 Churches

Weekend Attendance	Percentage of Church Sample
Base Size	1007
Less than 101	3%
101 – 250	23%
251 – 500	25%
501 – 1,000	27%
1,001 – 2,500	15%
2,501 – 5,000	5%
5,001 or more	2%

CHART A3-2: The 1,007 churches represented in *Move* are diverse in size, with more than half reporting between 250 – 1,000 in weekend attendance.

Weekend attendance shows a distribution concentrated in the midsize range of church size. Slightly more than half (52 percent) report weekend attendance between 251 – 1,000 adults, and 26 percent are in the smallest categories (250 or less). We realize this is not necessarily representative of the national distribution of all churches, since a much higher percentage of all churches fall in the 100 or under range.

Denominations and Styles

Churches in the survey represent a wide mix of denominations and styles (charts A3-3 and A3-4). Nondenominational and Baptist churches account for 45 percent of the 1,007 churches, though we did achieve a solid mix of other denominations, like Methodist, Lutheran, and Presbyterian. The style descriptions reflect the three words chosen by each participating church as those that best describe their church. Contemporary, evangelical, and seeker friendly lead the way as the most popular choices, though it is important to point out that a large percentage of churches *did not* describe themselves as contemporary, evangelical, or seeker friendly.

In summary, the demographic mix of the 1,007 churches included in the findings reported in *Move* represents the diversity of churches that have subscribed to the REVEAL Spiritual Life Survey since it was first made available in 2007. It was not weighted or redistributed in any way to create a particular profile.

Denominations Represented in the 1,007 Churches

Church Denomination	Percentage of Church Sample
Base Size	1007
Nondenominational	28%
Baptist	17%
Methodist	9%
Lutheran	8%
Presbyterian/Reformed	7%
Christian Church/Church of Christ/ Disciples of Christ	4%
Assembly of God/Church of God/ Pentecostal	4%
Association of Vineyard	3%
Other	20%

CHART A3-3: The denominations represented in the 1,007 churches in *Move* range from nondenominational at 28 percent to Baptists at 17 percent and the Association of Vineyard at 3 percent.

Styles Represented in the 1,007 Churches

Church Style (Multiple Responses Allowed)	Percentage of the Church Sample
Base Size	1007
Contemporary	64%
Evangelical	63%
Sensitive to seekers (Seeker friendly)	54%
Missionary-minded	39%
Innovative	34%
Visionary	32%
Conservative	24%
Traditional	18%
Mainline	15%

CHART A3-4: When asked to select three words that best describe the style of their church, almost two-thirds of the 1,007 churches represented in *Move* chose *contemporary* or *evangelical* as one of those words. However, significant percentages also chose *missionary-minded* (39 percent), *conservative* (24 percent), and *traditional* (18 percent).

4. Who Are the Best-Practice Churches?

These churches achieved a Spiritual Vitality Index (SVI) that placed them in the top 5 percent of the 500 churches taking the REVEAL survey in the fall of 2007. Since that time, a number of additional churches have recorded SVI scores in the top 5 percent. While we have not undertaken another thorough review of best-practice stories and strategies, our more limited exploration since 2008 has affirmed the four principles discovered in the best-practice work based on the churches below.

Church	Senior Pastor	Church Profile	Weekend Adult Attendance (2008)
Bethlehem Assembly of God Valley Stream, New York	Steven Milazzo	Assembly of God Multicultural Suburban	850
The Bridge Community Leadington, Missouri	Tim Gray	Nondenominational Rural	400
Christian Gospel Center Church of God in Christ Detroit, Michigan	Marcus Ways	Pentecostal African-American Urban	350
The Citadel of Faith Detroit, Michigan	Harvey Carey	Evangelical Covenant Multicultural Urban	220
East Valley Four-square Church East Helena, Montana	Jeff Richards	Pentecostal Rural	320

Church	Senior Pastor	Church Profile	Weekend Adult Attendance (2008)
Faith Chapel Christian Birmingham, Alabama	Michael Moore	Nondenominational African-American Urban	3,500
First Baptist of Orlando Orlando, Florida	David Uth	Baptist Suburban	6,000
Full Gospel Tabernacle Far Rockaway, New York	Jorge Vega	Nondenominational Multicultural Urban	350
Gateway Church Southlake, Texas	Robert Morris	Nondenominational Multicultural Suburban	9,000
Gloucester County Community Church Sewell, New Jersey	Bruce Sofia	Nondenominational Suburban	2,500
Harbor Light Fremont, California	Terry Inman	Assembly of God Multicultural Suburban	900
Palm Valley Church Mission, Texas	Rick Gannon	Nondenominational Multicultural Suburban	3,000
Spirit of God Fellowship South Holland, Illinois	John Sullivan	Nondenominational Multicultural Suburban	400
Tennessee Valley Community Church Paris, Tennessee	Steve Gallimore	Baptist Rural	400
Tri-County Church Du Bois, Pennsylvania	David Bish	Nondenominational Rural	850
Watermark Church Dallas, Texas	Todd Wagner	Nondenominational Suburban	4,800

5. What Are the Spiritual Belief and Attitude Statements and Where Do They Come From?

The purpose of our research is to uncover insights about what advances spiritual growth and what gets in the way of that growth. Our working definition of spiritual growth is based on Christ's teaching about the greatest commandment — to love God and to love others (Matthew 22:36–40). In order to assess where people are spiritually, we used statements about spiritual beliefs and attitudes and asked them to describe how strongly they agreed with those statements. Here are the statements we used:

- *Salvation by Grace*: I believe nothing I do or have done can earn my salvation (Ephesians 2:8–9).

- *The Trinity*: I believe the God of the Bible is the one true God — Father, Son, and Holy Spirit (2 Corinthians 13:14).

- *Personal God*: I believe God is actively involved in my life (Psalm 121).

- *Christ Is First*: I desire Jesus to be first in my life (Matthew 6:33).

- *Authority of the Bible*: I believe the Bible has decisive authority over what I say and do (2 Timothy 3:16–17).

- *Identity in Christ*: I exist to know, love, and serve God (John 1:12–13).

- *Stewardship*: I believe a Christian should live a sacrificial life that is not driven by pursuit of material things (1 Timothy 6:17–19).

- *Giving Away My Life*: I am willing to risk everything that is important in my life for Jesus Christ (Romans 12:1–2).

- *Giving Away My Faith*: I pray for non-Christians to accept Jesus Christ as their Lord and Savior (Ephesians 6:19–20).

- *Giving Away My Time*: I give away my time to serve and help others in my community (Colossians 3:17).

- *Giving Away My Money*: My first priority in spending is to support God's work (2 Corinthians 8:7).

These statements are based on Scripture and derived from the *Christian Life Profile Assessment Tool* created by Randy Frazee, senior minister of Oak Hills Community Church in San Antonio, Texas. Dozens of church leaders, theologians, and others engaged in a rigorous process of biblical inquiry to find the core, repeatable characteristics of a follower of Christ. The statements were then tested and refined in multiple forums, including *The Spiritual State of the Union*, an ongoing benchmark of the "spiritual temperature" in America, sponsored by The University of Pennsylvania and The Gallup Organization. Among the experts contributing to this comprehensive effort were Dallas Willard, J. I. Packer, and Larry Crabb. The thoroughness of this approach, as well as the caliber of people engaged in the process, prompted us to adopt these statements for use in our research.

6. Willow's Response to REVEAL

"So, what's Willow doing in response to all the REVEAL findings?" That's one of the most common questions we get from pastors and church leaders. You too might be wondering how this research has impacted our ministry. In the spirit of continuing to share what we are doing and learning in order to benefit other churches, the following is a summary of the most significant changes our church has made in response to what we learned from REVEAL.

Willow Creek Community Church has undertaken two rounds of change in response to its REVEAL results. The first took place between 2004 and 2007, and the second began in 2008 and is ongoing.

What We Did First (2004 – 2007)

In 2004, once Willow Creek's senior leaders processed the church's first survey results, three things became clear right away: we needed to recognize that the responsibility for spiritual growth belongs to both the church and the individual; we needed to better support our Christ-Centered congregants; and we needed to designate a leader who would focus on the unique needs of those who were Close to Christ and Christ-Centered.

Shifting the Responsibility for Spiritual Growth

Before REVEAL, our church staff felt the responsibility to design and implement a world-class spiritual-growth strategy that essentially communicated to the congregation, "We know what is best for you. Participate in these various programs and activities and you will grow spiritually." Those activities included attending weekend and midweek services, participating in a small group, and serving in one (or many) of the hundreds of available opportunities. We were confident that these activities would help anyone and everyone in the church grow spiritually, regardless of where they were on their spiritual journey.

In hindsight, that strategy—assuming most of the responsibility for providing experiences that fostered the congregants' spiritual growth—set unrealistic expectations for what a church could reasonably provide. Taking too much responsibility for others' spiritual growth fostered an unhealthy dependence of congregants on the church staff. So one of the first changes we made was to shift our "we know what is best for you" approach to a message like this: "We are all on a spiritual journey, and each of us must take responsibility for our own spiritual growth. Your spiritual journey is unique, and you will need something different at each stage of your spiritual growth. Leaders are here to help you as you identify what you need and then help you take the next step on your journey." Instead of trying to mastermind the ultimate spiritual growth strategy that would work for everyone, we shifted the primary responsibility back to the individual, where it belonged. The role of leadership became that of coach, encourager, and equipper.

Supporting Christ-Centered Congregants

Our Christ-Centered congregants had relatively high levels of dissatisfaction with how the church was helping them grow—and they wanted more in-depth Bible teaching. Their dissatisfaction was a significant concern, because our survey results clearly showed that our most mature congregants were the best evangelists and volunteers. We depended on them to advance Christ's mission and we sincerely wanted them to thrive spiritually. So we began several initiatives to address their concerns. We created resources based on the weekend service teaching that enabled people to do deeper study during the week. In addition to teaching biblical messages on felt-need topics at weekend services, we added more messages that presented expository teaching on books of the Bible. Our survey results indicated that our midweek services were meeting the needs of the Growing in Christ and Close to Christ segments, but that the satisfaction levels fell among those in the Christ-Centered segment. They wanted to go even deeper in their biblical knowledge. So we adjusted the midweek messages to include greater challenge for those who were Christ-Centered. We believed we could do that without adversely impacting the less spiritually mature segments in the audience because the research clearly showed that *everyone's* desire was to understand the Bible in greater depth.

Declaring a Leader

During our defining retreat in the summer of 2004, when the leadership team first processed Willow's REVEAL results, Senior Pastor Bill Hybels quickly identified one of our biggest problems—we did not have a leader whose job was focused on meeting the unique needs of the Close to Christ and Christ-Centered attenders—*half* of our congregation. Willow has always believed that selecting the right leader with the right gifts, abilities, and spiritual maturity is the first step toward making something happen. We needed someone who could coordinate our existing activities and then create additional opportunities to catalyze the ongoing development of our most spiritually mature congregants.

We eventually brought in a proven leader, Randy Frazee, to lead that effort. Randy had been the senior pastor of Pantego Bible Church in the Dallas area; he had a passion for discipleship and could also help lead our small-group system. Randy led the charge to create a biblical literacy course, he championed further changes to the midweek service, and his team began work on a personal spiritual growth assessment tool that would help individuals determine next steps in their spiritual journey. The desire was to move from a one-size-fits-all strategy to a personalized spiritual-growth plan. That work is now coming to fruition in an initiative called *Engage*. *Engage* is a web-based system where congregants receive personalized spiritual growth plans in response to a short REVEAL survey that gauges the best next steps for their spiritual development. These next steps range from a customized Bible engagement plan to other opportunities like classes or serving experiences. *Engage* will be available not just for Willow Creek, but for any interested churches.

These may not sound like big changes, but frankly it took a while to absorb what we were learning and to get others up to speed on what we were discovering. We spent time in meeting after meeting, walking staff and key lay leaders through the REVEAL findings. They needed time to assimilate the implications and ask questions before they were ready to change the way they ran their ministries. But little by little we started to see people's thoughts, attitudes, and actions shift.

2007: Wake-Up Call Number Two

Although we had considered the first survey in 2004 as a wake-up call, we didn't really come to grips with the depth of change we needed to make until 2007, when we resurveyed the congregation. How much of an impact had the changes up to that point really made? As it turns out, not much. In fact, we made no significant movement in the key areas we were hoping to improve. That was hard to take. What made these results even harder to take was that, for the first time, we could compare Willow's results to twenty other churches who had also taken the survey. Clearly, in some areas, we had a long way to go.

Comparing ourselves with other churches wasn't about competing with them; it was about getting a clear picture of what was actually possible for us as a community that seeks to serve God fully. We could now see what the potential was for our own church. Benchmarking ourselves to other churches helped prioritize our next set of actions, making it clear where we were excelling (like in evangelism and serving those in need) and helping us focus on the critical things that still needed improvement (like Bible engagement and weekend services).

It was clear that incremental changes were not going to deliver the results we were hoping for. It was time to really shake things up, because staying where we were was not an option. Our mission of turning irreligious people into fully devoted followers of Jesus Christ drove us to make some of the biggest changes in Willow's history.

What We're Doing Now (2008 through Today)

In January 2008, our senior leadership team gathered again for a strategic planning retreat. We spent three days discussing our survey results, and this time, the ideas were much more radical and involved wholesale change of Willow's core strategy. Following the retreat, we implemented five major initiatives.

1. We fully embraced the REVEAL spiritual continuum as the spiritual growth framework for our church.

Up until this time, we did not talk much to the congregation about the REVEAL findings. But starting at weekend services in 2008, Bill drew the four-segment continuum on a flipchart for several weeks in a row. He referenced each segment and challenged people in the congregation to not only assess where they were, but to choose a specific next step they could take to move closer to Christ. We shared survey results with the congregation and made explicit the steps we were taking to equip them in their spiritual journeys.

We also let the church staff know that REVEAL was here to stay—that senior leadership accepted its results and conclusions 100 percent, and they needed to do everything possible to align their ministries with its findings. You see, some wondered if the whole REVEAL thing was just a fad—a passing idea that would get some attention for a season and then just quietly fade away. This had led many to adopt a "wait and see" posture; now senior leadership needed to make it clear that REVEAL was here to stay.

2. We ended our two-service model, morphed our midweek service into a university classroom format, and made significant changes to the weekend service.

For the first thirty-three years of the church, Willow Creek offered two distinct services each week: a weekend service targeted primarily to spiritual seekers and a midweek service targeted primarily to more mature Christ-followers. It was clear from the data, however, that our congregation wanted more options that could address their various spiritual needs. In addition, busy schedules made it increasingly difficult for folks to attend the Wednesday night midweek service. If that was the only place they could get deeper teaching, we were not going to be able to realize our mission. The two-service model needed to change.

We decided to morph the midweek service into a university classroom format, where attendance was encouraged for those who needed a particular next step. This idea was developed through dialogue with several churches who had used a similar approach and whose churches rated very high in the REVEAL research. We now start our new Wednesday-night experience (not service) with thirty minutes of worship for those who want to come early. Then attenders are released to one of a dozen classes designed for people at each stage of the spiritual journey, similar to a format in which there are 101-, 201-, and 301-level classes.

Classes range from those designed for people exploring Christianity to those that help participants understand how the Bible is put together or how they can discover their spiritual gifts. Local seminary professors teach in-depth classes on books of the Bible. And in order to help those who can't make it to church on Wednesday night, almost all classes are subsequently available online. We continue to make changes in the format and class offerings, but overall, we find that this approach is helping people advance in their spiritual journey, as evidenced by recent surveys of the congregation.

Because not everyone would attend a Wednesday night service — either in person or online — we realized we also needed to make changes to the weekend service. It needed to catalyze the spiritual movement of people in all four segments of the spiritual continuum equally, not with a primary bias toward the spiritual seekers. Services needed to be more challenging for everyone, providing more in-depth biblical content and specific next steps. We increased the amount of corporate worship and put together services designed to help everyone have a significant encounter with God.

3. We changed our small-group strategy.

Starting in 1993, our goal had been to get everyone into a small group, believing that, as we repeatedly stated, "Life change happens best in a small group." (We even made small-group participation a requirement for church membership!) Between 1993 and 2003 the number of people in small groups increased from around 4,000 to more than 15,000. But the REVEAL analysis made it clear that this goal was misplaced. Based on the churches we have studied, including our own, there is no evidence that getting 100 percent of a congregation into small groups is an effective spiritual formation strategy.

What we *did* validate, though, was that *spiritual community* is vital for everyone's ongoing growth. So we shifted the emphasis from getting everyone into a small group to getting everyone involved in some kind of spiritual community. You see, we discovered that the majority of Close to Christ and Christ-Centered folks were already experiencing spiritual community through things like mentoring relationships, spiritual friendships, and "rogue" small groups that they created on their own. But we were continuing to insist that they be in an "official" church small group, placing an unnecessary burden on their backs.

Our new strategy necessitated new language. We now say that life change happens best in community (not necessarily a small group). And beyond that, we tell our congregation that while spiritual community is essential to each person's spiritual growth, it is your responsibility to find and build it. We have lots of small groups with trained leaders available for you to join, if that would be of help to you. But the responsibility remains with the individual to pursue spiritual community.

4. We established daily Bible reading as a normal expectation for our entire congregation.

We have always known that daily Bible reading is an essential spiritual discipline for Christ-followers, but REVEAL tells us that even those who are Exploring Christ should be reading their Bibles regularly. With the added insight that Bible engagement is the single most spiritually catalytic activity a person can engage in, this became one of our church's most significant priorities.

At any weekend service, it's now fairly common to hear Bill Hybels say, "We can't read your Bible for you!" We seek to inspire an appetite for God's Word through more in-depth weekend teaching and more frequent use of Scripture reading and meditation during worship. In addition, midweek options have a strong biblical focus and include many advanced classes. Moreover, the changes are not just limited to the adults. Our children's ministry curriculum has shifted its goal from teaching kids what the Bible says to teaching them how to read and understand it for themselves. Our high school ministry changed its curriculum as well, to ensure that after four years, students will have cultivated a daily habit of Bible reading—one of several lifelong spiritual practices taught and reinforced by this ministry.

5. We put even more energy and investment toward serving our local community.

Responding to the REVEAL findings has not just been about fixing areas that need attention; it has also been about leveraging our strengths and continuing to join God where he is clearly moving. The research verified that serving those in need is one of the most catalytic things a church can do to move people closer to Christ. This was very good news for Willow, because for over ten years one of our main strategic initiatives had been to reach out and serve those in need throughout the Chicagoland area. We take this so seriously that we track each month how many volunteers serve through one of our compassion and justice ministries. This number has grown steadily over the years. For example, in 2010, over 70,000 acts of service—a 30 percent increase over 2009—occurred through our volunteers. And when asked, 77 percent of our congregation is very satisfied with how Willow provides opportunities for them to serve those in need, which is 28 percent higher than the average of all the churches in the REVEAL database. But we want to do even more.

Willow Creek's Care Center is currently the largest food pantry in the Chicago region, serving over 17,000 unique families in 2010. Over 650 volunteers serve weekly, supported by two full-time and one part-time staff members. We also have a CARS ministry that gives away cars and does free car repairs for those in need. Both ministries are housed offsite in rented facilities. At our church's thirty-fifth anniversary in October 2010, we announced that the Care Center and CARS ministry would be relocated to the South Barrington campus, creating a new, expanded, and coordinated care ministry that, in addition to food and transportation assistance, would also provide children's clothing, a medical clinic, job training, and several other care and support services. A $10 million Compassion Campaign was kicked off that weekend to fund the vision. We believe this new ministry, when it is fully operating in late 2012, will provide even more opportunities for the congregation to serve our local community, while catalyzing the spiritual growth of our congregation.

Where We're Going ... One Step at a Time

Obviously, we can't do everything at once and we still have lots of things we are motivated to change. But we are absolutely committed to doing what we must do to help everyone in our church experience a vibrant and deepening relationship with Christ. The most recent survey of our congregation (2010) has encouraged us to keep on going. Since 2007, we have:

- Increased Bible engagement by 35 percent, putting Willow on par with the best-practice churches.

- Increased overall satisfaction with weekend services among congregants in all four segments on the spiritual continuum. The number of attenders who say these services are helping them to grow spiritually has grown by 29 percent.

- Increased satisfaction with how congregants are challenged to grow and take next steps in their spiritual lives by 27 percent.

- Increased overall satisfaction with how congregants feel the church helps them to grow spiritually by 34 percent.

Willow is still not a top-5 percent REVEAL church, but the changes undertaken since 2004 have created solid momentum, demonstrated by meaningful positive increases in our Spiritual Vitality Index. The numbers, however, are less important; as Paul might say, "What is more, I consider everything a loss because of the surpassing worth of knowing Christ Jesus my Lord" (Philippians 3:8). That is truly the biggest change at our church: REVEAL has changed our conversation. We still talk about attendance and church activities, to be sure. But everyone within the organization knows those numbers don't necessarily measure what we're really after, which is changing hearts and lives for Jesus.

Facts really have been our friends. Thanks to REVEAL and the determination and hard work of Willow's staff, those facts are helping us do a better job of helping people grow in their relationship with Christ.

7. Research Approach and Methodology

We began with a simple question: Could scientific research help us understand and perhaps measure spiritual growth? In other words, could the same research tools used in the marketplace to measure consumer attitudes and behaviors also be used by local churches to measure the spiritual beliefs and behaviors of their congregations? We believed the answer was yes.

We have refined our research since completing the first survey at Willow Creek Community Church in 2004. Today our database includes survey responses from approximately 250,000 congregants attending 1,000 churches. After so many years conducting this research, we feel confident that the research survey tool and analyses have proven capable of producing valid and valuable insight for church leaders.

Here is a brief overview of our research approach and methodology.

Approach

Our approach focused on three key areas and questions:

- *Segments*: What are the different groups/segments of people the church might be looking to serve?
- *Needs*: What spiritual growth needs are being met, not being met well, or not being met at all for each segment?
- *Drivers and Barriers*: What are the drivers of spiritual growth, and what are the barriers to spiritual growth?

These three areas provided the framework around which we organized the information we collected.

Methodology

Broadly speaking, there are two types of research methodology: qualitative and quantitative. We used both qualitative and quantitative methodologies, and then employed analytical techniques and processes to review the data.

Qualitative (Gathering Insights)

This is typically a one-on-one process in which a researcher poses questions directly to an individual. The questions often ask not only for information and opinions but also allow the interviewer to probe the richness of emotions and motivations related to the topic. Researchers use qualitative data to help clarify hypotheses, beliefs, attitudes, and motivations. Qualitative work is often a first step because it enables a researcher to fine-tune the language that will be used in quantitative tools.

Quantitative (Establishing Statistical Reliability and Validity)

This process utilizes detailed questionnaires often distributed to large numbers of people. Questions are typically multiple choice with participants choosing the most appropriate response among those listed for each question. Quantitative research collects a huge amount of data, which can often be generalized to a larger population and allow for direct comparisons between two or more groups. It also provides statisticians with a great deal of options for methods to use in analyzing the results.

Analytical Process and Techniques (Quantifying Insights and Conclusions)

Quantitative research involves an analytical plan designed to process the data to yield empirically based insights. Several analytical techniques were used in our four research phases:

- *Correlation Analysis*: Measures the extent to which two variables are related (if at all). Finding a correlation does not mean that one variable causes the other; it means their patterns of movement are connected.

- *Discriminant Analysis*: Determines which variables best explain the differences between two or more groups. We can't infer that these variables directly cause the differences to occur between the groups.

Instead, we know that there are significant differences between the groups on the variables.

- *Regression Analysis*: Used to investigate relationships between variables. This technique is typically utilized to determine whether or not the movement of an outcome (or dependent) variable can be predicted from one or more independent variables.

- *Hierarchical Cluster Analysis*: Used to determine which survey items are most similar to each other in their statistical properties and group them accordingly. The validity of the grouping could then be tested using Confirmatory Factor Analysis.

- *Confirmatory Factor Analysis*: Used to test a model that theorizes that a group of items on a survey measure one or more shared underlying constructs. The model is tested to determine how well the data fit the theory. Good fit validates the theory.

- *Path Analysis*: An advanced technique related to regression analysis used to determine the relative effect of multiple variables on an outcome (or dependent) variable. Indirect effects (where the effect of one or more variables on the outcome variable is mediated by another variable) can be calculated. A theoretical model of direct and indirect effects is developed and tested to determine how well the data fit the theory. Acceptable fit validates the theory.

We used both qualitative and quantitative methods in 2004 when we focused exclusively on Willow Creek Community Church and also in our 2007 research involving hundreds of churches. Here is a summary of the methodology used in our most recent work.

Qualitative Phases

December 2006

- *One-on-one interviews with sixty-eight congregants.* We specifically recruited people in the more advanced stages of spiritual growth. Our goal was to capture language and insights to help guide the development of our survey questionnaire.

- *Interview duration*: 30–45 minutes.

- *Focused on fifteen topics.* Topics included spiritual life history, church background, personal spiritual practices, spiritual attitudes and beliefs, etc.

April/May and September 2008

- *In-depth interviews with sixteen churches.* We specifically recruited churches that were in the top 5 percent of the REVEAL database based on their Spiritual Vitality Index (SVI). Our goal was to better understand what makes these churches stand out and determine if there were similarities across these churches that could be categorized as best practices.

- *First phone interview duration*: 60–90 minutes.

- *Second in-person discussion duration:* Two-day group gathering.

- *Focused on a number of areas.* Topics included church history and background, overall church purpose, church processes, current church programs, expectations for the congregation, how they focus on spiritual growth, how they measure success, how they select staff, etc.

Quantitative Phases

Phase 1 (January–February 2007)

- Online survey fielded with seven churches diverse in geography, size, ethnicity, and format.

- Received 4,943 completed surveys.

- Utilized fifty-three sets of questions on topics such as:
  –Attitudes about Christianity and one's personal spiritual life.
  –Personal spiritual practices, including statements about frequency of Bible reading, prayer, journaling, etc.
  –Satisfaction with the role of the church in spiritual growth.
  –Importance and satisfaction of specific church attributes (e.g., helps me understand the Bible in depth) related to spiritual growth.
  –Most significant barriers to spiritual growth.
  –Participation and satisfaction with church activities, such as weekend service, small groups, youth ministries, and serving.

Phase 2 (April–May 2007)

- Online survey fielded with twenty-five churches diverse in geography, size, ethnicity, and format.

- Received 15,977 completed surveys.

- Utilized refined set of questions based on Phase 1.

Phase 3 (October–November 2007 and January–February 2008)

- Online survey fielded with 398 US churches diverse in geography, size, ethnicity, and format, plus an additional ninety-one churches in seventeen countries.
- Received 116,239 completed surveys.
- Utilized a refined set of questions based on Phase 2 research.
  - –Expanded survey to include twenty statements about core Christian beliefs and practices from *The Christian Life Profile Assessment Tool Training Kit*.[1]
  - –Added importance and satisfaction measures for specific attributes related to weekend services, small groups, children's and youth ministries, and serving experiences.

Phase 4 (September 2008–March 2010)

- Online survey fielded with 609 US churches diverse in geography, size, ethnicity, and format.
- Received 131,814 completed surveys.
- Utilized a refined set of questions based on Phase 3 research and qualitative data from interviews with best-practice churches.
  - –Expanded survey to include seventeen items measuring importance and satisfaction with aspects of the senior pastor's leadership.
  - –Added eight items measuring importance and satisfaction with aspects of the church's role in spiritual growth.

Analytical Process and Resources

Each phase of our research included an analytical plan executed by statisticians and research professionals. These plans utilized many analytical techniques, including correlation, regression, discriminant analysis, cluster analysis, confirmatory factor analysis, and path analysis. To put our analytical approach into perspective, here are three points of explanation about the nature of our research philosophy.

---

[1] Randy Frazee, *The Christian Life Profile Assessment Tool Training Kit* (Grand Rapids, Mich.: Zondervan, 2005).

Our Research Is a Snapshot in Time

Because this research is intentionally done at one point in time—like a snapshot—it is impossible to determine with certainty that a given variable, such as valuing spiritual guidance from the church, causes movement from one segment to another (for example, from Growing in Christ to Close to Christ). To establish causality, we would have to assess the spiritual development of the same people over a period of time (longitudinal research).

However, the fact that increased levels of valuing spiritual guidance occur in the Close to Christ segment compared with the Growing in Christ segment strongly suggests that valuing spiritual guidance from the church does influence spiritual movement between segments. While it does not determine conclusively that spiritual guidance "causes" movement, discriminant analysis does identify the most differentiating characteristics between segments. So we infer from the findings that certain factors are more "predictive" and consequently more influential to spiritual growth than others.

Our ultimate goal is to measure the same people over multiple points in time (longitudinal research) in order to more clearly understand the causal effects of spiritual growth. Longitudinal research is challenging to conduct because it involves tracking people as they move or change churches over time. It is usually undertaken after "snapshot" research has identified the key variables to focus on measuring long term. However, even with longitudinal findings, we know there will be much left to learn, and much we will never understand about spiritual formation. The attitudes and behaviors we measure today should not be misinterpreted as defining spiritual formation. Instead they should be considered instruments used by the Holy Spirit to open our hearts for his formative work.

The Purpose of This Research Is to Provide a Diagnostic Tool for Local Churches

Our intent is to provide a diagnostic tool for churches that is equivalent to the finest marketplace research tool at a fraction of the marketplace cost. This is "applied" research rather than "pure" research, meaning that its intent is to provide actionable insights for church leaders, not to create social science findings for academic journals.

In a nutshell, while we intend to reinforce our research base with longitudinal studies, we chose to draw conclusions about what people need and want from the church and from their senior pastor based on point-in-time research using appropriate statistical analyses. This approach meets the most rigorous standards of market research that routinely influences decision making at some of the most respected and successful organizations in the country.

Research Is an Art as Well as a Science

While the data underlying our findings is comprehensive and compelling as *science*, we have also benefited from the *art* of experts whose judgment comes from years of experience. The three research experts closest to this work represent more than fifty years of wide-ranging applied research projects. Eric Arnson began his career in quantitative consumer science at Procter & Gamble, and ultimately became the North American leader of brand strategy for McKinsey and Company. Terry Schweizer spent twenty years with the largest custom-market research organization in the world, running its Chicago office before joining the REVEAL team full-time in 2007. Nancy Scammacca Lewis holds a PhD in quantitative methods from the University of Texas at Austin. She has served part-time on the pastoral staff of a local church for the past seven years while consulting on research projects in education and the social sciences. Eric, Terry, and Nancy poured the benefit of their expertise and judgment into every finding in this book, which gives us confidence that both the art and the science components of our research are on very solid ground.

Research Standards

In summary, we have employed the highest applied research standards available, including a robust qualitative process and four waves of quantitative surveys with over a thousand diverse churches. While there is much more work yet to do, we are confident that the insights and findings in *Move* reflect a very high level of research excellence.

Acknowledgments

In essence, *Move* is the story of how spiritual growth — defined as increasing love of God and others — seems to happen. Based on our research, spiritual growth occurs in tandem with an increasing willingness to sacrifice material and emotional treasures fully into God's care.

Reflecting that spirit, we want to sincerely thank a few individuals who truly sacrificed to ensure that this work would be completed:

- Eric Arnson, who was a tireless champion and extraordinary contributor of wisdom and encouragement every step along the way
- Terry Schweizer, who left a longstanding marketplace career to dedicate his significant talent and expertise exclusively to REVEAL
- Bill Hybels, who has championed this work and courageously led Willow Creek to respond to all we have learned
- Jim Mellado, whose advocacy and leadership support for REVEAL has never waned
- Christine Anderson, who has project-managed every publication related to REVEAL and overcame multiple obstacles that threatened to keep this work from seeing the light of day
- Judy Keene, who contributed in mighty ways through her editorial and writing expertise, giving *Move* a fresh voice and taking us to a new level of professional language and expression
- Mel Probst and Nancy Scammaca, who offered their incredible gifts in our earliest days to help a fledgling research effort become so much more than it would have been without them
- Lori Meyers, whose administrative skills and good humor buoyed the team and kept us on track in good times and bad
- The Willow Creek Leadership Team, who decided unanimously to turn church strategies and ministries upside down in response to REVEAL

- Our families, who accepted less than our best at times on the home front, never ceasing to cheer us on with great love and patience

Finally, we would be beyond remiss if we didn't acknowledge the REVEAL church leaders, whose pioneering spirits and love for their congregants have inspired us time and again to take the next hill. Because they believed, even when we had our doubts, that this work could make a difference for Jesus.

WILLOW CREEK ASSOCIATION

This resource is just one of many ministry tools published in partnership with the Willow Creek Association. Founded in 1992, WCA was created to serve churches and church leaders striving to create environments where those still outside the family of God are welcomed—and can more easily consider God's loving offer of salvation through faith.

These innovative churches and leaders are connected at the deepest level by their all-out dedication to Christ and His Kingdom. Willing to do whatever it required to build churches that help people move along the path toward Christ-centered devotion; they also share a deep desire to encourage all believers at every step of their faith journey, to continue moving toward a fully transformed, Christ-centered life.

Today, more than 10,000 churches from 80 denominations worldwide are formally connected to WCA and each other through WCA Membership. Many thousands more come to WCA for networking, training, and resources.

For more information about the ministry of the
Willow Creek Association, visit: **willowcreek.com.**

Share Your Thoughts

With the Author: Your comments will be forwarded to the author when you send them to *zauthor@zondervan.com*.

With Zondervan: Submit your review of this book by writing to *zreview@zondervan.com*.

Free Online Resources at
www.zondervan.com

Zondervan AuthorTracker: Be notified whenever your favorite authors publish new books, go on tour, or post an update about what's happening in their lives at www.zondervan.com/authortracker.

Daily Bible Verses and Devotions: Enrich your life with daily Bible verses or devotions that help you start every morning focused on God. Visit www.zondervan.com/newsletters.

Free Email Publications: Sign up for newsletters on Christian living, academic resources, church ministry, fiction, children's resources, and more. Visit www.zondervan.com/newsletters.

Zondervan Bible Search: Find and compare Bible passages in a variety of translations at www.zondervanbiblesearch.com.

Other Benefits: Register to receive online benefits like coupons and special offers, or to participate in research.

ZONDERVAN®

ZONDERVAN.com/
AUTHORTRACKER
follow your favorite authors